THE ART of ASKING

THE ART of ASKING

or *How I Learned to
Stop Worrying and
Let People Help*

AMANDA PALMER

Foreword by Brené Brown

GRAND CENTRAL
PUBLISHING

NEW YORK   BOSTON

Grand Central Publishing
Hachette Book Group
1290 Avenue of the Americas
New York, NY 10104

www.HachetteBookGroup.com

Printed in the United States of America

RRD-C

First Edition: November 2014
10 9 8 7 6 5 4 3 2 1

Grand Central Publishing is a division of Hachette Book Group, Inc.
The Grand Central Publishing name and logo is a trademark of
Hachette Book Group, Inc.

The Hachette Speakers Bureau provides a wide range of authors for speaking events.
To find out more, go to www.hachettespeakersbureau.com or call (866) 376-6591.

The publisher is not responsible for websites (or their content) that are not owned
by the publisher.

Library of Congress data has been applied for.

ISBN 978-1-4555-8108-5 (Hardcover ed.); ISBN 978-1-4555-3377-0
(Autographed ed.); ISBN 978-1-4789-8288-3 (Audiobook ed.);
ISBN 978-1-4789-2740-2 (Audiobook downloadable ed.);
ISBN 978-1-4555-8107-8 (Ebook ed.)

THIS BOOK IS DEDICATED TO MY MUTTI,
who, through her love, first taught me how to ask

Foreword

A decade or so ago in Boston, Amanda performed on the street as a human statue—a white-faced, eight-foot-tall bride statue to be exact. From a distance, you could have watched a passerby stop to put money in the hat in front of her crate and then smile as Amanda looked that person lovingly in the eye and handed over a flower from her bouquet. I would've been harder to spot. I would have been the person finding the widest path possible to avoid the human statue. It's not that I don't throw my share of dollars into the busking hats—I do. It's just that I like to stay at a safe distance, then, as inconspicuously as possible, put my money in and make a beeline for anonymity. I would have gone to great lengths to avoid making eye contact with a statue. I didn't want a flower; I wanted to be unnoticed.

From a distance, Amanda Palmer and I have nothing in common. While she's crowdsurfing in Berlin wearing nothing but her red ukulele and combat boots, or plotting to overthrow the music industry, I'm likely driving a carpool, collecting data, or, if it's Sunday, maybe even sitting in church.

But this book is not about seeing people from safe distances—that seductive place where most of us live, hide, and run to for what we think is emotional safety. *The Art of Asking* is a book about cultivating trust and getting as close as possible to love, vulnerability, and connection. Uncomfortably close. Dangerously close. Beautifully close. And uncomfortably close is exactly where we need to be if we want to transform this culture of scarcity and fundamental distrust.

Distance is a liar. It distorts the way we see ourselves and the way we understand each other. Very few writers can awaken us to that reality like Amanda. Her life and her career have been a study in intimacy and connection. Her lab is her love affair with her art, her community, and the people with whom she shares her life.

I spent most of my life trying to create a safe distance between me and anything that felt uncertain and anyone who could possibly hurt me. But like Amanda, I have learned that the best way to find light in the darkness is not by pushing people away but by falling straight into them.

As it turns out, Amanda and I aren't different at all. Not when you look close up—which is ultimately the only looking that matters when it comes to connection.

Family, research, church—these are the places I show up to with wild abandon and feel connected in my life. These are the places I turn to in order to crowdsource what I need: love, connection, and faith. And now, because of Amanda, when I'm weary or scared or need something from my communities, I ask. I'm not great at it, but I do it. And you know what I love more than anything about Amanda? Her honesty. She's not always great at asking either. She struggles like the rest of us. And it's in her stories of struggling to show up and be vulnerable that I most clearly see myself, my fight, and our shared humanity.

This book is a gift being offered to us by an uninhibited artist, a courageous innovator, a hardscrabble shitstarter—a woman who has the finely tuned and hard-fought ability to see into the parts of our humanity that need to be seen the most. Take the flower.

*W*HO'S GOT A TAMPON? I JUST GOT MY PERIOD, I will announce loudly to nobody in particular in a women's bathroom in a San Francisco restaurant, or to a co-ed dressing room of a music festival in Prague, or to the unsuspecting gatherers in a kitchen at a party in Sydney, Munich, or Cincinnati.

Invariably, across the world, I have seen and heard the rustling of female hands through backpacks and purses, until the triumphant moment when a stranger fishes one out with a kind smile. No money is ever exchanged. The unspoken universal understanding is:

Today, it is my turn to take the tampon.

Tomorrow, it shall be yours.

There is a constant, karmic tampon circle. It also exists, I've found, with Kleenex, cigarettes, and ballpoint pens.

I've often wondered: are there women who are just TOO embarrassed to ask? Women who would rather just roll up a huge wad of toilet paper into their underwear rather than dare to ask a room full of strangers for a favor? There must be. But not me. Hell no. I am totally not afraid to ask. For anything.

I am SHAMELESS.

I think.

. . .

I'm thirty-eight. I started my first band, The Dresden Dolls, when I was twenty-five, and didn't put out my first major-label record until I was twenty-eight, which is, in the eyes of the traditional music industry, a geriatric age at which to debut.

For the past thirteen years or so, I've toured constantly, rarely sleeping in the same place for more than a few nights, playing music for people nonstop, in almost every situation imaginable. Clubs, bars, theaters, sports arenas, festivals, from CBGB in New York to the Sydney Opera House. I've played entire evenings with my own hometown's world-renowned orchestra at Boston Symphony Hall. I've met and sometimes toured with my idols—Cyndi Lauper, Trent Reznor from Nine Inch Nails, David Bowie, "Weird Al" Yankovic, Peter from Peter, Paul and Mary. I've written, played, and sung hundreds of songs in recording studios all over the world.

I'm glad I started on the late side. It gave me time to have a real life, and a long span of years in which I had to creatively figure out how to pay my rent every month. I spent my late teens and my twenties juggling dozens of jobs, but I mostly worked as a living statue: a street performer standing in the middle of the sidewalk dressed as a white-faced bride. (You've seen us statue folk, yes? You've probably wondered who we are in Real Life. Greetings. We're Real.)

Being a statue was a job in which I embodied the pure, physical manifestation of asking: I spent five years perched motionless on a milk crate with a hat at my feet, waiting for passersby to drop in a dollar in exchange for a moment of human connection.

But I also explored other enlightening forms of employment in my early twenties: I was an ice cream and coffee barista working for $9.50 an hour (plus tips); an unlicensed massage therapist working out of my college dorm room (no happy endings, $35 per hour); a naming and branding consultant for dot-com companies ($2,000 per list of domain-cleared names); a playwright and director (usually unpaid: in fact, I usually lost my own money, buying props); a waitress in a German beer garden (about 75 deutsche marks a night, with tips); a vendor of clothes recycled from thrift shops and resold to my college campus center (I could make $50 a day); an assistant in a picture-framing shop ($14 per hour); an actress in experimental films (paid in joy, wine, and pizza); a nude drawing/painting model for art schools ($12 to $18 per hour); an organizer and hostess of donation-only underground salons (paid enough money to cover the liquor and event space); a clothes-check girl for illegal sex-fetish loft parties ($100 per party), and, through that job, a sewing assistant for a bespoke leather-handcuff manufacturer ($20 per hour); a stripper (about $50 per hour, but it really depended on the night); and—briefly—a dominatrix ($350 per hour—but there were, obviously, very necessary clothing and accessory expenses).

Every single one of these jobs taught me about human vulnerability.

Mostly, I learned a lot about asking.

Almost every important human encounter boils down to the act, and the art, of asking.

Asking *is*, in itself, the fundamental building block of any relationship. Constantly and usually indirectly, often wordlessly, we *ask* each other—our bosses, our spouses, our friends, our employees—in order to build and maintain our relationships with one another.

Will you help me?

Can I trust you?

Are you going to screw me over?

Are you suuuure I can trust you?

And so often, underneath it all, these questions originate in our basic, human longing to know:

Do you love me?

. . .

In 2012, I was invited to give a talk at the TED conference, which was daunting; I'm not a professional speaker. Having battled my way—very publicly—out of my major-label recording contract a few years earlier, I had decided that I'd look to my fans to make my next album through Kickstarter, a crowdfunding platform that had recently opened up the doors for thousands of other creators to finance their work with the direct backing of their supporters. My Kickstarter backers had spent a collective $1.2 million to preorder and pay for my latest full-band album, *Theatre Is Evil*, making it the biggest music project in crowdfunding history.

Crowdfunding, for the uninitiated, is a way to raise money for ventures (creative, tech, personal, and otherwise) by asking individuals (the Crowd) to contribute to one large online pool of capital (the Funding). Sites like Kickstarter, Indiegogo, and GoFundMe have cropped up all over the world to ease the transaction between those asking for help and those answering that call, and to make that transaction as practical as possible.

Like any new transactional tool, though, it's gotten complicated. It's become an online Wild West as artists and creators of all stripes try to navigate the weird new waters of exchanging money for art. The very existence of crowdfunding has presented us all with a deeper set of underlying questions:

How do we ask each other for help?
When can we ask?
Who's allowed to ask?

My Kickstarter was dramatically successful: my backers—almost twenty-five thousand of them—had been following my personal story for years. They were thrilled to be able to aid and abet my independence from a label. However, besides the breathless calls from reporters who'd never heard of me (not surprising since I'd never had an inch of ink in *Rolling Stone*) asking about why all these people helped me, I was surprised by some of the negative reactions to its success. As I launched my campaign, I walked right into a wider cultural debate that was already raging about whether crowdfunding should be allowed at all; some critics were dismissing it out of hand as a crass form of "digital panhandling."

Apparently, it was distasteful to ask. I was targeted as the worst offender for a lot of reasons: because I'd already been promoted by a major label, because I had a famous husband, because I was a flaming narcissist.

Things went from dark to darker in the months after my Kickstarter as I set off to tour the world with my band and put out my usual call to local volunteer musicians who might want to join us onstage for a few songs. We were a tight community, and I'd been doing things like that for years. I was lambasted in the press.

My crowdfunding success, plus the attention it drew, led TED to invite me, a relatively unknown indie rock musician, to talk for twelve minutes on a stage usually reserved for top scientists, inventors, and educators. Trying to figure out exactly what to say and how to say it was—to put it mildly—scary as shit.

I considered writing a twelve-minute performance-art opera, featuring ukulele and piano, dramatizing my entire life from The Womb to The Kickstarter. Fortunately, I decided against that and opted for a straightforward explanation of my experience as a street performer, my crowdfunding success and the ensuing backlash, and how I saw an undeniable connection between the two.

As I was writing it, I aimed my TED talk at a narrow slice of my social circle: my awkward, embarrassed musician friends. Crowdfunding was getting many of them excited but anxious. I'd been helping a lot of friends out with their own Kickstarter campaigns, and chatting with them about their experiences at local bars, at parties, in backstage dressing rooms before shows. I wanted to address a fundamental topic that had been troubling me: *To tell my artist friends that it was okay to ask. It was okay to ask for money, and it was okay to ask for help.*

Lots of my friends had already successfully used crowdfunding to make new works possible: albums, film projects, newfangled instruments, art-party barges made of recycled garbage—things that never would have existed without this new way of sharing and exchanging energy. But many of them were also struggling with it. I'd been watching.

Each online crowdfunding pitch features a video in which the creator explains their mission and delivers their appeal. I found myself cringing at the parade of crowdfunding videos in which my friends looked (or avoided looking) into the camera, stammering, *Okay, heh heh, it's AWKWARD TIME! Hi, everybody, um, here we go. Oh my god. We are so, so sorry to be asking, this is so embarrassing, but... please help us fund our album, because...*

I wanted to tell my friends it was not only *unnecessary* to act shame-ridden and apologetic, it was *counterproductive.*

I wanted to tell them that in truth, many people enthusiastically *loved* helping artists. That this wasn't a one-sided game. That working artists and their supportive audiences are two necessary parts in a complex ecosystem. That shame pollutes an environment of asking and giving that thrives on trust and openness. I was hoping I could give them some sort of cosmic, universal permission to stop over-apologizing, stop fretting, stop justifying, and for god's sake...just ASK.

. . .

I prepared for more than a month, pacing in the basement of a rented house and running my TED talk script past dozens of friends and family members, trying to condense everything I had to say into twelve minutes. Then I flew to Long Beach, California, took a deep breath, delivered the talk, and received a standing ovation. A few minutes after I got off the stage, a woman came up to me in the lobby of the conference center and introduced herself.

I was still in a daze. The talk had taken so much brain space to deliver, and I finally had my head back to myself.

I'm the speaker coach here, she began.

I froze. My talk was supposed to have been exactly twelve minutes. I'd paused a few times, and lost my place, and I'd gone well over thirteen. *Oh shit*, I thought. *TED is going to fire me.* I mean, they couldn't really *fire* me. The deed was done. But still. I shook her hand.

Hi! I'm really, really sorry I went so over the time limit. Really sorry. I got totally thrown. Was it okay, though? Did I TED well? Am I fired?

No, silly, you're not fired. Not at all. Your talk... And she couldn't go on. Her eyes welled up.

I stood there, baffled. Why was the TED speaker coach looking as if she was going to cry at me?

Your talk made me realize something I've been battling with for years. I'm also an artist, a playwright. I have so many people willing to help me, and all I have to do is... but I can't... I haven't been able to...

Ask?

Exactly. To ask. So simple. Your talk unlocked something really profound for me. Why the hell do we find it so hard to ask, especially if others are so willing to give? So, thank you. Thank you so much. Such a gift you gave.

I gave her a hug.

And she was just the first.

Two days later, the talk was posted to the TED site and YouTube. Within a day it had 100,000 views. Then a million. Then, a year later, eight million. It wasn't the view counts that astounded me: it was the stories that came with them, whether in online comments or from people who would stop me in the street and ask to share a moment, not because they knew my music, but because they recognized me from seeing the talk online.

The nurses, the newspaper editors, the chemical engineers, the yoga teachers, and the truck drivers who felt like I'd been speaking straight to them. The architects and the nonprofit coordinators and the freelance photographers who told me that they'd "always had a hard time asking." A lot of them held me, hugged me, thanked me, cried.

My talk had resonated way beyond its intended audience of sheepish indie rockers who found it impossible to ask for five bucks on Kickstarter without putting a bag over their heads.

I held everybody's hands, listened to their stories. The small-business owners, solar-panel designers, school librarians, wedding planners, foreign-aid workers...

One thing was clear: these people weren't scared musicians. They were just...a bunch of people.

I'd apparently hit a nerve. But WHAT nerve, exactly?

I didn't have a truly good answer for that until I thought back to Neil's house, to the night before our wedding party.

• • •

A few years before this all happened, I met Neil Gaiman.

Neil's famous, for a writer. He's famous for an anyone.

For years, Neil and I had chased each other around the globe in the cracks of our schedules, me on the Endless Road of Rock and Roll, him on the parallel road of Touring Writer, falling in love diagonally and at varying speed, before finally eloping in our friends' living room because we couldn't handle the stress of a giant wedding.

We didn't want to disrespect our families, though, so we promised them that we would throw a big, official family wedding party a few months later. We decided to do it in the UK, where the bulk of them live. (Neil is British, and so are a lot of my cousins.) Furthermore, the setting was magic: Neil owned a house on a teeny island in Scotland, which was coincidentally the birthplace of my maternal grandmother. It is a windswept, breathtaking-but-desolate grassy rock from which my ancestors fled in poverty-stricken terror in the early 1900s, seeking a brighter, less-breathtaking-but-less-desolate future overseas in the promising neighborhoods of the Bronx.

The night before the wedding party, Neil and I bedded down early to get a full night's sleep, anticipating an epic day of party organizing, eating, drinking, and nervously introducing two hundred family members to one another. Neil's three grown-up kids were staying in the house with us, along with Neil's mother and an assortment of Gaiman relatives. They were all snuggled away in their beds across the hall, up the stairs, a few stray young cousins roughing it in tents on the back lawn.

And on the second floor of the house, while Neil slept beside me, I was having a full-blown panic attack.

Somewhere down there I suppose I was freaking out about getting married, full stop. It was feeling very real all of sudden, with all the family around. What was I doing? Who *was* this guy?

But mostly, I was freaking out about money.

My Kickstarter was about to launch and I was pretty confident it would bring in plenty of cash—I'd crunched the numbers—but I wasn't on tour, I was in northern Scotland, throwing a wedding party and putting a new band together, earning nothing. I'd just had a talk with my accountant, who had informed me that I wasn't going to have enough money to cover my office staff, band, road crew, and regular monthly expenses unless I dropped everything and went back on the road immediately—or unless I took out a loan to bridge the gap for a few months before the Kickstarter and new touring checks arrived.

This wasn't an unfamiliar situation. To the recurring dismay of my managers, I'd already spent most of my adult life putting all of my business profits straight back into the next recording or art project once I had recovered my costs. In the course of my rocking-and-rolling career, I'd been rich, poor, and in-between . . . and never paid much attention to the running tally as long as I wasn't flat broke, which occasionally happened due to an unforeseen tax bill or the unexpected tanking of a touring show. And that was never the end of the world: I'd borrow money to get through a tight spot from friends or family and promptly pay it back when the next check came in.

I was an expert at riding that line and asking for help when I needed it, and, far from feeling ashamed of it, I prided myself on my spotless interpersonal credit history. I also took comfort in the fact that a lot of my musician friends (and business friends, for that matter) went through similar cycles of feast and famine. In short, it always worked out.

Only this time, there was a different problem. The problem was that *Neil* wanted to loan me the money.

And I wouldn't take the help.

We were *married*.

And I still couldn't take it.

Everybody thought I was weird not to take it.

But I *still* couldn't take it.

I'd been earning my own salary as a working musician for over a decade, had my own dedicated employees and office, paid my own bills, could get out of any bind on my own, and had always been financially independent from any person I was sleeping with. Not only that, I was celebrated for being an unshaven feminist icon, a DIY queen, the one who loudly left her label and started her own business. The idea of people *seeing* me taking help from my husband was...cringe-y. But I dealt, using humor. Neil would usually pick up the tab at nice restaurants, and we'd simply make light of it.

Totally fine with me, I'd joke. *You're richer.*

Then I'd make sure to pay for breakfast and the cab fare to the airport the next morning. It gave me a deep sense of comfort knowing that even if we shared some expenses here and there, I didn't *need* his money.

I knew the current gap I had to cover was a small one, I knew I was about to release my giant new crowdfunded record, I knew I was due to go back on tour, and everything logically dictated that this nice guy—to whom I was married—could loan me the money. And it was no big deal.

But I just. Couldn't. Do. It.

I'd chatted about this with Alina and Josh over coffee a few weeks before the wedding party. They were true intimates I'd gone to high school with, at whose own wedding I'd been the best man (our mutual friend Eugene had been the maid of honor) and we'd been sharing our personal dramas for years, usually while I was crashing on ever-nicer couches in their apartments as they moved from Hoboken to Brooklyn to Manhattan. We were taking turns bouncing their newborn baby, Zoe, on our laps, I had just told them that I didn't want to use any of Neil's money to cover my upcoming cash shortage, and they were looking at me like I was an idiot.

But that's so weird, Alina said. She's a songwriter and a published author. My situation wasn't foreign to her. *You guys are married.*

So what? I squirmed. *I just don't feel comfortable doing it. I don't know. Maybe I'm too afraid that my friends will judge me.*

*But, Amanda...**we're** you're friends,* Alina pointed out, *and **we** think you're crazy.*

Josh, the tenured philosophy professor, nodded in agreement, then looked at me with his typically furrowed brow.

How long do you think you'll keep it this way? Forever? Like, you'll be married for fifty years but you'll just never mix your incomes?

I didn't have an answer for that.

.   .   .

Neil wasn't the type to attach strings, or play games, but it was my deepest fear that I'd be somehow beholden, indebted to him.

This was a new feeling, this panic, or rather, an old one: I hadn't felt this freaked out since I was a teenager battling constant existential crises. But now my head was a vortex of questions: *How could I possibly take money from Neil? What would people think? Would he hold it over my head? Maybe I should just put this album off another year and tour? What would I do with the band I just hired? What about my staff? How would they deal? Why can't I just handle this gracefully?* **Why am I freaking out?**

I left the bed after an entire night of tossing and fretting. I went into the bathroom and turned on the light.

What is WRONG with you? I asked the puffy-eyed, snot-leaking, deranged person that was staring back at me from the mirror.

I dunno, she answered. *But this is not good.* I was scaring myself. What was happening to me? Was I crazy?

It was six a.m., the sun was just beginning to rise, and the sheep were baa-ing mournfully. We had to be awake at eight to drive to the wedding party.

I went back to bed and crawled into Neil's armpit. He was out cold, and snoring. I looked at him. I loved this man so much. We'd been together for over two years and I'd learned to trust him completely—trust him not to hurt me, not to judge me. But something still felt stuck shut, like a door that should open but just doesn't budge. I tossed my body to the other side of the bed and tried to sleep, but the cyclone of thoughts didn't stop. *You have to take his help. You can't take his help. You have to take his help.* And then I started to bawl, feeling completely out of control and foolish. I was tired of crying alone, I guess, and ready to talk.

Darling, what's wrong?

He's British. He calls me *darling.*

I…I'm freaking out.

I can see that. Is it the money thing? He put his arms around me.

I don't know what I'm going to do for these next few months, I snorfled. *I think I should put off making the record if I can't afford to pay everyone right now. I'll just tour for the next year and forget about the Kickstarter until…I don't know, I can probably borrow the money from someone else to get through the next few months… maybe I can…*

Why someone else? he interrupted quietly. *Amanda…we're married.*

So what?

So just get over it and borrow the money from me. Or TAKE the money from me. Why else did we get married? You'd do the same thing for me if I were in an in-between spot. Wouldn't you?

Of course I would.

So, what is HAPPENING? I'd much rather you let me cover you for a few months than see you in this state, it's getting disturbing. All you have to do is ASK me. I married you. I love you. I want to HELP. You won't let me help you.

I'm sorry. This is so weird—I've dealt with this shit so many times and it's never bothered me like this. It's crazy. I feel crazy. Neil, am I crazy?

You're not crazy, darling.

He held me. I *did* feel crazy. I couldn't rid myself of this one pounding, irritating thought, reverberating through my head like a bitter riddle, an impossible logic puzzle that I just couldn't shake off or solve.

I was an adult, for Christ's sake.

Who'd taken money from random people, on the street, for years.

Who openly preached the gospel of crowdfunding, community, help, asking, and random, delightful generosity.

Who could ask any stranger in the world—with a loud, brave laugh—for a tampon.

Why couldn't I ask my own husband for help?

. . .

We ask each other, daily, for little things: A quarter for the parking meter. An empty chair in a café. A lighter. A lift across town. And we must all, at one point or another, ask for the more difficult things: A promotion. An introduction to a friend. An introduction to a book. A loan. An STD test. A kidney.

If I learned anything from the surprising resonance of my TED talk, it was this:

Everybody struggles with asking.

From what I've seen, it isn't so much the act of asking that paralyzes us—it's what lies beneath: the fear of being vulnerable, the fear of rejection, the fear of looking needy or weak. The fear of being seen as a burdensome member of the community instead of a productive one.

It points, fundamentally, to our separation from one another.

American culture in particular has instilled in us the bizarre notion that to ask for help amounts to an admission of failure. But some of the most powerful, successful, admired people in the world seem, to me, to have something in common: they ask constantly, creatively, compassionately, and gracefully.

And to be sure: when you ask, there's always the possibility of a *no* on the other side of the request. If we don't allow for that *no*, we're not actually asking, we're either begging or demanding. But it is the fear of the *no* that keeps so many of our mouths sewn tightly shut.

Often it is our own sense that we are undeserving of help that has immobilized us. Whether it's in the arts, at work, or in our relationships, we often resist asking not only because we're afraid of rejection but also because we don't even think we *deserve* what we're asking for. We have to truly believe in the validity of what we're asking for—which can be incredibly hard work and requires a tight-rope walk above the doom-valley of arrogance and entitlement. And even after finding that balance, *how* we ask, and how we receive the answer—allowing, even embracing, the *no*—is just as important as finding that feeling of valid-ness.

When you examine the genesis of great works of art, successful start-ups, and revolutionary shifts in politics, you can always trace back a history of monetary and nonmonetary exchange, the hidden patrons and underlying favors. We may love the modern myth of Steve Jobs slaving away in his parents' garage to create the first Apple computer, but the biopic doesn't tackle the potentially awkward scene in which—probably over a macrobiotic meatloaf dinner—Steve had to *ask his parents for the garage.* All we know is that his parents said yes. And now we have iPhones. Every artist and entre-preneur I know has a story of a mentor, teacher, or unsung patron who loaned them money, space, or some kind of strange, ass-saving resource. Whatever it took.

I don't think I've perfected the art of asking, not by a long shot, but I can see now that I've been an unknowing apprentice of the art for ages—and what a long, strange trip it's been.

It started in earnest the day I painted myself white, put on a wed-ding gown, took a deep breath, and, clutching a fistful of flowers, climbed up onto a milk crate in the middle of Harvard Square.

You may have a memory of when you first, as a child, started connecting the dots of the world. Perhaps outside on a cold-spring-day school field trip, mud on your shoes, mentally straying from the given tasks at hand, as you began to find patterns and connections where you didn't notice them before. You may remember being excited by your discoveries, and maybe you held them up proudly to the other kids, saying:

*did you ever notice that **this** looks like **this**?*
the shapes on this leaf look like the cracks in this puddle of ice
which look like the veins on the back of my hand
which look like the hairs stuck to the back of her sweater...

Collecting the dots. Then connecting them. And then sharing the connections with those around you. This is how a creative human works. Collecting, connecting, sharing.

All artists work in different mediums, but they also differ when it comes to those three departments. Some artists love the act of *collecting*. We might call this experiencing, or emotionally and intellectually processing the world around us: the ingredients—the puddles of ice, the sweater—that go into the poetic metaphor. Or the wider and longer-term collection: the time it takes to fall in and out of love, so that you can describe it in song, or the time it takes a painter to gaze at a landscape before deciding to capture it on canvas. Or the nearly three years Thoreau needed to live simply on the side of a pond, watching sunrises and sunsets through the seasons, before he could give *Walden* to the world.

Some artists devote more time to *connecting* the dots they've already collected: think of a sculptor who hammers away for a year on a single statue, a novelist who works five years to perfect a story, or a musician who spends a decade composing a single symphony—connecting the dots to attain the perfect piece of art. Thoreau himself needed another three years *after* his time in the cabin to distill and connect his experiences into the most beautiful and direct writing possible.

Like most stage performers, I've always been most passionate about the final phase: the *sharing*. There are lots of ways to share. Writers share when someone else reads or listens to their words in a book, a blog, a tweet. Painters share by hanging their work, or by sliding the sketchbook to a friend across the coffee-shop table. Stage performers also collect and connect (in the form of experiencing, writing, creating, and rehearsing), but there is a different kind of joy in that moment of human-to-human transmission: from you to the eyes and ears of an audience, whether fireside at a party or on a stage in front of thousands. I'm a sharing addict. But no matter the scale or setting, one truth remains: the act of sharing, especially when you're starting out, is fucking difficult.

There's always a moment of extreme bravery involved in this question:

. . . will you look?

It starts when you're little. Back in the field: the veins of the leaf looked like your hand, and you said it, out loud, to the kids walking next to you.

You may have seen the lights go on in their eyes, as you shared your discovery—*Whoa, you're right! Cool*—and felt the first joys of sharing with an audience. Or you may have been laughed at by your friends and scolded by the teacher, who explained, patiently:

Today isn't "looking for patterns" day.

This is not the time for that.

This is the time to get back in line, to fill in your worksheet, to answer the correct questions.

But your urge was to connect the dots and share, because *that,* not the worksheet, is what interested you.

This impulse to connect the dots—and to share what you've connected—is the urge that makes you an artist. If you're using words or symbols to connect the dots, whether you're a "professional artist" or not, you are an artistic force in the world.

When artists work well, they connect people to themselves, and they stitch people to one another, through this shared experience of discovering a connection that wasn't visible before.

*Have you ever noticed that **this** looks like **this**?*

And with the same delight that we took as children in seeing a face in a cloud, grown-up artists draw the lines between the bigger dots of grown-up life: sex, love, vanity, violence, illness, death.

Art pries us open. A violent character in a film reflects us like a dark mirror; the shades of a painting cause us to look up into the sky, seeing new colors; we finally weep for a dead friend when we hear that long-lost song we both loved come unexpectedly over the radio waves.

I never feel more inspired than when watching another artist explode their passionate craft into the world—most of my best songs were written in the wake of seeing other artists bleed their hearts onto the page or the stage.

Artists connect the dots—we don't need to interpret the lines between them. We just draw them and then present our connections to the world as a gift, to be taken or left. This IS the artistic act, and it's done every day by many people who don't even think to call themselves artists.

Then again, some people are crazy enough to think they can make a living at it.

THE PERFECT FIT

I could make a dress
A robe fit for a prince
I could clothe a continent
But I can't sew a stitch

I can paint my face
And stand very very still
It's not very practical
But it still pays the bills

I can't change my name
But I could be your type
I can dance and win at games
Like backgammon and Life

I used to be the smart one
Sharp as a tack
Funny how that skipping years
    ahead
Has held me back

I used to be the bright one
Top in my class
Funny what they give you
    when you
Just learn how to ask

I can write a song
But I can't sing in key
I can play piano
But I never learned to read

I can't trap a mouse
But I can pet a cat
No, I'm really serious!
I'm really very good at that

I can't fix a car
But I can fix a flat
I could fix a lot of things
But I'd rather not get into
    that

I used to be the bright one
Smart as a whip
Funny how you slip so far
    when
Teachers don't keep track
    of it

I used to be the tight one
The perfect fit
Funny how those compliments
    can
Make you feel so full of it

I can shuffle, cut, and deal
But I can't draw a hand
I can't draw a lot of things
I hope you understand
I'm not exceptionally shy
But I've never had a man
That I could look straight in
    the eye
And tell my secret plans

I can take a vow
And I can wear a ring
And I can make you promises
    but
They won't mean a thing

Can't you just do it for
    me, I'll pay you well
Fuck, I'll pay you anything if
    you could end this

Can't you just fix it for
    me, it's gone berserk,
Fuck, I'll give you anything if
You can make the damn thing
    work

Can't you just fix it for
    me, I'll pay you well,
Fuck, I'll pay you anything
If you can end this
Hello, I love you won't you
    tell me your name?
Hello, I'm good for nothing

will you
love
me
just
the
same

—from *The Dresden Dolls*, 2003

I was twenty-two, I'd just graduated from college, and I really, *really* didn't want to get a job.

Don't get me wrong: I wasn't lazy. I wanted to *work*. But I had no desire to get a JOB job.

Growing up as an über-emotional teenage songwriter and theater nerd, I faced a bewildering and bottomless chasm between what I wanted to become—*a Real Artist*—and how one actually, well... *becomed* it. Though I worshipped daily at the altar of MTV, I didn't know any famous musicians, so I couldn't ask them how they had becomed. I didn't even know any non-famous musicians. All the adults I'd ever encountered—my parents, my friends' parents—all had "grown-up" jobs: mysterious, complicated, white-collar jobs, jobs in tall buildings, jobs that involved computers, jobs about which I understood absolutely nothing and in which I had no interest.

When people asked me What I Wanted To Be When I Grew Up, I'd lie and try to just give them the most impressive answer I could think of: A lawyer! A doctor! An architect! An astronaut! A veterinarian! (I liked my cat. I figured I qualified.)

The truth just sounded too stupid. I wanted to be a Rock Star. Not a pop star. A ROCK STAR. An artistic one, a cool one. Like Prince. Like Janis Joplin. Like Patti Smith. Like the dudes in The Cure. The ones who looked like they Lived Their Art. I loved playing the piano, I loved writing songs, and I knew that if I had any choice in the matter, THAT'S the job I wanted.

But I had no clue how anybody got such a job, or what being a wage-earning artist meant in practical terms. I'd barely caught a glimpse of a working artist in his or her natural habitat until I attended my first rock concert at the age of eleven and saw that Cyndi Lauper was a real person. Until that moment, I had been suspicious that Cyndi Lauper, Prince, and Madonna were, in fact, being convincingly played by actors.

Furthermore, the liberal arts education that my parents had generously broken their backs to be able to afford, because they considered it a crucial necessity for "survival in the real world," had done a shocking amount of nothing to prepare me for the cold truth of my chosen career path.

Not that college was all impractical theory or wasted time, and I harbor no regrets. I learned how to hand-develop my own film in a darkroom. I learned the basics of theatrical lighting design. I studied Chaucer, John Cage, postmodern performance art, post-WWII German experimental filmmakers and Post-Apocalyptic/Eschatological Beliefs Throughout A Variety Of World Religions And Fictional Genres. I even learned—not in the classroom, of course—how to construct a potato cannon that could shoot as far as 250 feet (the distance to the rival dorm across the street) using a long piece of PVC piping, and a bottle of Aqua Net extra-hold hairspray. (And a potato.)

I also learned over those four years that a diet of hummus, cookies, and cereal makes you fat, that it's impossible to tap a keg unless it's been properly chilled, and that DJ-ing a college radio show from three to five in the morning doesn't expand your social circle one iota. And that heroin kills people.

But I did *not* learn how to be a rock star, or, for that matter, an employable, wage-earning bohemian; Wesleyan University did not offer any practical courses in that department. And there didn't seem to be anybody hanging around that I could ask.

Now I was done, I had the degree, I'd made my family happy. And after enrolling, panicking, and quickly withdrawing from a full-ride scholarship to get my master's degree in "anything I wanted" at Heidelberg University (I'd figured out, by that point, that academia was making me miserable, and drunk), I flew home to Boston from Germany with two giant suitcases and no real plan about how to Start My Real Life.

I considered my situation:

I knew I wanted to be a musician.

I knew I didn't want a Real Job.

I knew I had pay for food and a place to live.

I took a barista job, rented a room in a dilapidated share house in Somerville, Massachusetts, and decided I'd be a statue.

• • •

Toscanini's Ice Cream, where I worked as a sorbet-scooping espresso puller along with a motley bunch of twentysomethings, was a local operation with three Cambridge locations owned and lovingly managed by an incredible guy named Gus Rancatore. A humble press quote permanently etched into the front window of the store read:

"THE BEST ICE CREAM IN THE WORLD"—THE NEW YORK TIMES.

The baristas were assured four shifts a week at $9.50 an hour plus tips, which was enough to live on, and everyone who worked there ate a lot of ice cream, which was free to the employees.

My expenses included rent ($350 a month), food other than ice cream (I could survive on about $100 a month), and the extras: cigarettes, beer, records, bike repairs, and occasionally, clothes. I'd never had expensive taste and bought most of my wardrobe at the dollar-a-pound section of a used clothing store in Cambridge called The Garment District, which is where I found The Dress.

Building the statue was easy: I poked around the vintage shops trying to spot an inspiring, long-sleeved, high-necked, monochromatic costume fit for a statue, and found an antique bridal gown that fit the bill and cost only $29. *PERFECT*, I thought. I'd be a *bride*. All white. Easy. Sorrowful. Mysterious. *Coy. Compelling.* WISTFUL! How could anyone hate a bride?

I also bought some white face paint, a full-length lace veil, and a pair of long, white opera gloves. Then I went to the wig shop and completed my ensemble with a black Bettie-Page-style bob. I bought a glass vase from a thrift shop and spray-painted it white on the sidewalk outside of my apartment.

I started the next day.

I decided it would be perfect to hand out flowers as little tokens of gratitude, but I didn't know exactly how many I would need. I certainly wasn't going to *buy* flowers when they were growing freely all up and down the Charles River—I had spent the last of my savings on the getup and was pretty much broke.

So I took an hour-long amble along the banks of the river that flowed gracefully alongside the Harvard dorms, feeling very entrepreneurial, resourceful, *and* bohemian, picking any flower with an actual blossom that looked presentable until I had about fifty. I harvested three stray milk crates from an alleyway, ducked into the employees-only bathroom in the basement of Toscanini's, and donned my costume.

Then, heart slamming, I ventured into the main intersection of Harvard Square. Please picture this moment: I was walking on a standard city sidewalk, on a hot summer day, in a bridal gown with my face painted white, carrying three milk crates, wearing a black wig and clompy, black German combat boots. I got stares.

I selected a relatively well-trafficked spot on the brick sidewalk in front of the subway station, arranged my milk crates in a pyramid, covered the crate-pedestal with a spare white skirt, clambered atop, straightened my back, raised my spray-painted vase full of wildflowers in the air, and . . . stood still.

．　．　．

The first few moments up there were terrifying.

I felt stupid, actually.

Vulnerable. Silly.

It was lucky that I was covered in white face paint—my face burned bright red beneath it for the first ten minutes, I could feel it.

The sheer absurdity of what I was doing was not lost on me.

You're painted white and standing on a box.
You're painted white and standing on a box.
You are painted white and you are STANDING ON A BOX.
You are so full of shit.

My mantra of masochism broke the minute the first few people curiously wandered up to me. A small crowd formed at a respectful distance and a five-year-old boy approached me, wide-eyed. Into the empty hat at my feet, he cautiously placed the dollar his mother had given him.

I jerked my arms alive, as if in shock, dramatically hovered my hand above my white-painted vase, gazed at him, then selected and silently handed him one of the flowers.

He shrieked with delight.

It worked.

Then somebody else put a dollar in.

Then another.

Then another.

At the end of an hour, the bouquet of flowers was gone.

I climbed down. I schlepped my crates back to Toscanini's, stashed them furtively in the basement, said hi to my co-workers, slipped behind the counter to make myself an iced coffee with a scoop of free hazelnut ice cream, and sat down at one of the little metal tables outside the shop to count my hat. There was some loose change, but mostly bills. Someone had thrown in a five.

I had made $38 in an hour. On a good tip day at the store, I made $75. In six hours.

I washed my face in the bathroom and walked back to the center of the Square, with the wad of dollar bills in my pocket.

Right at the intersection of Mass Ave and JFK Street, it hit me. I stopped short, stunned by the realization of what had just happened:

I can do this as a job.

I can do this every day that it's warm and not rainy.

If I just made thirty-eight dollars in an hour, I can work three hours and make about a hundred dollars in a day.

I don't have to scoop ice cream anymore.
I can make my own schedule.
I don't have to have a boss.
Nobody can ever fire me.
I WILL NEVER HAVE TO HAVE A REAL JOB AGAIN.
And technically?
I never really did.

. . .

I had dipped my toe into the living statuary experience before, albeit briefly. While drinking seriously, studying casually, and waitressing part-time at a beer garden (free beer!) during a year abroad in a sleepy little German town called Regensburg, I'd decided to try supplementing my income with a beta-version of The Bride: a trippy, white-faced, wheel-of-fortune ballerina statue I named Princess Roulette. I stood frozen in the center of a chalk pie chart I drew in the cobblestoned town square. I'd divided it up into eight sections, each with its own little prop or basket, and I'd wait for a stranger to place a coin in my hat, at which point I'd close my eyes, spin in a circle, and land with a jerk, pointing at a random space. I'd then mechanically proffer up a small gift (an exotic coin, a candy, an antique key), unless, of course, I'd landed in one of the "suicide" spots, in which case I mimed a clownish mini-tragedy, killing myself with a variety of prop weapons. I would spin, stop, open my eyes, trudge slowly over to the waiting bottle of poison while looking incredibly somber, wipe an imaginary tear from my eye, pick up the bottle, drink its invisible contents, and then fall to the cobblestones, gagging and twitching. (I also had a toy gun.) Once I had achieved full corpse pose, I would hope for applause, get up, dust off my glittery tutu, and jauntily return to my frozen position in the center.

It was whimsical but grisly, sort of *Harold and Maude* meets Marcel Marceau. The Germans didn't quite know how to react.

One landing spot was neither gift nor suicide: it was the "tea set," which was supposed to be a jackpot of sorts. If I landed there, I'd grab the hand of my victim, whom I would wordlessly invite to sit on the ground to enjoy an imaginary cup of mime-tea using a vintage collection of cracked cups and saucers I'd bought at a flea market. I assumed that this activity would be utterly thrilling to every passerby. I was sorely disappointed by the fact that not every German took me up on my theatrical offer to enjoy a cup of mime-tea. What gave?

It never occurred to me that staging my own comic suicide with different props in the middle of a small-town plaza and inviting strangers to sit on the ground probably wasn't the most effective way to win the hearts and deutsche marks of Bavarian families out on their Sunday strolls.

Princess Roulette quickly taught me a lot about the practicalities and economics of being a living statue/performance artist, and a little bit about Germans. The biggest takeaways:

1- It is *not* profitable to give someone a Thing that cost you two deutsche marks if the person you are giving it to only gives you fifty pfennigs.

2- If you are Performing an Action in exchange for Money, and each Action takes two minutes, and obnoxious eight-year-old Bavarian boys are putting ten-pfennig coins in your basket one after the other while people with real deutsche marks look on with amusement, you are not Maximizing your Performance Time.

3- Germans wearing nice clothes do not like to sit on the ground.

Although I performed as Princess Roulette only four or five times, I quickly learned that the relationship between a street performer and the street audience is a delicate one, one that adheres to a different contract than the one that exists between the stage performer and the ticket-buying audience. There's a much greater element of risk and trust on both sides.

I learned this the hard way on my very first day, when a friendly-looking man in his thirties walked by with his toddler daughter. Parents out on walks with their curious children are a godsend to street performers; they take great pleasure in supplying their kids with hat money and watching as their offspring experience a spontaneous, magical, and fully supervised interaction-with-a-stranger.

This one, however, went a bit pear-shaped. The dad put a coin into my hat and I began spinning. As I opened my eyes, I saw that the little girl had wandered over to one of my roulette baskets and had helped herself to a huge handful of my gift candy. Upon seeing this, I was at a loss. This child was stealing my candy. I had never anticipated this problem. After considering, briefly, what the correct action was for my character, I looked the little three-year-old girl straight in the eye and, breaking my mime-silence, pretended to cry. Quietly, but committedly, I emitted a high-pitched, but measured, anguished whine of agony over the loss of my candy.

This was *not* the correct thing to do.

The little girl proceeded to burst into ACTUAL tears and let forth her own (far less measured) wail, and for a split second, our collective, pack-like moan of anguish in that little town square in Germany sounded like some kind of epic, Wagnerian cry of broken, senseless human loss and suffering...

WHY??

I stood frozen, in shock, as the horrified father scooped his emotionally assaulted daughter into his arms and flashed me that universally heartbreaking glare that says, *WHAT HAVE YOU DONE TO MY CHILD?*

I felt really guilty, like I'd scarred this child for life and drained the joy out of any future trust-based interactions she might have with any street performers, actors, mimes, or human beings.

I also felt—and this was a new emotion—like a bad *artist*.

In that moment, something seismic shifted. I'd been viewing my role on the street as a performance artist who would share the gift of her weird, arty impulses with the amenable public. I'd grown up an experimental theater kid, writing, directing, and acting in my own surreal and morbid plays on school stages. I wasn't an entertainer— I was making *art,* dammit. And though I wasn't afraid to disturb people, I never wanted to *hurt* them.

This interaction made me realize that working in The Street wasn't like working in the theater. The Street is different: nobody's buying a ticket, nobody's choosing to be there. On the street, artists succeed or fail by virtue of their raw ability to create a show in unexpected circumstances, to thoroughly entertain an audience that did not expect to be one, and to make random people *care* for a few minutes. The passersby are trusting you to give them something valuable in exchange for *their* time and attention, and (possibly) their dollars. Something skilled, unexpected, delightful, impressive, something moving. With few exceptions, they're not giving you a dollar to confront and disturb them.

That dad and his little girl didn't want *theater.*

They didn't want to be provoked.

They wanted to be entertained.

But they also wanted something more. They wanted *connection.*

It dawned on me, standing there in my white face paint and tutu, that I was effectively working in a service position: A strange combination of court jester, cocktail hostess, and minister. A strange, coin-operated jukebox of basic, kind, human encounters.

．　．　．

I learned a lesson on my first day of Bride-ing: standing on a plastic milk crate becomes REALLY uncomfortable after a few minutes as you sink slowly into the middle. It's hell on your knees.

I would stand with my combat-boot-clad feet locked in place for half an hour, until the position became intolerable and I had to move. I would wait until I was between crowds, and then imperceptibly shift my weight from foot to foot, finding a new part of the crate to stand on. A few days later, I figured out that I could solve this problem by capping the milk crate with a square of hard plywood.

In my mute, frozen state, time and space took on a fascinating new quality, measured from one liberated movement to another, and I created an internal spoken dialogue with the world around me. I figured that if I said things loud enough in my head, the message would shoot out through my eyes.

Hi.

I'd blink my eyes a bit, and regard my new human friend, while they regarded me.

As they dropped money in my hat, I would lock my eyes onto theirs, and think:

Thank you.
blink
Here. Take a flower.
blink
And if I was in a particularly good mood:
I love you.
blink

•   •   •

What I hadn't anticipated was the sudden, powerful encounters with people—especially lonely people who looked like they hadn't connected with anyone in ages. I was amazed by the intimate moments of prolonged eye contact happening on the busy city sidewalk as traffic whizzed by, as sirens blared, as street vendors hawked their wares and activists thrust flyers at every passerby, as bedraggled transients tried to sell the local homeless community newspaper to rushing commuters...where more than a second or two of a direct, silent gaze between strangers is usually verboten.

My eyes would say:
Thank you. I see you.

And their eyes would say:
Nobody ever sees me.
Thank you.

. . .

Late one night at a yoga retreat a few years ago, a teacher asked a group of us to try to remember the first instance in our childhoods when we noticed that things were, for lack of a more clinical term, "not okay." My answer was so quick to come and so deeply revealing that it made me laugh out loud. It is, in fact, my earliest intact memory. I was three.

There was a tall wooden staircase in our home, and one day I toppled all the way from the second floor to the first. I sharply remember that *Am I going to die?* slow-motion panic as I tumbled head over heels in a bouncing, cartoon blur. I was uninjured, but the fall had been traumatizing, and I ran, weeping and discombobulated, into the kitchen to recount the epic incident to my family.

Here's what I remember.[1] The kitchen was full of people: my mother, probably my stepfather, maybe my three older siblings, maybe some other random adults.

And none of them believed me.

They thought I was making it up. Trying to get attention. Exaggerating. Dramatizing.

And there I was, thirty-two years old, at a yoga retreat, desperately trying to find myself, and realizing that everything I'd been doing in my life, artistically, could be summed up like this:

PLEASE BELIEVE ME. I'M REAL. NO REALLY, IT HAPPENED. IT HURT.

---

1. Writer disclaimer: My mother is totally going to read this book and she's probably going to call me after she reads this part and so I am going to preemptively tell her right here that I love her and this probably didn't even happen even though I think I remember it and it's really important to the story. HI MOM.

And I sat there and laughed and laughed.

And cried. And laughed. At myself.

It was so embarrassing.

I laughed thinking about all the ridiculous stunts I'd pulled as an introverted, angry, punk teenager, dressing like an outlandish freak but being too insecure and afraid to talk to anybody. I laughed thinking about myself as an antisocial college senior who plonked her naked-and-covered-in-stage-blood body onto different spots around campus pretending to be dead as part of her postmodern performance art thesis, attempting to elicit *some* sort of reaction from the other students.

PLEASE. BELIEVE ME. I'M REAL. IT HURTS.

I laughed at the canon of heart-wrenching piano songs I'd written as a teenager, which added up to one screaming, pounding, screaming, pounding manifesto with a single, unified theme:

PLEASE. BELIEVE ME. I'M REAL.

I laughed thinking about the hundreds of hours I'd spent standing on a box, gazing silently and wistfully at passersby, handing them flowers in exchange for money. I laughed thinking about working in strip clubs during that same period, gyrating to Nick Cave and staring into the eyes of lonely, drunken strangers, challenging them to look into my soul instead of my crotch:

PLEASE. BELIEVE ME. I'M REAL.

I laughed thinking about all the nights I'd howled on concert hall stages, screaming those same old teenage songs at the top of my lungs, as aggressively and honestly and *believably* as I possibly could, to the point that I lost my voice almost every single night for a year and had to get surgery to cut away the rough, red nodes that had grown on my vocal cords as a result of too much yelling:

PLEASE. BELIEVE ME.

I laughed thinking about every single artist I knew—every writer, every actor, every filmmaker, every crazed motherfucker who had decided to forgo a life of predictable income, upward mobility, and simple tax returns, and instead pursued a life in which they made their living trying to somehow turn their dot-connecting brains inside out and show the results to the world—and how, maybe, it all boiled down to one thing:

BELIEVE ME.

Believe me.

I'm real.

. . .

Here's the thing: all of us come from some place of wanting to be seen, understood, accepted, connected.

Every single one of us wants to be believed.

Artists are often just...louder about it.

. . .

At that same yoga retreat, we stood and faced each other in pairs, really looking at each other from a close distance. We were told to simply BE with the other person, maintaining eye contact, with no social gestures like laughing, smiling, or winking to put ourselves at ease.

Grown women and men cried. Really and truly sobbed.

When we were finished with the exercise, we talked about how it had felt. The thread echoed again and again: many people had never felt so *seen* by another person. Seen without walls, without judgment....just seen, acknowledged, accepted. The experience was—for so many—painfully rare.

. . .

Even cynical people got caught up in the romance of The Bride. People have a Thing with Brides.

I suppose I banked on this when I bought the dress. Who could hate a BRIDE?

There's something magical, pure, beautiful. The virgin. The holy. The hopeful. Whatever.

I spent a lot of time on that box enjoying the irony of the fact that

I was a bride for a living, stuck in this dress, while philosophically I knew I didn't want to get married. Ever.

All my parents, stepparents, and exes-of-stepparents, the whole lot of them, looked crazy to me. Why keep getting married and divorced, people? Why not just DATE?

I would not make their mistake. Even if I was in love.

I wanted to be free. Unfettered.

Marriage always looked like hell to me.

. . .

When a stranger put money into the hat, I would try to emanate an immense amount of gratitude for this savior who had momentarily freed me from my frozen pose. I wouldn't look at the donor immediately. I would be coy. I would look at the sky. I would look at the crowd. I would look at the street. I would look at my vase. And then, once I had selected the perfect flower with as much graceful fluidity as possible, I would finally gaze at my new friend, never smiling with my mouth but always with my eyes, and lean my body forward ever so slightly, holding out the flower delicately clutched between my thumb and forefinger.

This always reminded me of the act of communion: that small, quiet, intimate moment when the priest proffers the wafer, intimately instructing you to ingest the body of Christ. (I was pretty bored in church as a kid, but I always loved that ritual. I also liked the singing bits.)

So, a dollar into the hat. I would gaze lovingly at my new human friend, my head filling up with a little silent monologue that sounded something like this:

The body of Christ, the cup of salvation.

Regard this holy flower, human friend.

Take it, it's for you. A gift from my heart.

Oh, you want a picture? Okay! We can take a picture.

I'll just hold this flower and wait while your girlfriend gets out her camera.

The body of Christ, the cup of salvation. The flower of patience.

Oh. I see your girlfriend's camera batteries are dead.

Now your other friend is getting his camera out.

This is all fine. Because I am the picture of Zen and in the moment.

The body of Christ, the cup of salvation, the flower of forgiveness.

So come to me, human friend! Nuzzle into the folds of my white gown, we will pose together. With love.

Oh, new human friend, your friend with the camera is drunk, isn't he?

May he find peace. May he find solace. May he find the shutter button.

Okay. Now you finally have your picture and you have high-fived your drunken friend.

Now please take this flower I have been holding out to you. My sacrament.

The body of Christ, the cup of salvation, the flower of oneness and joy and . . .

HEY.

Why are you walking away?

I have a flower for you!

A gift! A holy token of love!

The body of Christ!!

TAKE THE FUCKING FLOWER.

For real, dude . . . you don't want my flower?

Jesus okay fine.

I will just hang my head in sorrowful shame for all that is wrong with the world.

As he walked away, I would hang my head in sorrowful shame for all that was wrong with the world.

And if I was, by my own estimation, nailing my job, everybody watching this interaction on the sidewalk would shout after the dude, as he walked away with his drunk friend and girlfriend:

HEY! HEY YOU!! SHE'S GOT A FLOWER FOR YOU!!! TAKE THE FLOWER!!!!

The dude would usually bend to the peer pressure and come back to take it. But not always.

Sometimes I just had to let him go.

Girls, for the record, almost always took the flower. The ones who refused? Sometimes they seemed to think they were doing me a favor by rejecting the flower, gesturing:

No, no! I couldn't possibly! Keep it for someone else!

But they didn't understand that they were breaking my heart. Gifting them my flower—my holy little token—was what made me feel like an artist, someone with something to offer, instead of a charity case.

Over the years, though, I got used to it, and instead of taking it personally, I began to understand:

Sometimes people just don't want the flower.

Sometimes you have to let them walk away.

• • •

Joshua Bell, a world-class violinist, teamed up with the *Washington Post* for a social experiment in which he played his $3.5 million Stradivarius one morning in the L'Enfant Plaza subway station in Washington, DC. During his performance, which ran about forty-five minutes, seven people stopped to listen for a minute or more, twenty-seven contributed money, and he made a total of $32 (not counting the $20 thrown in his hat by the one woman who recognized him). More than a thousand people had walked by him without stopping.

In the aftermath, it was easy for many people to shake their heads at the perceived shame of it all: how could music so *valuable*—some of these same people might be paying as much as $150 a ticket to watch him play the same program at the local symphony hall the following night—become so *worthless* on the street?

But if you watch the hidden camera footage of the stunt, and note the time of day (morning rush hour) and the demographics (busy government employees on their way to work), it starts to make more sense. Those mindless barbarians who had no idea what they were witnessing were commuters on their way to work who couldn't afford to stop at that exact moment to appreciate art. Certain art hungers for context. We can't blame these passersby; we can simply applaud and feel gratitude for the few people who slowed and cocked their heads, heard the voice of god speaking via Bach speaking via Josh Bell's Stradivarius, and feel joy and hope that a few folks actually threw in a dollar or two.

As for me, it took a few months of hardcore statue work to really find my footing and develop this sense of deep gratitude for the sliver of the population, however small, that was willing to tune their head frequencies to the Art Channel for a moment, interrupting their march to work.

That ongoing sense of appreciation shaped my constitution in a fundamental way. I didn't *just* feel a fleeting sense of thanks for each generous person who stopped; I had been hammered into a gratitude-shaped vessel and would never take for granted those willing to slow down and connect.

• • •

There is a certain sense of indiscriminate gratitude that is essential to hone if you're going to survive in the arts. You can't really afford to be choosy about your audience, nor about how they wish to repay you for your art. In cash? In help? In kindness?

Each of these currencies possesses a distinct value. Dita Von Teese, a star in the contemporary burlesque scene, once recounted something she'd learned in her early days stripping in LA. Her colleagues—bleach-blond dancers with fake tans, Brazilian wax jobs, and neon bikinis—would strip bare naked for an audience of fifty guys in the club and be tipped a dollar by each guy. Dita would take the stage wearing satin gloves, a corset, and a tutu, and do a sultry striptease down to her underwear, confounding the crowd. And then, though forty-nine guys would ignore her, one would tip her fifty dollars.

That man, Dita said, was her audience.

This is exactly what I learned standing on the box, then while playing in bars in my first band, and, later, when I turned to crowd-funding. It was essential to feel thankful for the few who stopped to watch or listen, instead of wasting energy on resenting the majority who passed me by.

Feeling gratitude was a skill I honed on the street and dragged along with me into the music industry. I never aimed to please everyone who walked by, or everyone listening to the radio. All I needed was...*some* people. Enough people. Enough to make it worth coming back the next day, enough to make rent and put food on the table. And enough so I could keep making art.

• • •

It is an interesting thing, a white-painted face. It's a historically rich signifier, the onion layer of clown-white cream covering the skin like a paper-thin mask, a universal invitation from one human being to another that says:

Staring at my face and making eye contact is acceptable and encouraged.

Only now do I realize why it made so much sense to keep the white face paint as I transitioned from being a statue to being in a rock band. Our Weimar-cabaret-inspired makeup was a signature of The Dresden Dolls. Often mocked (especially by the other plaid-clad indie Boston bands who referred to us as "the gay mime band"), often misunderstood (by the journalists who asked what our alter egos, à la Ziggy Stardust or Alice Cooper, were supposed to "represent"), and often seen reproduced on the faces of our hardcore fans as a symbol of solidarity, the white face paint functioned as a freak flag.

I liked giving permission to people to look at my face. Not so much because I wanted them to LOOK AT ME LOOK AT ME LOOK AT ME, but because I wanted them to feel invited to meet my gaze and share a moment. And I knew the game worked. I knew that, having invited them into my face like a host invites a guest into a kitchen, I would be equally invited to look back into theirs. Then we could see each other. And in that place lies the magic.

I see you.

BELIEVE ME.

Ask any great actor: sometimes the mask is the tool that lets you get at the truth.

. . .

There is something about silence.

One night in a candlelit restaurant in San Francisco, shortly after we got married, I asked Neil if we could just write each other notes during the whole meal. In real time, like texting, but with pens and paper.

The waiter thought we were slightly strange, but by the end of the meal we'd shared a degree of intimate information that we probably wouldn't have if we'd just been sitting there chatting. And we could illustrate our points with pie charts and cartoons. And we really enjoyed our food, because we weren't literally talking through it.

The couple next to us asked what we were doing, and when we told them, they ordered a pad of paper and two pens from the waiter.

. . .

One of the things I loved best about The Bride was how, though she was silent, she could make it possible for people to talk to one another.

I was a ready-made conversation piece. And nothing delighted me more than to see people with nothing in common chatting about The Bride the way they'd chat about an ambulance pulling up, or a flash thunderstorm.

Excuse me, is that a person?

Dude, is that a real person?

Wow, is that a real statue?

Oh, look! What does he do when you give him money?

There are ingredients that create safe space for communion. It would make me absolutely beam with joy when I saw strangers giving each other money, saying:

Wait, hey! Take this dollar, put it in her hat! You gotta see this! That's a real person!

It gave me faith in humanity. Even if they thought I was in drag.

*　•　•　•*

Anthony was my best friend.

I've been trying, since I was a kid, to explain to people exactly WHAT he was to me when I was growing up. He wasn't quite my guru, wasn't quite my parent, wasn't quite my teacher.

I usually attempted to describe him by mumbling something that included the word "mentor," but I mostly found myself satisfied with this run-on portrait: *Anthony met me when I was nine and taught me everything I know about love and knows me better than anybody and we still talk almost every single day even if I'm touring in Japan.*

He loved telling the story of one of our first interactions, soon after he moved in next door to my parents' house on the quiet road where I grew up in Lexington, Massachusetts.

It was a winter night, after a big snowfall in our little suburban neighborhood, and he and his wife, Laura, were throwing a dinner party. I ambled across my lawn over to his and started pelting their window with snowballs. I thought it was funny. He did, too, sort of.

He came to the door.

I want a snowball fight, I said.

I can't, he said. *But I'll get you back later.*

And he returned to the dinner party, back into the warmth and fire and wine of the adult world behind him.

Then, according to the story, I returned about twenty minutes later, and started pelting their giant picture window with snowballs a second time.

He came to the door again.

What the hell?

You said you'd get me later, I said. *I'm here to get gotten.*

Amanda, it's been twenty minutes, he said. *I meant later... like... tomorrow.*

I don't actually remember this happening, but I know the story by heart, because he's told it so many times. I also don't remember the first time I hugged him, but he tells that story, too.

I was thirteen, and our relationship had evolved from occasional next-door-neighbor snowball enemies to full-on pals. He claims we were standing in his driveway and something had happened that merited An Actual Hug.

But we had never hugged, and I was, according to him, *interested* in the idea, but wasn't used to hugging. So I leaned my body against his, he says, like a slowly falling pine tree, letting my head rest on his chest while the rest of my body kept a terrified distance.

Anthony and Laura didn't have children, and I was gradually spiritually adopted. Anthony was a professional therapist, and a good listener. I desperately needed someone to listen. And once I'd unloaded all my teenage pain on him, he knew the way to win my trust. He never told me what to do.

Instead, he told me stories.

Stories about his life, stories about Zen masters, stories about his grandfather.

Here's one of my favorites.

A farmer is sitting on his porch in a chair, hanging out.

A friend walks up to the porch to say hello, and hears an awful yelping, squealing sound coming from inside the house.

"What's that terrifyin' sound?" asks the friend.

"It's my dog," said the farmer. "He's sittin' on a nail."

"Why doesn't he just sit up and get off it?" asks the friend.

The farmer deliberates on this and replies:

"Doesn't hurt enough yet."

Through the years, Anthony would tell me this one whenever I was suffering from particularly bad bouts of self-destructiveness. Those were pre-cell-phone days, and I used to call him from the dorm, from my squalid sublets, from boyfriends' apartments, and collect from pay phones all over Europe the year I backpacked and studied abroad. I'd leave messages that filled his answering machine and mail him typewritten letters that were too long to stuff into an envelope without bursting the seams.

WHY DO I KEEP DOING THESE THINGS TO MYSELF? I'd ask him, moaning about my latest killer hangover, brush with death, lost wallet, or on-again-off-again relationship with the latest drug-abusing (but really good-looking) boyfriend.

I could hear him smiling through the phone.

Ah, beauty. Doesn't hurt enough yet.

. . .

I've had a problem feeling real all my life.

I didn't know until recently how absolutely universal that feeling is. For a long time, I thought I was alone. Psychologists have a term for it: imposter syndrome. But before I knew that phrase existed, I coined my own: The Fraud Police.

The Fraud Police are the imaginary, terrifying force of "real" grown-ups who you believe—at some subconscious level—are going to come knocking on your door in the middle of the night, saying:

We've been watching you, and we have evidence that you have NO IDEA WHAT YOU'RE DOING. You stand accused of the crime of completely winging it, you are guilty of making shit up as you go along, you do not actually deserve your job, we are taking everything away and we are TELLING EVERYBODY.

I mentioned The Fraud Police during a commencement speech I recently gave at an arts college, and I asked the adults in the room, including the faculty, to raise their hands if they'd ever had this feeling. I don't think a single hand stayed down.

People working in the arts engage in street combat with The Fraud Police on a daily basis, because much of our work is new and not readily or conventionally categorized. When you're an artist, nobody ever tells you or hits you with the magic wand of legitimacy. You have to hit your own head with your own handmade wand. And you feel stupid doing it.

There's no "correct path" to becoming a real artist. You might think you'll gain legitimacy by going to art school, getting published, getting signed to a record label. But it's all bullshit, and it's all in your head. You're an artist when you say you are. And you're a good artist when you make somebody else experience or feel something deep or unexpected.

When you've "made it" in academia, you become a tenured professor. It's official. Most of the time, though, "outside" appointment and approval (*Congratulations! You're an official Professor/CEO/President/ etc.*) in any field doesn't necessarily silence The Fraud Police. In fact, outside approval can make The Fraud Police louder: it's more like fighting them in high court instead of in a back alley with your fists. Along with all the layers of official titles and responsibilities come even deeper, scarier layers of *oh fuck they're gonna find me out.*

I can imagine a seasoned brain surgeon, in the moment before that first incision, having that teeny moment where she thinks:

For real? I dropped my cell phone in a puddle this morning, couldn't find my keys, can't hold down a relationship, and here I am clutching a sharp knife about to cut someone's head open. And they could die. Who is letting me do this? This is BULLSHIT.

Everybody out there is winging it to some degree, of this we can be pretty sure.

In both the art and the business worlds, the difference between the amateurs and the professionals is simple:

The professionals know they're winging it.

The amateurs pretend they're not.

. . .

On an average day, working two bouquets of flowers, I could make over a hundred dollars. Sometimes more, sometimes less, but it was certainly more than the $9.50 an hour I was earning at Toscanini's.

The consistency of the income really did amaze me. If the weather held, I could count on making about $40 to $50 an hour from random people walking by and making random decisions to give me a random amount of money.

How was it possible that it was so predictable? That's a question for the economists, I suppose. When I asked my Twitter followers about this, and the statisticians started weighing in about entropic probabilistic synchronicity, I gave up and settled on a simpler theory:

Given the opportunity, some small consistent portion of the population will happily pay for art.

. . .

Sometimes, up on the box, I would fall in love with people. Pretty often, come to think of it. It was easy, given how safe and swaddled I was up there in my cloud of pretty, white, untouchable stillness. No commitment. Just this, just now, just us.

Occasionally one of the more broken-looking homeless people of Harvard Square would approach me, drop a dollar in, and I would offer my flower. We'd look at each other, and sometimes their faces would crumple and tears would appear.

Hi.

I see you there.

I can't believe you just gave me a dollar.

You probably need it more than me.

I've been watching you circle the plaza all day asking people for money and I hope to god you know that you and I are, in this moment, exactly the same.

I never felt guilty about those dollars, though, because there was such a beauty and humanity in the fact that these homeless people were, right along with the rich tourists, stopping to connect with me. They saw value in what I was doing. They saw the power and necessity of the human connection.

Was it *fair*? I don't know. It felt fair.

There was something conspiratorial about it; their money felt symbolically valuable to me in a way that made me swell with pride—they approved of me, and their approval somehow meant more to me than anybody else's.

I started to realize there was a subterranean financial ecosystem in Harvard Square involving all of us street freaks. I found it impossible to pass the other street performers—a revolving cast of puppeteers and musicians, jugglers and magicians—or the homeless folk, without giving them my own dollars, sometimes dollars from my own hat that I'd been given just minutes before. The gift circulated.

One day a really old, raggedy-looking Japanese guy watched me for a very long time.

He made himself a little perch on one of the cement benches across the sidewalk, surrounded by rolled-up sleeping bags and a colorless, tattered collection of garbage sacks, and sat there, looking at me with his weathered face. I watched him out of the corner of my eye. After about an hour, he dug into his pocket and fished out a dollar, and he shuffled over to me, put the dollar in my hat, and looked up.

Here's your flower.

I see you.

His eyes narrowed, and he looked at my face, like he was looking for the answer to a question that I couldn't hear him asking, and I just stared right back. And then he nodded slightly, took the flower, and shuffled away. I loved him.

The next day he came back and left a note in the hat.

He wanted to know if I would marry him.

I don't know how he expected me to answer.

I never saw him again.

. . .

I wanted to be seen.

That was absolutely true. All performers—all humans—want to be seen; it's a basic need. Even the shy ones who don't want to be *looked at*.

But I also wanted, very much, to *see*.

I didn't quite grasp this until I had been up on the box for a while. What I loved as much as, possibly even more than, being seen was *sharing* the gaze. Feeling connected.

I needed the two-way street, the exchange, the relationship, and the invitation to true intimacy that I got every so often from the eyes of my random street patrons. It didn't always happen. But it happened enough to keep me up on the box.

And that's why stripping, even though it often paid way better, when I tried my hand at it a few years later, just didn't do it for me. I was being *looked* at. But I never felt seen. The strip joint was like Teflon to real emotional connection. There was *physical* intimacy galore: I witnessed hand jobs being given under tables,[2] and lots of legs and tits and more being covertly rubbed at the bar. I danced for endless hours, stark naked on a stage, and talked for even more hours with the loneliest men in the world while pretending to drink champagne. We strippers were experts in dumping our drinks back into ice buckets when the customers weren't looking—it was a job skill you actually had to acquire working at The Glass Slipper. If I'd actually drank all the absurdly overpriced champagne (from which I earned a 15 percent cut) that was purchased for me on a good night by lonely men who wanted to chat, I would have consumed, in the

---

2. My mother will be happy to know I never gave one. HI MOM.

course of my six-hour shift, enough to have brought me to a blood-alcohol level of approximately five-point-dead.

Sometimes I would get home and have a nice little breakdown, having no idea what to do with all the loneliness I'd collected. I tried to capture it in a lyric, years later, in a song called "Berlin" (my chosen stripper name):

```
It's hard to work on an assembly line of broken hearts
Not supposed to fix them, only strip and sell the parts
```

People would look straight into your crotch.
But nobody would look you in the eye.
And that drove me crazy.

. . .

Sometimes people would hold my gaze and try to give the flower *back* to The Bride, as if to somehow repay me for the flower I had just given them.

And I would gesture:
No no, it's yours to keep.

A few times people came back to my spot, fifteen minutes later, to lay a whole store-bought bouquet at my feet. Some people would pick flowers or rhododendron stems from Harvard Yard and hand me their gift, and then I'd give them one of my flowers, and we'd keep trading, and it would all get really funny and confusing.

On a good day, I couldn't tell who was giving what to whom.

. . .

Asking is, at its core, a collaboration.

The surgeon knows that her work is creative work. A machine can't do it because it requires human delicacy and decision making. It can't be done by an automaton because it requires critical thinking and a good dose of winging-it-ness. Her work requires a balance of self-confidence and collaboration, a blend of intuition and improvisation.

If the surgeon, while slicing that vulnerable brain, hits an unexpected bump in the process and needs to ask the person beside her for something essential—and quickly—she has absolutely no time to waste on questions like:

Do I deserve to ask for this help?

Is this person I'm asking really trustworthy?

Am I an asshole for having the power to ask in this moment?

She simply accepts her position, asks without shame, gets the right scalpel, and keeps cutting. Something larger is at stake. This holds true for firefighters, airline pilots, and lifeguards, but it also holds true for artists, scientists, teachers—for anyone, in any relationship.

Those who can ask without shame are viewing themselves in collaboration with—rather than in competition with—the world.

Asking for help with shame says:

You have the power over me.

Asking with condescension says:

I have the power over you.

But asking for help with gratitude says:

We have the power to help each other.

• • •

Sometimes I had to sneeze. Statues should not sneeze. It became a dramatic internal activity: I'd spend an entire minute just concentrating on the feeling in my throat and nose, playing with the strange twilight zone of sneeze-not-sneeze.

And sometimes I'd just fucking sneeze. Nothing to be done.

It was a formidable Zen practice.

Sometimes a mosquito or a fly or a bee would land on my cheek, and we'd just sort of hang out together.

Sometimes the sun would beat down directly on my face and a bead of sweat would cling to the tip of my nose until it got fat enough to start dripping into the street.

Sometimes I'd have to wipe my nose because I had a cold. Or because it *was* cold.

I would be so freezing sometimes that I would hyperextend the dance of flower-giving and draw out the entire gesture arduously, so some poor person would wait there patiently for minutes while I enacted a bizarre-looking, overdramatic, avant-garde modern dance, trying to warm up my body.

This would culminate in the eventual giving of the flower and a climactic flourish in which, with my gloved hand, and as subtly as possible, I could also wipe away the long, graceful string of clear snot that was hanging out of my white-painted nose.

. . .

The art of asking can be learned, studied, perfected. The masters of asking, like the masters of painting and music, know that the field of asking is fundamentally improvisational. It thrives not in the creation of rules and etiquette but in the smashing of that etiquette.

Which is to say: there are no rules.

Or, rather, there are plenty of rules, but they ask, on bended knees, to be broken.

. . .

Gus, our boss at Toscanini's Ice Cream, was a true patron of the arts—a perfect example of the sort of person who lives a life committed to the creativity of patronage, and expands the boundaries of what we are empowered to give one another.

He was a beloved local Celebrity Ice Cream Chef, obsessively passionate about music, culture, Cambridge politics, and new frontiers in frozen dessert making. He would devise, like an inspired mad scientist, ice creams and sorbets made out of pink peppercorns, basil, and beer.

Gus was an avid connector: He printed information about local dance companies on the store's takeaway coffee cups. He gave away crates of ice cream to science activists from MIT. He provided ice-cream gift certificates to silent auctions to rebuild city parks. He was like an ice-cream Santa Claus. It was almost a rite of passage for a young indie musician in Boston to work at either Toscanini's or Pearl Art & Craft (the other flexible-schedule job in Cambridge that didn't consider it a customer service liability to rock a blue Mohawk behind the counter).

Even though I'd hit the jackpot with my newfound hundred-dollar-a-day street-performance career, I still needed a place to store my bridal rig. Carting it back and forth between my crappy apartment and the store would have been impossible. So I kept one weekly shift at the ice-cream shop, plucked up my courage, and casually asked Gus:

Um, do you mind if I keep my bride stuff in the basement? It's just a couple of milk crates and some clothes and makeup and stuff.

Sure! said Gus, cheerfully. *You can store the creepy bride down there.* (That's what he called her.) *Don't scare the customers.*

The basement of Toscanini's was an ancient, dank cave with a low-slung ceiling tangled in pipes and a brick-and-dirt floor, crammed with cardboard boxes containing cups, spoons, and napkins. There was a tiny employees-only bathroom and a huge walk-in freezer where the five-gallon ice-cream tubs were kept. (That walk-in freezer became a very handy subzero reverse-sauna after a long, hot day statue-ing in the sun, and I'd often freak the bejeezus out of employees who accidentally stumbled upon me hanging out in there, naked, when they came in to restock tubs of French Vanilla.)

I got the entire bridal transformation down to about nine minutes: I'd sit down on the toilet in the basement, powder-whiten my face, pull the wedding dress over my jeans and boots, tuck my hair into a wig cap, and arrange the veil atop my head with a mess of bobby pins. Then I'd pull on the long white gloves, gather up my crates and giant train of gown into my arms, ascend the basement stairs, exchange salutes with my co-workers behind the counter, and bask in the what-the-fuck expressions on the faces of the ice-cream customers as I passed through the shop like a Dickensian hallucination and headed out onto the street.

All I have to say is: thank Christ I didn't work at Baskin-Robbins.

. . .

My boyfriend Joseph would stop by sometimes to watch me statueing. He was an actor.

He would hang back for a while, then ceremoniously put his dollar into the hat with a flourish, and look deep into my eyes while I dramatically picked out his flower. Then I would gesture to him, as the crowd watched, curious about this stranger who was getting extra attention. I would gesture to him to come closer, then coyly withhold my flower. People would laugh, and I would gesture to him to come right up to my face, then I'd kiss him, slowly, on the lips, and then tuck the flower in his hair.

The crowd always went wild with affectionate sounds. I loved that they didn't know anything.

He could have been anyone.

. . .

After my TED talk, I started discussing some of the finer points of my experience as a street performer on my blog, and I was surprised at the number of people who said in the comments: *Before I saw your talk, I always thought of street performers as beggars. But now I see them as artists, so I always give them money.*

Reading things like this broke and burst my heart at the same time, and pierced the core of the very issue I was trying to grapple with in the talk itself. If the mentality was so easily shifted, how could this be taken from the street to the Internet, where so many artists I knew were struggling to accept the legitimacy of their own calls for help?

I opened a discussion on my blog, one that I'd already seen reflected in the crowdfunding hall of mirrors over the past few years:

What was the difference between *asking* and *begging*?

A lot of people related their experience with their own local buskers: they saw their tips into the hat not as charity but as payment for a service.

If asking is a collaboration, begging is a less-connected demand: Begging can't provide value to the giver; by definition, it offers no exchange. Here are the words that the blog commenters used over and over when trying to describe begging:

Manipulation, desperation, base, animal, last-ditch, manipulative, guilt, shame.

The key words that kept appearing in relation to asking:

Dignity, collaboration, exchange, vulnerability, reciprocity, mutual respect, comfort, love.

The top-voted comment on the blog, from a reader named Marko Fančović, nails it:

Asking is like courtship; begging, you are already naked and panting.

Asking is an act of intimacy and trust. Begging is a function of fear, desperation, or weakness. Those who must beg *demand* our help; those who ask have faith in our capacity for love and in our desire to share with one another.

On the street or on the Internet, this is what makes authentically engaging an audience, from one human being to another, such an integral part of asking.

Honest communication engenders mutual respect, and that mutual respect makes askers out of beggars.

* * *

People would put all *sorts* of weird shit in the hat. I never knew what I was going to find at the end of the day in addition to the collection of coins and bills; it was a little like opening up a fucked-up Christmas stocking. Every random gift made me giddy; people would throw in hand-scrawled thank-you notes on the backs of ATM receipts, little drawings they'd done while watching me, sticks of gum, phone numbers, photographs they'd taken of me, fruit, rocks, hand-woven bracelets, badly rolled joints, love poems.

. . .

Gus wasn't my only patron in those early days; I had a whole collection. I became a kind of street-performing institution, and the locals had even given me a name: The Eight-Foot Bride, which I took as a compliment since I barely cleared seven foot six atop the milk crates.

There was the guy who managed a sandwich shop on the other side of the square, who loved The Eight-Foot Bride. One day I came in to get a burrito in between statue-ing shifts. My white face (I didn't bother to remove my makeup between shows) was a dead giveaway. He asked me, full of excitement:

OOH! Are you the statue girl??

Yep. I'm the statue girl.

Your burritos are free forever. What you do is incredible.

You're kidding.

The free burritos saved me at least $40 a week in food costs.

There was the guy who owned the old-fashioned tobacco shop next to Toscanini's, which had a hidden balcony lined with tables reserved for chess players to rent for $2 an hour. He let me sit there without paying during my breaks, out of the sun, drinking my free coffee and musing in my journal, without being stared at or asked by any passing strangers why I was covered in makeup.

There was the florist. After my first day up on the box, I realized that the routine of picking flowers by the side of the river wouldn't be very sustainable (and I didn't want to single-handedly clean out Cambridge of flora), so I wandered into the local flower shop. I was faced with a puzzle: what kind of flower was pretty and substantial enough to give away, easy enough to hold, and not too expensive? I settled on daisy poms—which are sort of like daisies but not so willowy, and way cheaper. The shop was run by a mother-and-son team, and after buying flowers in there for a few consecutive days, I felt like I was a good enough customer to ask the son:

Do you maybe have any flowers you don't… need? Like—any seconds or irregulars? Slightly banged up flowers that maybe you can't sell…?

What do you need them for? he asked.

Well, it's kind of weird. I'm a statue. I give them away when I move, to people who give me money.

He smiled.

Oh, you're THAT girl.

He took me down to the basement and showed me a huge bucket of yesterday's flowers, which were starting to just barely brown at the edges.

Knock yourself out, statue girl. Pick what you want. I'll give you a great price.

After that, every few days, I'd walk to the florist and patiently wait for him to deal with whatever real customers he had. Then he'd examine his current daisy pom situation and give me the ones that were too wilted to sell but still fit for a street performer—for about a third of the regular price. Some days there just weren't any rejects, but he'd still hand me a few bunches and make up a cheap price. He liked helping me. Sometimes he would throw in a few slightly wilting roses, and I'd make those the centerpiece of my bouquet for each show—saving a rose for the very last person who gave me a dollar, as a little floral finale.

. . .

People yelled abuse at me occasionally—sometimes from the sidewalk, sometimes from passing traffic.

The most common insults hurled my way included, but weren't limited to (and it really helps to imagine these in a Boston accent, as that's usually how they came packaged):

Nice costume, ya fuckin' reetahd!

Hey baby, I'll marry your ass!

Get off the sidewalk, freak!

What is this, Halloween? Hahahaha!!!

A very eighties-flavored insult was used a few times:

Get a life!

And then there was this one, shouted from a passing car:

GET A JOB!

Of all the insults hurled in my direction, **GET A JOB** hurt the most. It was an affront. I took it personally.

I had a job. I was *doing* my job. I mean, sure. It was a *weird* job. And a job I'd created out of thin air with no permission from a higher authority. But I was *working*, and people were *paying* me. Didn't that make it *a job*? And, I would think as my face burned with resentment, I was making a consistent income, which made the **GET A JOB** insult hurt even more.

I'm making plenty of money. Maybe more than you, asshole, I'd think, all hurt and defensive.

· · ·

Brené Brown, a social scientist and TED speaker who has researched shame, worthiness, courage, and vulnerability, recently published a book called *Daring Greatly*, which I fortuitously picked up at a Boston bookstore when I was just beginning to write this book. I was so blown away by the commonalities between our books that I twittered her, praising her work and asking her if she would give me a foreword for this book.[3] She writes:

> The perception that vulnerability is weakness is the most widely accepted myth about vulnerability *and* the most dangerous. When we spend our lives pushing away and protecting ourselves from feeling vulnerable or from being perceived as too emotional, we feel contempt when others are less capable or willing to mask feelings, suck it up, and soldier on. We've come to the point where, rather than respecting and appreciating the

---

3. She said yes. If you haven't read it, go back and read it now. It's wonderful.

courage and daring behind vulnerability, we let our fear and discomfort become judgment and criticism.

Following this logic, we can assume that the likelihood of someone yelling **GET A JOB** from their passing car is indirectly proportionate to their own crippling fear about getting up on the figurative box themselves.

Or to strip it down to its essence:

Hate is fear.

* * *

I broke up with Joseph.

My boyfriend Jonah would stop by sometimes to watch me statue-ing. He played the cello.

I loved giving flowers to people I loved.

I'd saved $400 to buy a ticket to go on a vacation with him and his family, and I'd given him the cash to book my flight along with theirs. But then we started breaking up, and we decided that I shouldn't go in the middle of our off-again-on-again drama; it would be too awkward.

I'd had a good day of Bride-ing: some nice guy had hand-folded me an origami crane, which I had tucked in the folds of my dress, Jonah had come by to blow me an on-again kiss and say hello, and it had rained but only for about two minutes, so I didn't get too wet. I went down the stairs to the basement of Toscanini's to sit on the dark brick floor and count my hat for the day, and to my astonishment, there was a wad of cash wound up in a rubber band. I ran upstairs and grabbed the shop telephone and called Jonah.

You're never going to believe this but somebody put FOUR HUN-DRED DOLLARS in my hat today.

Oh, Amanda, he said.

What? It's amazing! Can you believe someone cared that much?

Oh, Amanda.
What?
Oh...Amanda.
WHAT?

. . .

Lewis Hyde published a beautiful dot-connecting book in 1983 called *The Gift*, which tackles the elusive subject of what Hyde calls "the commerce of the creative spirit."

He explains the term "Indian Giver," which most people consider an insult: someone who offers a gift and then wants to take it back. But the origin of the term—coined by the Puritans—speaks volumes. A Native American tribal chief would welcome an Englishman into his lodge and, as a friendly gesture, share a pipe of tobacco with his guest, then offer the pipe itself as a gift. The pipe, a valuable little object, is—to the chief—a symbolic peace offering that is continually regifted from tribe to tribe, never really "belonging" to anybody. The Englishman doesn't understand this, is simply delighted with his new property, and is therefore completely confused when the next tribal leader comes to *his* house a few months later, and, after they share a smoke, looks expectantly at his host to gift him the pipe. The Englishman can't understand why anyone would be so rude to expect to be given this thing that *belongs to him*.

Hyde concludes:

The opposite of "Indian giver" would be something like "white man keeper"...that is, a person whose instinct is to remove property from circulation...The Indian giver (or the original one, at any rate) understood a cardinal property of the gift: whatever we have been given is supposed to be given away again, not kept...The only essential is this:

The gift must always move.

· · ·

And then there was Lee.

I was going crazy in my crappy Somerville share house; my roommate and I were ready to kill each other. I wanted, secretly, to start some kind of freaky art commune, but I had about $300 to my name and no idea where to start. Instead, I stumbled into one that already existed when Rob Chalfen, my local coffee-shop friend who boasted Cambridge's largest collections of New Directions paperbacks and old-time jazz on vinyl, invited me to his friend's going-away party at a commune-collective across the river in Boston proper. He knew I was art-house hunting and thought I might be able to finagle my way in the door.

The Cloud Club is a four-story brick townhouse wrapped protectively in a winding vine of leafy wisteria, the root of which is as wide as a human torso and curves smack across the huge oak front door, hanging low enough that you have to duck under to get inside.

I walked up a winding, rickety staircase into a hallway covered with faded mirrors, surreal drawings, and blinking Christmas lights. Empty gilded frames and upside-down paintings hung at odd angles. A crowd was gathered in a cozy, low-lit kitchen warmed by a wood-burning fireplace with fixtures from the 1890s. All around me were the clinking of glasses, the lighting of cigarettes, and the buzzing conversation of musicians, filmmakers, sex workers, activists, and painters.

On the top floor, in a room brimming over with antlers, plants, swords, and old hooked rugs, the party was in full swing. Guests used a huge tree situated in the middle of the room to climb up to a bedroom loft capped with a handmade glass geodesic dome; a sliding door led to a roof covered with discarded sinks and rotting sculptures that overlooked the glittering Boston night skyline. And the crown jewel: in the corner of the room was a rickety spinet piano. I took a deep breath. I was home.

Rob introduced me to Annie-the-writer, the woman who was going away, and I mentioned to her that I was looking to rent an apartment. Was this one available?

Go talk to Lee. She laughed. *It might be.*

I passed through a hallway of billowing, spiraling, white plaster shapes hand-sculpted onto the walls, and through a set of double doors that looked like they had been repurposed from a fin de siècle Parisian bar. I was so in love with this house already, I wanted to kiss every floorboard and mismatched doorknob. I grew up in a collapsing Colonial fixer-upper that my parents spent the entirety of my childhood trying to make heatable and habitable. This place felt as familiar to me as my own fingers.

I knocked tentatively, went in through the door, and there, engulfed in a cave-like room stuffed with anthropomorphic sculptures and piles of spiral notebooks, was Lee, seated on one of his own hand-carved chairs, writing a little sign on a piece of yellowed paper that said, "Room for Rent, Market Price or DIS-COUNT FOR VISIONARY ARTISTS." Clearly he was planning on taking it down to the party and posting it on Annie's door. He looked like Gandalf in a cowboy hat, with a kindly smile, a flowered shirt, a huge, white beard, and the kind of rugged, careful hands that had done a lot of heavy lifting and intricate craftsmanship.

WAIT, I said.

Yes? he said, looking up and smiling.

DON'T WRITE THAT SIGN.

Why not? he asked.

I'M HERE. I'M MOVING IN.

At this, he giggled, took my phone number, and told me to come back tomorrow.

We'll see, he said.

Lee didn't just accept tenants off the bat, even when they came referred by friends. You had to show up with luggage, hang out and chat with him for some unspecified period of time, and then, only after you had passed what my future housemates would come to refer to as the "mystery aesthetic" test, would you be allowed to consider yourself an official member of the household.

I showed up the next day with two boxes of clothes, a toothbrush, and a pile of books, determined never to leave. It worked.

Back in the 1970s, Lee had created the Cloud Club because he wanted an art family around him. He didn't have any money back in those days. He'd been living out of his van (painted, he likes reminding us, with images from *Alice in Wonderland*—and the van after that was covered with Blue Meanies from *Yellow Submarine*) and needed to borrow the down payment for the house—about $9,000—from his friend Brian, who had the money.

Brian and Lee are both over seventy now, and still great friends. That $9,000 loan was the seed for a house that's now been called home by more than a hundred different artists over the past forty years, with Lee in the role of magical landlord-trickster-conductor. His favorite place to be is in any corner, hidden from view, where he can capture things happening on video. Lee is an outsider artist in his own right, a self-taught architect, painter, and sculptor: the Cloud Club *is* his art, and we get to live in it.

There are about eight of us living there at any given time, and we all have our own little apartments with our own kitchens and bathrooms. Mostly, nobody leaves their doors locked. We share a car, we share the washer and dryer and take turns buying laundry detergent, we share the back garden. My housemate Mali, who's a singer, is the one with the green thumb—she plants kale and distributes it around the house.

Since he started the Cloud Club, Lee has deliberately charged his tenants about a third of the market value rent for each apartment. He not only *allows*, he *encourages* the musicians in the house, and our friends' bands, and our friends' bands' drummers' poet girlfriends, to use the communal space for parties, meetings, and concerts. He never charges anyone for that; instead, he takes an extreme glee in seeing the space used and filled with life. He films the goings-on and uploads them to YouTube. He wants to feel things happening. He makes enough money to cover the expenses.

People like Lee have a different relationship with the spotlight: they not only prefer playing a support role, they *thrive* doing it, taking pleasure in holding the light for others to run around in. Lee's like a combination Art Butler (he'll often surprise me with a plate of fruit while I'm in the middle of composing) and all-purpose fixer-upper resource (if you ask him, he'll teach you all about plumbing, soldering, or wiring. I never ask). At his core, he loves to feel useful to all of his tenants, and he beams with pride when he sees our art succeed. His patronage can come in strange, unpredictable forms (*No, Lee, I don't need seventy reams of pink paper that you just found in the dumpster. Why did you put them in my kitchen?*).

But beyond the cheap rent, eccentric space, and reams of paper, Lee's gift to me, and the never-ending parade of art tenants that he houses, is bigger, deeper, harder to see. The Cloud Club, in all its artistic, ramshackle glory, is his version of the offered flower, his gift to the world—and anybody who lived there or who walks under the front vine and in through the creaky, salvaged front door feels that gift. Lee himself is an introvert (he even calls himself a "hermit"), but the house speaks for him: it is, itself, the container he's created so that we might all have a moment of real connection with one another.

. . .

I broke up with Jonah.

My boyfriend Blake would stop by sometimes to watch me statue-ing. He was an undergrad at MIT with a passion for painting and who doted on his dorm-room collection of huge saltwater aquariums filled with clown fish. He also had an octopus.

Blake graduated and landed a job as a full-time engineer, and the salary was hefty, but it didn't leave him any time to make art, so he quit and decided to commit to his painting.

But painting didn't pay the rent. He needed something practical. So to make money, he became a living statue of a white-winged angel on the other side of Harvard Square.

He wore a long white robe and gloves, dyed his hair a shocking white blond, and engineered and constructed the giant wings himself, out of papier-mâché and feathers. They were beautiful.

* * *

Since The Bride was such a conspicuous freak, I felt loudly ignored by those who walked by me without a single glance. I didn't take it personally. At least, I *tried* not to.

So many people were hurrying to school or racing to work, chatting with their partners and otherwise occupied. I was ignored by probably 99 percent of all those who passed me on that sidewalk over my five or six years of Bride-ing. Which amounts to being deliberately ignored—while actively "performing"—by, I dunno, a few million people. This is why I highly recommend street performing over attending a conservatory to any musician, especially if they're going into rock and roll: it wears your ego down to stubbly little nubs and gives you performance balls of steel.

Sometimes it was just a bad day, and it felt like nobody, and I mean *nobody*, would stop. Who knows why.

When that happened, I'd start performing for my own amusement, letting the melancholy of loneliness wash over me, tilting my head to one side sadly, slumping my shoulders a bit, and raising my hands up to heaven in a pitifully grand gesture:

Why, god, has everyone forsaken me?

I could convince myself so thoroughly that none of humanity was any good that I actually let a few sincere tears stream down my face, letting the people briskly walking by me serve as unwitting universal examples of just how cold and cruel the world really was.

・ ・ ・

I took The Bride on the road. The costume fit in a rolling tool-
box that I could also stand on, and I carried her—she paid my
way, in fact—to Australia, to Key West, to Los Angeles, to Vegas,
to New York, to Germany. Busking in different environments
was hard because I'd gotten into such a cozy rhythm in Harvard
Square; some cities were more hospitable than others. My first day
in the center of the French Quarter in New Orleans, I was not
only yelled at by the other, highly territorial street performers, but
some random jerk came up behind me and whispered that he was
going to set my veil on fire, and a few minutes later, a horse drawing a touristy carriage stopped right next to me and peed all over
my dress.

・ ・ ・

My hands were usually raised, herald-like, to one side, or piously
clasped to my heart, or palms up to the sky like a star-shaped ballerina...but they were never outstretched for money. If people put
money directly into my hand, which they would often try to do, it
always felt wrong and uncomfortable. My hat was out for money,
but my hands were out for something bigger.

Madelein Du Plessis sent me this story in the blog comments:

When I was a kid there was an article about a woman who
went to India to help with a charity thing. All the beggar
children would come for food and they would beg with their
hands, palms up. After a long day, she went home and there
was this little kid, stretching his arms out towards her. At first
she thought the kid was begging, but then she saw that his
palms were facing towards each other. Then she realized the
kid was asking to be picked up and hugged. She ended up
adopting the kid.

Madelein's realization: They all needed food. This kid wanted more than food.

He also wanted love.

· · ·

Anthony made me feel real.

He was born in 1948, and he regaled me with tales from the sixties that made my heart ache to turn back the clock and live in a time when everybody hitchhiked and smoked hash while listening to Joni Mitchell on crackly vinyl records. Anthony's stories drew pictures in my teenage mind of wild, vital human beings creating a new reality in an upheaved world, protesting a war, running around with feathers in their hair and knives in their boots, tearing down the system and trying to score as many girls, drugs, and adventures as they could. I was jealous.

Anthony was raised in Boston in a big Italian-American family who'd made their fortune in the liquor and real estate businesses. The combination of his calm, Buddhist approach to life (he taught and introduced me to yoga, meditation, and the general concept of mindfulness), *and* the fact that he was a martial arts expert, would arm me with pepper spray before I went on long trips alone, and displayed an arsenal of exotic self-defense weapons in the study above the office where he saw his patients, never struck me as strange.

In my Hollywood biopic, he'd be Mr. Miyagi from *The Karate Kid*, but played by Robert De Niro. In an overdramatic teenage flashback scene, I would confide in him that I'd been sexually assaulted by a boy from the high school. He would then narrow his eyes, make an Italian gesture in which he bit his folded tongue in half while wrinkling his nose, and say:

I'm going to find that guy and beat him to a pulp...

Then he'd put his hands in yoga prayer position over his heart, bow his head, and calmly add:

...with compassion.

We shared our stories on the phone, in long letters sometimes typewritten, sometimes handwritten, and eventually (once it existed) over email. Whenever we could, we connected in person, on long walks, over food, over coffee.

We made up absurd, fictional skits and scenarios about my lovers, our friends, our neighbors, ourselves. One of the skits starred a particularly skinny boyfriend of mine (who had a real-life penchant for wearing skirts) hitchhiking a ride on an eighteen-wheel truck to visit me in college and getting forcibly ejected from the passenger seat when the truck driver realizes he isn't a girl, then being blown into the air by the blast of tailpipe exhaust as the truck pulls away, then magically being picked up by a passing breeze for a few hundred miles and floating through the metal grate above my basement dorm window, into the room, and onto my bed. We would tack on details of these skits over dozens of phone calls, making up absurd new characters, cracking each other up. We were ridiculous.

But as I got older, we shared more of the real things. Not just the entertaining stories, but the sad ones. The mean ones. The embarrassing ones. The scary ones. He told me his whole life, and I told him mine. Our love ran deep.

Anthony was also one of my patrons. He gifted me books on Buddhism and pocket knives. Occasionally, when he knew I was broke, he'd include a crisp hundred-dollar bill in a letter. When I was just out of college, surviving from statue paycheck to stripper paycheck, making my living in one-dollar bills, Anthony would sometimes front my rent money if I was tight on cash. I was once wiped out by a three-hundred-dollar speeding ticket I got on the Massachusetts Turnpike while racing to a gig as an artist's model at a local art college. I had $250 in my bank account and my $350 rent was due. I borrowed the money from Anthony.

I swear I'll pay you back, I promised.

I know you will, he answered. I would.

We used to talk about what would happen if he died. He's more than twenty-five years older than me, and I worried about it. I once asked him, while we were lying on the adjacent couches of his study, what I should say at his funeral. Since I'd probably have to say something.

He gave this some thought. He said he'd like me to walk up to the front of the wake or memorial or whatever, carrying a stick.

What kind of stick?

Whatever kind of stick, he said. *You know, a branch, a stick. A big one. One you can hold and everyone can see.*

So you mean, like, a NATURAL stick. Not like...a martial arts stick. You mean like a...

WHATEVER kind of stick, he said, sounding annoyed. *A stick from a tree. An ALL-PURPOSE stick. I'm trying to tell you something important here, clown.*

Okay, I said, breathing out. *You're dead, I'm at the funeral. What do I do with the stick?*

Don't say anything, he told me. *Just hold that sucker up in the air, break it in half, and throw it on the floor.*

Everything breaks.

. . .

I had a hard time keeping boyfriends. They usually lasted about a year, then things would start to get real—or appear to start going in a potentially real direction—and I would flee in terror. But I wasn't very good at being independent either. I couldn't stand to spend the night alone and was a serial drunk-dialer of exes.

They all told me I had a fear of intimacy, but I vehemently disagreed; I craved intimacy like a crack addict.

The problem was that I craved intimacy to the same burning degree that I detested commitment.

Being a statue was such a perfect job.

. . .

I loved all the handwritten notes people took the time to write and leave in the hat.

You're beautiful.
Thank you for changing my day.
I've been watching you for an hour.
I love you.
The Bride was so easy to love.

She was silent.

She was blank, harmless, beatific... just loving people and giving them flowers.

She was perfect.

Because... who knew?

She could be anything.

Anyone.

In real life, I was the furthest thing from quiet, and the furthest thing from perfect. I gabbed nonstop, dressed flamboyantly, dyed my hair purple and red and green, repeatedly crashed my bike into cars, started prying conversations with strangers, and hammered on a piano in my bedroom while screeching angry songs about my pain at maximum volume in my spare time.

There was one very sweet-looking guy in his forties or fifties who, for an entire statue summer, gave me a twenty-dollar bill every time he saw me. My peripheral vision was excellent, and I could usually see what size bill people were dropping in my hat—unless they were going out of their way to hide it.

Day after day, I came to recognize him, and even expect him, and eventually we shared a tiny smile every time he passed by. It was a sweet, silent, secret little relationship.

Towards the end of the summer, he kicked around one day until my flowers ran out, and shyly approached me—would I have a cup of coffee with him?

Sure, I said.

I figured I owed it to him. I was impressed he'd even asked.

I went back to the ice-cream shop, changed into my civilian clothes, and we sat together in an outdoor café and chatted about life. He was a chemical engineer, from MIT, and slightly sad. He was nervous, not easy to talk to. I told him about my life: about writing music, about my wonderful crazy art-housemates at the Cloud Club, about living in Germany, what it was like to be a statue. He told me about his failed marriage. Two flawed human beings, sitting at the Au Bon Pain, exchanging mundane details. He'd clearly fallen in a forlorn sort of love with The Bride. Meeting me must have been such a disappointment.

I walked away from our coffee date feeling like I'd broken something beautiful.

I wanted to stay anyone.

It was easier.

. . .

Even if The Bride was slow-moving, it sometimes felt like life happened at light speed; thirty little secret love affairs with passersby in just under seventy minutes, and all the heartache that goes along with it.

I'm in love.

Nobody loves me.

I'm in love.

Nobody loves me.

I'd stand there like a dry plant, passively waiting to be watered.

Any source of nourishment would do. It was so simple, really, like the entirety of the human condition distilled down to a single idea:

Feeling alone. And then, not.

Every pair of gazing eyes that locked with mine, a reminder:

Love still exists.

. . .

When Neil and I first met, long after my street-performing days were over, we were both in relationships with other people, and we didn't find each other all that attractive. I thought he looked like a baggy-eyed, grumpy old man, and he thought I looked like a chubby little boy. (A photograph taken on the day we first met provides credible evidence.) I now think he's smashingly handsome, and he calls me "the most beautiful woman in the world." Ain't love grand?

We were introduced over email by my friend Jason Webley, whom I'd met when we were both busking at an Australian festival—me as The Bride, him scream-singing over his pirate-y accordion songs. I was crashing in Jason's houseboat in Seattle the week Neil posted one of Jason's homemade stop-motion videos to his own blog, causing the view-counts to soar into the tens of thousands.

Do you know Neil Gaiman? Jason asked. We were working on a songwriting collaboration: a weird side-project record based completely on puns called *Evelyn Evelyn*, in which we wrote, played, and sang as conjoined twin sisters with the same first name.

Neil Gaiman. Doesn't he write comics? Isn't he the Sandman *dude?* I'd never read anything he'd written, but I'd definitely heard his name.

Yes, him! He posted my "Eleven Saints" video on his blog yesterday and it got like fifty thousand hits. I just wrote him a thank-you note and he wrote back ten minutes later. He seems really nice.

A few days later, Jason and I were working on a radio-play-style script for our album, a ten-minute spoken account of the fictional twins' horrific upbringing (their mother died in childbirth, then came a stint in the circus and a string of unseemly guardians, etc.). We were having a blast writing it, coming up with absurd details, but we wanted to run the text by someone to make sure the storyline was clear. Jason suggested we ask Neil.

But isn't he kinda famous? I asked. *Why not? Go for it. Ask.*

It couldn't hurt. He asked. Neil said yes, took a look at the radio play, and suggested a few changes. I wrote him a thank-you note. He was in Ireland at that time, he said in his response, alone in a borrowed house trying to finish a book about a little boy who grows up in a graveyard, and he had been sick with the flu for a full week. A few days later, I emailed and asked him how he was getting on. And a few days after that, I emailed and asked him who he actually was.

He started telling me about his life, his book, his flu, his divorce. I told him about my life, my career, my record label troubles.

I was slaving over a book for the fans at the time, a compilation of macabre photographs to go along with my new album *Who Killed Amanda Palmer*. I'd gotten excited about the concept, and already had five or six great dead/naked-Amanda photos (I was, of course, mining my past and including the pictures from my dead/naked-Amanda performance-art college thesis), but had been told by my label that they didn't have any budget to add artwork to the CD packaging. Instead of fighting them, I decided to simply publish the photos separately, in a book, and sell it directly from my website as a companion to the record. I figured it would be fun—and useful—to get a famous writer to create clever captions for the photos. I asked Neil. He said yes. A few months later, he came to Boston to work on the book. He didn't want to write captions, he said; the photos looked more like whole stories to him, which would take more time to write. And he wanted to meet the corpse in person.

On our first day together, we took a walk to the Public Garden to get to know each other a bit before we hunkered down to work on the book. I asked him how his life was unfolding, how it felt to be him, and I was surprised at how readily forthright he was; he seemed so shy and guarded at first glance. He was going through a rough time. Our week was friendly and platonic.

We finished the book and stayed in touch every so often, getting on with our real lives and respective relationships. I released my album and embarked on a long tour. A few months later, Neil and I both happened to be in New York on his birthday and agreed to meet up for coffee. I was flummoxed about what to give him for a birthday present. What does one get Neil Gaiman, Celebrated Writer Of Fantasy And Science Fiction Novels? A special pen? A fancy journal? A fossil of a Tyrannosaurus rex tooth? A map of a black hole?

The Bride.

It was *perfect*. When I'd told him about my years as The Bride, he'd been delighted, and emailed me a story he'd written years before about a male living statue who stalks a woman, writing her creepy letters that he mysteriously leaves in her apartment.

He was having lunch with his literary agent that day, and would be free at four o'clock, so I asked him to come to Washington Square Park when he was done. I told him I'd be reading on a bench. It was November, and cold, so I waited a bit before setting down a locally filched milk crate in front of an empty fountain, ducking behind a tree, and putting on my Bride getup for the first time in a few years, inhaling its familiar cakey smell of sweat and makeup, and feeling floaty. I stepped up on the box at ten minutes to four, figuring I wouldn't have long to wait.

After twenty minutes, I started to shiver and kept wondering if I should give up, but I didn't want to get down and ruin the surprise, and I'd already suffered too long to let it go. There was construction in the park. Maybe he couldn't find me. A few people stopped to get a flower. After thirty minutes, my fingers went numb, then my hands went numb, then my legs and arms froze. After about an hour, he appeared, accompanied by a woman, and approached me cautiously.

...Amanda? Is that you?

The Bride stayed silent. I stared at him and cocked my head. This was weird. He had come *with* someone, and I felt like I was embarrassing him. I'd noticed he was easily embarrassed.

He put a dollar in my hat and I gave him a flower. I tried to make eye contact with him, and he smiled goofily while the woman stepped back and laughed at our little exchange. I hopped down. I still felt like I was embarrassing him.

Well, er, Amanda, this is Merrilee, my literary agent! Merrilee, this is Amanda, you know, the... rock star lady. With the dead naked book... and all that. Merrilee smiled at me.

I pushed the veil out of my face, reached out my numb, gloved fingers, and shook her hand.

Hi.

The uncomfortableness lasted a few more minutes before Neil and I walked off to a nearby café, where I told Neil I would buy him a birthday hot chocolate. I took off my wig and Neil helped me carry the three milk crates.

My god, you're freezing, he said. *Your teeth are chattering.* He took off his overcoat and draped it over my shoulders.

I didn't have any cash in my wallet, and the café was cash only. But I had made eight dollars doing The Bride, and I insisted on buying our hot chocolate with those crumpled-up bills, which I fished out of the can I'd used to collect them. The bill for two hot chocolates came to eleven dollars. Fucking New York. Apologizing, I hit Neil up for the rest of the money.

It's okay, he said. *What you did out there was wonderful.*

Ah, thanks. Yeah. Sorry it got all fucked up. I should have planned the surprise better.

No, he said. *It was perfect. I think it's the nicest thing anyone's ever done for me, actually.*

What? Really? I said.

Really. And I've decided something.

What's that?

I've decided that I'm not going anywhere.

Sorry. What?

I'm not going anywhere, he repeated.

I don't know what you mean, Neil.

I mean, he said, speaking more slowly, *that I'm not. Going. Anywhere. Even if it takes years. I think I'll stay right here.*

Like…here at the corner table? I joked nervously. *You mean you're never going to leave Cafe Gitane ever? That sounds very Neil Gaiman-y.*

No, he said, plainly. *I'll leave this café. But I won't leave you. That's what I mean. I'm not going anywhere.*

Oh, I said. *I see. I think.*

And I couldn't think of anything to say after that.

We were both still in other relationships, though it was no secret that they were both foundering.

We parted ways, and I walked down the street thinking:

Did what I think just happened actually happen? Does Neil Gaiman, Celebrated Writer Of Fantasy And Science Fiction Novels want to date me? God, he's so much older than me, I thought, doing the math. *Sixteen years. No way. That's too much. And he's famous. Which is kind of great but kind of not. And he's so... awkward and... British... and... I don't know. He'd hate me and my life and friends.*

We have practically nothing in common, I reasoned. But still, there was something about him. He was so... what was he? He was so...

... kind.

. . . .

Sometimes people—almost always men—would walk up to The Bride and, with dramatic ceremony that ranged from the corny to the sublimely tasteful, offer me their wedding rings.

I would clasp my heart, saying with my fluttering eyes:

For meeee?

And I would touch my fingers to my lips, speechless, shrug my shoulders upwards in extreme delight, smile slightly, take the ring, and slip it lovingly onto my gloved pinky.

Thank you for this beautiful wedding ring. I love you.

Then I'd go back to standing still.

Then things would get kind of awkward.

The person would want the wedding ring back.

So we'd stand there, staring at each other.

I'd shake my head.

A pause. A really nervous pause.

Then I'd reconsider, and remove the ring, and start to return it— much to the relief of my new human friend.

Then I'd change my mind.

This game could go on for a while if business was slow.

. . .

Despite the fact that the majority of passersby ignored me (and occasionally sent me into spirals of existential despair), I had come to have a sort of faith in the street, and in the general public, because they would instinctively protect me. I was truly vulnerable up there, but I felt a benevolent force field of human energy around me.

A few times some jerk would grab my money-filled hat and run away with it. But somebody always chased him (and it was always a him) down the street and grabbed the hat back and returned it, often feeling the need to apologize to me, as if to apologize for all of humanity.

I'd thank them with some flowers. They would take them. They understood.

One day, while I was surrounded by a small audience, a mentally ill guy approached me and started spitting and screaming at me in a foreign language. Things reached a whole new level of frightening when he reached up and grabbed my frozen, outstretched arm, trying to pull me off my pedestal. My feet were bound by the skirt beneath my dress. If I fell over, I couldn't break my own fall.

I didn't speak or scream, I just looked him right in the eye, as fiercely and imploringly as I could, thinking:

Please, oh god, please let go of me.

But he didn't. Just as I was about to break character and wrestle myself free, someone from the crowd moved in and grabbed the guy, pulling him off me and dragging him a safe distance away. I didn't break character. I watched the whole scene play out like a movie. The crowd applauded. I gave the Samaritan a flower, pressing my hands together, a gesture of heartfelt gratitude. Then I got back to work.

A teenage girl once whipped an apple at me from about twenty feet away, just barely missing my face and hitting my collarbone. I kept my balance while one of my friends, who happened to be watching, chased her for three blocks and set her straight.

Drunk people were always a pain in the ass. Friday and Saturday nights could be lucrative but intolerable. One night, a group of wasted frat boys walked by me and one of them stopped, looked up, grabbed me around my legs, and buried his face in my crotch, making drunkenly ecstatic "yummy" sounds.

I looked down and shook my head sadly.

What can you do?

People made me sad sometimes.

But mostly I just got sad if they didn't want the flower.

. . .

One day I really got the shit scared out of me. I heard a car screech up onto the curb behind my pedestal, and a pair of hands grabbed me around the waist from behind. I heard a voice say,

GET HER!

And three people dressed in black, wearing ski masks, started to tie my hands together. Another snatched all my milk crates and money. They threw me in the back of a van and the driver revved the engine and pulled away, speeding down Mass Ave. One of the black-clad guys took his mask off, giggling uncontrollably: it was E. Stephen, one of my screwball artist pals, who constructed apocalyptic sculptures and devices out of found objects and dead animals. He kept jars of his own toenail clippings for use in future projects.

I sighed and looked at him, rolling my eyes.

Dude... I was WORKING.

. . .

I realize now that I felt chronically guilty about having chosen to be an artist. I didn't understand this at the time; I just felt a consistent kind of inward torture, pulled towards a life in art while simultaneously feeling foolish for having made that choice. The Fraud Police ate away at me persistently through my twenties; the needling voices simmered below the surface and gnawed at my subconscious in an endless, grating loop:

When are you going to grow up, get a real job, and stop fucking around?

What makes you think you deserve to earn money playing your little songs to people?

What gives you the right to think people should give one shit about your art?

When are you going to stop being so selfish and start doing something USEFUL, like your Sister the Scientist?

If you take those questions and turn them into statements, they look like this:

Artists are not useful.

Grown-ups are not artists.

Artists do not deserve to make money from their art.

"Artist" is not a real job.

•   •   •

I've played in every venue imaginable over the last fifteen years, in fancy old theaters and shitty sports bars, in secret underground piano bars with capacities of forty people, to crowds of thousands in sports arenas.

But I maintain: no performing-art form can ever achieve the condition of The Eight-Foot Bride.

It was like breaking down a compound into its essential elements, then down to an atom, then down to an irreducible proton.

Such profound encounters—like the deeply moving exchanges I'd have with broken people who seemed to have found some sort of salvation in the accidental, beautiful moment of connection with a stranger painted white on a street corner—cannot happen on a safe stage with a curtain. Magical things can happen there, but not this. The moment of being able to say, unaccompanied by narrative:

Thank you . . . I see you.

In those moments I felt like a genie of compassion, able to pay attention to the hard-to-reach, hidden cracks of someone else's life— as if I were a specially shaped human-emotion tool that could reach way under the bed of somebody's dark heart and scrape out the caked-on blackness.

Just by seeing someone—really seeing them, and being seen in return—you *enrealen* each other.

What is possible on the sidewalk is unique. No song needed, no words, no lighting, no story, no ticket, no critic, no context.

It cannot get any simpler than a painted person on a box, a living human question mark, asking:

Love?

And a passing stranger, rattled out of the rhythm of a mundane existence, answering:

Yes.

Love.

. . .

It would rain, sometimes.

If I woke and saw the rain on a vaguely scheduled Statue Day, that meant a day off. I felt deeply in tune with nature—like my distant hunting-and-gathering forebears from ancient Scotland (or wherever my ancient forebears hunted and gathered). New England weather is known for its fickleness, and many days the rain would vanish as quickly as it came.

Sometimes I'd be up on the box when the rainclouds rolled in. I was usually happy to stay up there in the drizzle, but people were far less likely to stop. Trying to decide when to get down was always an interesting game I played with myself, and sometimes I'd just stay up there and get soaking wet, as some kind of random statement to the Performance Art Gods. I would fix my eyes downwards and watch the bricks on the sidewalk as they discolored with the rainwater, first a smattering of little specks, then lots of dark splotches, and eventually, they'd turn all-dark-red wet. The bridal costume, which I washed only occasionally in the Toscanini's bathroom sink, would emit an odor that you could smell for miles around.

Sometimes waiting it out was worth it. The rain would come,

then go, the sidewalk would dry and the sun would come out and dry me off, leaving only the faintest trace of Eau de Wet Bride.

. . .

Inviting my friends to watch The Bride was difficult, because there was never any set start or finish time. Just a noncommittal:

I'll be Bride-ing in the Square today, probably around fourish.

Anthony came by one day and set up a chair at the café across the sidewalk, a good thirty feet away. I was so excited he'd come; he could finally see what I was doing. I connected with people especially deeply that day, because I knew he was watching. I wanted him to see the seeing.

He watched for a long time. After I was finished, we went out for a falafel at Café Algiers, and he reported the conversations he'd overheard.

This one guy, this regular chess-player type who says he's there every day, says, "She is the Madonna of Harvard Square."

I laughed.

Then the guy next to him says, "Yeah, and she's Asian, I think she's actually Korean." And another guy leans over and whispers to me, "No word of a lie, she has combat boots on under that dress."

I laughed again.

And another guy tells me, "I'm in love with her."

Aww. You know, I said, *I think even **I'm** in love with her. She's... you know. She's perfect.*

I looked directly at him.

So you liked it? You really got it?

It was magnificent, clown. And I got behind you a couple times, so I could watch those faces, up close, of the people looking at you. I saw the love, the longing, all of it. I mean...it's the most powerful and basic of all things. You were right. It's the human encounter, all happening right there, beauty. And when that little kid came up, the scared one? Oof. I almost cried.

You almost cried? For real?

I almost cried, he said.
I WIN! I said.
You win. How do you feel?
LIKE A MILLION DOLLARS.
What you're doing up there is art, my girl. You're really doing it. I'm proud of you.

He paid the check. He always paid the check.

. . .

So I'd done it, sort of.

I felt like A Productive Member Of Society in my own weird way, a Real Artist.

But honestly? I didn't *want* to be a statue. I wanted to be a musician. I wanted to be vulnerable. Not as a character, but as myself.

Facing the street as a statue had its challenges, but truthfully, it all felt like cheating, because I wasn't actually showing myself. I was hiding behind a blank, white wall.

I loved the connecting. I loved the seeing. But it wasn't enough. People loved The Bride because she was perfect and silent.

Anyone.

I wanted to be loved for my songwriting, the musical dot-connection I'd been privately plugging away at for years, which showed me for what I actually was.

Imperfect.

And very, very loud.

GIRL ANACHRONISM

You can tell
From the scars on my arms
And the cracks in my hips
And the dents in my car
And the blisters on my lips
That I'm not the carefulest
    of girls

You can tell
From the glass on the floor
And the strings that are
    breaking
And I keep on breaking more
And it looks like I am shaking
But it's just the temperature
Then again
If it were any colder I could
    disengage
If I were any older I would
    act my age
But I don't think that you'd
    believe me
It's
Not
The
Way
I'm
Meant
To
Be
It's just the way the
    operation made me

And you can tell
From the state of my room
That they let me out too soon
And the pills that I ate
Came a couple years too late
And I've got some issues to
    work through
There I go again
Pretending to be you
Make-believing

That I have a soul beneath
    the surface
Trying to convince you
It was accidentally on purpose

I am not so serious
This passion is a plagiarism
I might join your century
But only on a rare occasion
I was taken out
Before the labor pains set in
    and now
Behold the world's worst
    accident
I am the girl anachronism

And you can tell
From the red in my eyes
And the bruises on my thighs
And the knots in my hair
And the bathtub full of flies
That I'm not right now at all
There I go again
Pretending that I'll fall
Don't call the doctors
Cause they've seen it all
    before
They'll say just
Let
Her
Crash
And
Burn
She'll learn
The attention just encourages
    her

And you can tell
From the full-body cast
That you're sorry that you
    asked
Though you did everything you
    could

(Like any decent person
   would)
But I might be catching so
   don't touch
You'll start believing
   you're immune to gravity
   and stuff
Don't get me wet
Because the bandages will all
   come off

You can tell
From the smoke at the stake
That the current state is
   critical
Well it is the little things,
   for instance

In the time it takes to break
   it she can make up ten
   excuses
Please excuse her for the day,
   it's just the way the
Medication makes her

I don't necessarily believe
   there is a cure for this
So I might join your century
   but only as a doubtful
   guest
I was too precarious removed
   as a caesarian
Behold the world's worst
   accident
I AM THE GIRL ANACHRONISM

—from *The Dresden Dolls*, 2003

So I started a band.
And we were **loud**.

We had no guitars; it was just me on the piano and the microphone and Brian Viglione, who stumbled into my life like a long-lost musical soul-twin, on the drums. Our minimal setup didn't limit our sonic power in the slightest: the drums alone deafened people, and I cranked my electronic piano to match. Brian had been reared on a steady diet of metal, jazz, and hardcore punk, and he hit the drums like a smoke-choked victim pounding on the exit door of a burning building; for him, commitment to the religion of drumming was his gateway to redemption. And I played piano the same way, seeking salvation through volume.

I met Brian during a Halloween party I threw at the Cloud Club. A few hundred people in costume were packed into the house, roving around all four floors. I'd been so busy organizing the party that I'd taken the lazy route and dressed as a temporary office worker in the two-piece suit my mother had insisted on buying me "for job interviews," which had been stuffed in a paper bag unironically marked "grown-up clothes" in the back of my closet for more than four years. Brian came as a severed head, dressed all in black with convincing-looking blood oozing down his neck.

Late that night, on the ancient upright piano, I played and sang four of my closeted songs to a small, drunk crowd of friends. Brian took me aside and declared: *I am destined to be your drummer.* I didn't argue. I'd been trying to start a band and was heading towards my twenty-fifth birthday, the deadline I'd superstitiously given myself to get my musical shit together or else face the inevitability of being a Total Failure.

We formed the band a week later and called ourselves The

Dresden Dolls, in a nod to Kurt Vonnegut's account of the Dresden bombing in *Slaughterhouse-Five* and the innocent, delicate porcelain figurines I always imagined strewn under the rubble of the decimated city. Dark, light, dark. That was us.

My sweet and patient mother had taught me piano basics and encouraged me to take lessons, to which I reluctantly trudged. I hated practicing and I found it incredibly frustrating to sight-read music off the page—as I still do—but I could figure out how to play anything I heard on the radio. I'd been amassing a pile of hypomanic songs for the piano since I was twelve, recording them into tape recorders and scribbling lyrics into notebooks in almost total privacy. Until I met Brian, I'd been a repressed performer of my own music, only venturing out once or twice a year to timidly share my not-so-timid songs with a live audience in a café, at an open mic night, at a party. My early teenage lyrics reflected and copied the music I loved: musical theater, The Beatles, New Wave— my songs were confessional and dark, drawing mostly from my confounded struggle to understand myself. I also wrote satirical songs about Starbucks. I couldn't handle any criticism, no matter how well-intentioned, and sharing my songs or playing live simply terrified me, since any rejection of the material felt like a direct rejection of *me*.

But now I was free to unleash my massive back catalog of unheard material onto Brian on the top floor of the Cloud Club, where Lee allowed us (of course) to rehearse for free. Brian sat at his drums and listened intently as I shared each song, and, without an ounce of judgment regarding the hyper-personal lyrical content, he orchestrated pounding, delicate, symphonic drum parts. Everything he did was perfect. One by one, I played Brian every song I'd ever written; we kept the best, we ditched the rest. We booked our first gig in a friend's art gallery.

Along with some thrown-together vintage costumes (to my delight, Brian loved to cross-dress) and our soon-to-be-signature white face paint (to my *extreme* delight, he loved wearing stage makeup), we had a magic chemistry that ambushed people with the sheer magnitude of our sincerity to emote. I was ecstatic. After spending half my life all but alone with a pile of weird little songs, I'd found a comrade, an outlet.

. . .

Date Neil Gaiman. *Date Neil Gaiman The Writer.* Date Neil Gaiman The Writer?

Why not? I figured I'd try.

Though I was nursing a broken heart from my last breakup, and he was still recovering from his, along with the shadowy aftershocks of his divorce, we edged towards each other, day by day, like two cautious but wounded animals, and started to poke experimentally at each other's hearts, opening up little doors one at a time. It was slow, self-conscious work; we both knew how damaged we were. At least we could joke about it. And bit by bit, we started to fall in love.

It wasn't a plummet to the bottom of the love well, which was the only way I'd experienced falling in love. I was used to relationships going from *Hi!* to *Fuck Me!* to *Fuck You!* in under three weeks. Those relationships tended to slam into painful realities when the initial rush was over. This one was different: it was more like that moment in Wonderland when Alice's dress poufs out like a parachute and she floats down to the bottom of the well like a delicate feather.

One thing, however, I just couldn't shake. I could deal with the fact that Neil was famous. I was famous, too, in my own small, indie-rock way. But rich? I was struggling with that one. I made plenty of money when I toured, but I spent every penny on my recordings, my road crew, and my office staff. I had no savings and barely owned anything at that point: no car, no real estate, no kitchen appliances. I owned a lot of books, records, and T-shirts. My net worth was roughly equivalent to the cost of the grand piano I'd bought for $15,000 when I finally signed a recording contract. My rent was $750 a month. Neil owned multiple houses.

To make things worse, I couldn't *talk* to anyone about how weird it felt. I mean, I *talked* to *everyone* about it—my close friends, my intimates, my touring mates—but none of them was in a similar position, and they couldn't really advise me. Plus, complaining to my broke-ass artist friends about how to adjust to dating a rich guy felt like it was in particularly poor taste. I needed someone to ask who I knew was in the same boat. I tried to figure out who that might be.

Kathleen Hanna. Singer of Bikini Kill, the seminal Riot Grrl band. *She* would know. She was a punk feminist icon who was used to being embroiled in controversy, cutting records, and touring; cult famous but never famous enough to fill a stadium. Like me, she'd spent years just working her ass off on her bands and projects, but had never been rich. Then she'd married Ad-Rock from the Beastie Boys, who *had* achieved stadium-sized success. From afar, they seemed really happy. I didn't know her, but I tracked down her email address and wrote her:

Hi. It's Amanda Palmer from The Dresden Dolls. I know you don't really know me, but I need to ask you for advice. It's a phone call, not an email.

She called me.

Honestly, Amanda? she said. *For a while it just sort of sucked. There was a month when I was so broke I barely had enough money for food. And I was dating Adam and crashing in his swank apartment in Manhattan while he was away on tour, and I was, like, scraping together money to walk to the corner and buy instant noodles and oatmeal. It was really weird. And the thing that sucked most of all was not being able to talk to anyone about it.*

You had my life! I said. *And I'm not even that poor anymore. I can afford food. But I'm still freaked out.*

Ha. I get it. You know, I'm glad you asked me...because I didn't have anyone I could ask. It was really lonely, and in this creepy way that sort of made you feel like a jerk for being upset about it.

That didn't sound familiar at *all*.

. . .

From the start, The Dresden Dolls functioned in an artistic community that depended on messy exchanges of goodwill and the swapping of favors. More than a decade later, when the outside world was trying to make sense of my million-dollar Kickstarter success, I found myself digging through the past, trying to explain how it worked.

The *New York Times* called. *Forbes* magazine called.

Tell us, Amanda, can you explain this relationship you have with your fans?

Are you married? I'd ask.

Actually, yes. My wife, Susan, and I just celebrated our tenth anniversary last week!

So tell me, can you explain this relationship you have with your wife?

At least I'd make them laugh.

Like all real relationships, my "special relationship" with my fans wasn't some shtick that I came up with at a marketing meeting. On the contrary, I've spent many marketing meetings banging my head against a long conference table.

Throughout my career, the fanbase has been like one big significant other to me, a thousand-headed friend with whom I have a real, committed partnership. I don't take vacations from communicating without warning. We share our art with one another. They help me run the business by feeding me constant information. I cop to my mistakes. They ask for explanations. We talk about how we feel. I twitter to say good night and good morning, the way I would with a lover. They bring me food and tea at shows when I'm sick. I visit them in hospitals and make videos for their friends' funerals. We trust one another. Occasionally, I've broken up with fans. Some have broken up with me.

In the band's first three years, we played in friends' illegal lofts, in makeshift art galleries, in crappy sports bars that were trying to lure in drink-buying customers with the promise of live music, in people's living rooms, in used clothing stores, at benefits for feminist sex-toy shops. Whether we were being paid or not, if it was a gig, we took it.

But mostly we just played at my house, since we could always get a gig there. I was already in the habit of throwing huge parties. Lee loved it when the Cloud Club came alive with guests, and my new housemate, the filmmaker Michael Pope, became a co-conspirator in organizing bashes at which we would cram people into the various floors of the house, and out into the back garden and onto the roof in the summer. We put a shoebox at the door of the house with a sign suggesting (but not requiring) a ten-dollar admission, and set up a bar in every kitchen, spending the rolling donation money on wine, beer, and vodka. Anybody could bring whatever they wanted to share, be it food, drink, art, or music. I was perfectly happy letting four hundred strangers waltz through my kitchen and bedroom; I had nothing so valuable in my apartment that I ever had to hide it.

The entirety of The Dresden Dolls' travel inventory (electric piano, five-piece drum kit, and a few old suitcases full of costumes and the band T-shirts we sold for $10 each) could be perfectly Tetris'd into the back of my beat-up Volvo station wagon (affectionately dubbed The Vulva). We started driving farther and farther distances from Boston to take gigs. Brian was the technical expert (he knew everything there was to know about gear, including where to buy it and how to set it up), and I was the band's manager, press agent, and booking agent. I'd just bought my very first cell phone.

It was 2001 and email was still coming into vogue (and slightly suspect—lots of people in my artistic social circle resisted it), but I was obsessive about maintaining an email-based newsletter for the band and for the house parties. I could send out an email to fifty Boston friends, they would spread the word, and two weeks later, hundreds of people would show up at our house for a party. So the band's email list began as the house-party inner circle, then grew every time we had a gig or a gathering—there was no distinction between fans and friends. Not only did most of our early fans know where I lived and where we practiced, but most of them had also been in my kitchen.

Eventually, since it seemed impolite to be extending Boston house-party invitations to our fans in St. Louis, we made one email list per city. I considered the email list our pride and joy—the Thing From Which All Other Things Stemmed. Any time I ran into an old college friend on the street, any time I got into a conversation with a stranger on the subway, any time someone expressed even a remote interest in the band, I'd ask, *DO YOU DO EMAIL?* If the answer was yes, I recorded their address onto whatever was handy— my journal, a napkin, my hand—and when I got home, I'd send a personal welcome note.

My own email address was front and center on our website. I emailed back and forth with individual fans daily—about our lives, our gigs, ideas for shows—and often included a few words of den-mother comfort, because much of the fan mail usually came with a harrowing personal story attached. People thanked me for the songs: "Half Jack" had helped someone come to terms with their own parents, "Coin-Operated Boy" was popular with dancers on the burlesque circuit, who used it for routines, "Girl Anachronism" spoke to people's own battles with self-doubt. While Brian drove us to out-of-town gigs, I managed the band from the passenger seat on my bulky, blue, constantly crashing Dell laptop. Managing the band didn't mean talking to labels, agents, or publishers; we didn't know any. Managing the band meant making friends with other freaks in other cities, finding performers to share the stage with, lining up couches to crash on, chasing down a gallery where a friend was hanging paintings and was happy to have a band play at the opening.

Slowly but surely we amassed a local, then regional, following as we convinced our art-party friends to follow us into the rock establishments of Boston and beyond. Like the Cloud Club parties, the early concerts were more like happenings than straight rock shows. We'd bike around town posting up flyers that read:

THE DRESDEN DOLLS live THIS SATURDAY
at THE MIDDLE EAST NIGHTCLUB.
Doors 9 p.m. $12.
ALL ARE WELCOME.
DRESS FOR THE END OF THE WORLD,
OR THE BEGINNING.

People got a kick out of dressing up for our shows, and we encouraged it. Top hats, zoot suits, body paint, feather boas, and wigs were de rigueur. Our email blasts, which I sent out every few weeks, were celebratory missives, written to our friends. I kept the tone personal: Come to a party at the house. Or come to a Dolls show at a club. Or come to a Dolls show at the house. It was all the same.

. . .

I told Anthony I was thinking about dating Neil Gaiman. I was nervous. Anthony never judged me, but he judged my boyfriends (and occasional girlfriends) as fiercely as a protective older brother would.

So who is he? Anthony asked.

He's a writer.

Never heard of him.

He's like . . . cult famous. He writes comic books and science fiction and stuff. He's forty-eight. And British.

Anthony emitted a guttural, rumbling sound of suspicion.

What? Which part? The Famous? The British? Or the forty-eight?

None of it. He sounds . . . like a contender. When do I get to meet him?

* * *

Describing how art and exchange play off each other in *The Gift*, Lewis Hyde says:

The spirit of an artist's gifts can wake our own.

In my darkest hours, I still go to my secret stash of medicine-music to comfort me, like a familiar childhood blanket, and cocoon myself in the songs of Kimya Dawson, Leonard Cohen, or Robyn Hitchcock, who seem to be expressing some inexpressible thing inside of me. And listening to those songs performed live, in concert, and sharing that blanket feeling with a crowd of strangers, gives me a feeling of humanhood that I don't often get to experience; it's the closest thing I have to church.

When the gift circulates, we feel the very essence of art and life not just in the words and songs, but also in our deep desire to share them with one another.

* * *

You probably don't know who Edward Ka-Spel is.

Edward Ka-Spel is the singer of my favorite band, The Legendary Pink Dots. They formed in the early eighties in the UK, and they've been recording and touring for more than thirty years. They still tour, playing to crowds of hundreds more often than thousands, and their fanbase is like a family. I'm in the family. I joined when I was fourteen and my first boyfriend, Jason Curtis, started making me Pink Dots mixtapes. The psychedelic mash of synthesizers, violins, and drum machines, plus the raw emotional honesty of the lyrics, stole me straight out of the clutches of the "standard" alternative music I'd been listening to (The Cure, R.E.M., and Depeche Mode, mostly). But along with the Pink Dots' music—which we had to hunt down in used record shops or mail-order from faraway Dutch distributors—came the community.

The first time I saw the band play live was at a small all-ages club in Boston. I was sixteen. I had barely experienced any live rock music, and certainly nothing like this: a band I loved, on a stage five feet in front of me. That night changed my life: I was finally experiencing, in *person,* the songs that had been the soundtrack of my life for the past few years, the lyric-images I'd memorized after hours of headphone-listening on walks to school, the worlds that had been direct-deposited into my heart through the channel of my ears—I was hearing them here, now, in a moment that would never exist again. I was also standing in a room with three hundred people who seemed to have formed a real, connected comradeship by virtue of Loving One Thing and, by extension, one another. It seemed that this whole scene of people had formed a sort of open secret society around their love of this strange music and the strange guys who played it. I hadn't even known this was possible. I certainly hadn't been expecting to meet the band after the show.

Meet the band? I asked Jason.

Yes, he said, *they always do this.* And he was right: there they were, selling their own CDs and shirts while holding court in the dim light of the club as the grumpy bar crew dismantled the stage. I stood in line, waiting to meet Edward, the main singer and songwriter, trying to think of what I could possibly say that could have any meaning to him whatsoever. My idol. And then, for a short moment, we were face-to-face.

It's my dream, I said, looking right into his eyes, *to make music as honest as yours.*

Edward smiled and took my hand. He was as kind and warm as if I were a long-lost friend. We chatted for a minute, what about I'll never remember. I was awestruck.

I'll never forget that brief encounter. I didn't feel like a fan meeting a rock star. I didn't feel like a groupie. I felt like a friend.

Two years later, when I was about eighteen, The Legendary Pink Dots came through Boston again on tour, and I was lucky enough to be invited to tag along to the after-party at my friend Alan's house, where the band was also crashing. Alan was an advanced-level computer geek who ran the fans' online bulletin board system. Late into the night, we sat in Alan's living room, sharing beer and stories. Jon, another member of the trusted Pink Dots family who hosted the band's official website, said, out of the blue, *Edward, did you know Amanda's a songwriter? She plays piano. She's pretty good.*

I froze. *No no no no no no no,* I thought.

Edward looked interested.

Really? he said. *Do you have anything we can hear?*

Alan, do you have Amanda's demo tape kicking around? Jon asked.

I'd made a four-track tape recording of a few of my piano songs with a few cheap microphones in my parents' living room, and Alan had one of the twelve copies in existence.

I think so, said Alan, rummaging around in a milk crate. *Yeah! Here it is . . .*

No no no no no no no no.

He popped the tape into the stereo, and I sat there trying not to throw up while Edward and the collected company listened to my piano songs warbling through the speakers.

Hearing my own singing voice paralyzed me, and another voice that I knew intimately rose up inside of me:

I can't write songs. I can't sing. I have a fucking phony English accent and THESE PEOPLE ARE ACTUALLY ENGLISH. How humiliating. And god, my lyrics are so pretentious and stupid and self-indulgent. Who the fuck do I think I am?

I wanted to run. I wasn't ready to be judged, and certainly not here, in this room, by my heroes. After two songs (one a fast-pounding punk rant about my nail-biting habit, the other a dirge about the loss of my virginity set in a metaphorical playground), Alan snapped off the tape player.

There! She's good, right? Edward and the band nodded affably and the conversation turned back to the show, politics, and other bohemian topics.

I was shaking. I stepped outside to smoke a clove cigarette, and was sitting on the steps in the cold autumn darkness, inhaling sharply and trying to calm myself down, when the door rattled shut behind me. It was Edward. He sat down next to me and lit his own hand-rolled cigarette. I'd never been alone with him before.

I want to tell you something, Amanda.

I had no idea what was coming, but I trusted him to be kind. God, I trusted him more than anyone or anything else in the world at that moment. But I was so afraid.

Yeah? I said, nonchalantly.

Your songs are good, Amanda. And I'm not just saying that.

I stared at him in disbelief.

I get given a lot of music, he continued. *It's like that on the road, you know, we get handed mountains of demo tapes every night. And they're, you know, not always good. Your songs are good. I don't know what your plans are. But I hope you keep going. I just wanted to say that.*

And he stubbed out his cigarette and went back into the house, leaving me on the porch, feeling an emotion I can only describe as ecstasy. I stayed on that cloud for days, walking around in a fog, thinking that my fate had somehow been decided for me.

Nobody had ever said that to me before. Nobody qualified, at least. Nobody who really counted. I try to recall the enormity of that feeling every time I'm talking to a younger musician who summons the courage to play me their stuff. I bear in mind that I may be the only full-time musician they've encountered who's ever directly said:

Yes. You're allowed to go do that. Go ahead.

• • •

The next time they came through Boston on tour, I was in college a few hours away and came back home for the show. I talked my parents, god bless them, into hosting five English and Dutch indie rock stars (plus a merch guy and a sound guy) in our suburban house. Some of them slept in the attic, some in the van outside, and I slept over at Jason's so they could take my bed. Early the next morning, I hurried back to fix them all breakfast before they drove off to the next tour stop. Seeing my favorite band eating in the dining room where my family celebrated Thanksgiving made my brain turn upside down. I had never put so much love into a batch of scrambled eggs.

I'd learned that it was pointless trying to tell these people what their music had *meant to me*. It meant everything. Their songs were the landscape of my inner life. I was modeling my own style of songwriting after theirs. It would just sound trite if I tried to explain it out loud.

But I could make them eggs.

. . .

By 2002, Brian and I were touring more and more, and we started earning real cash money at the shows. At the end of each night, the fans would ask us for CDs, but for a while we had nothing to sell besides some T-shirts and a bumper sticker that we had designed ourselves. No music.

The ability to burn CDs was a brand-spanking-new technology. So instead of taking our first cheap recording to a duplication house, we decided it would be more economical to just burn our own.

We made our first recording for free, thanks to a sound-engineer friend who snuck us into a studio after hours. I pasted together a collage I'd assembled out of old paper dolls to use as our album artwork, while Brian made endless OfficeMax runs in The Vulva to purchase boxes of blank CDs and empty jewel cases. We sat in the kitchen burning batches of our songs in a three-disc CD tower. On a good day we could make a few hundred discs, and we only needed a few dozen at a time to sell at shows: five songs for $5. The fans were eager to have them and they sold really well. Soon, my whole apartment in the Cloud Club—which was small to begin with—turned into a CD-assembly workshop. I got very friendly with the local post office, where we stood in line two or three times a week to ship batches of records to our fans with handwritten thank-you postcards. The fans used my home address to order everything.

They paid by personal check and we sent the CDs before the checks cleared (or didn't).

Meanwhile, I worked weekends as The Bride, got the stripping job as well, and Brian took shifts at the MIT student center branch of Toscanini's, where he asked for and received Gus's kind blessing to make a display stand for our CD at the register. At every shift, he wound up selling a few CDs to ice-cream customers.

GET THEIR EMAILS! I'd remind him.

He did. A good percentage of our initial hardcore fanbase was MIT grad students and professors, who stood happily at our gigs next to the twenty-two-year-old punk kids with their pierced septums and turquoise dreadlocks. Brian and I took great pleasure in the fact that we seemed to have created the most eclectic community of fans in Boston: art college students, vegan punks, drag queens, metalheads, academics, people who listened to National Public Radio. That meant the world to us. We didn't *want* to tap a particular crowd—we didn't want to be a hip indie band or a goth band. We wanted the people who came to the shows to feel like they were part of our weird little family, that they would never be turned away at the door for not being cool enough. Brian and I had both been insecure freaks in high school; we'd already spent our entire lives on the outside of that door, and we didn't just want to gain entrance. We wanted to smash the door down completely.

• • •

Things started to catch ablaze. We couldn't quit our jobs yet, but we were close. We won the local Boston battle of the bands. I quit smoking, because I wanted to take care of my voice, which I was constantly losing. We drove the van, we gigged, we drove, we ate metric tons of bad gas-station food, we drove, we soundchecked, we drove some more, and when we needed to sleep, we slept on the couches of old friends, out-of-town family, local fans, or crashed with other bands. In a pinch, we got a cheap motel or slept in the van, which was tricked out with a futon in the back.

In turn, we hosted countless musicians and friends at the Cloud

Club, whether they were playing shows with us or not—it was a karmic couch-circle. I'd get photos emailed to me on the road of bands in the back garden, bands on the roof, bands in the bathtub. Bands left thank-you notes, drawings, books, CDs behind as gifts.

Our fanbase grew slowly but steadily. We'd go to a city—Philly, Portland, Northampton, DC—and play to fifty people, then a hundred and fifty, then three hundred. Word spread. The email list grew. We still had no manager, no agent.

Sometimes, if we didn't have a place to crash, we'd just ask from the stage.

HANDS UP IF YOU CAN LET US SLEEP AT YOUR HOUSE TONIGHT.

We'd thank our hosts with CDs, T-shirts, tour stories, and our endless gratitude.

We made some wonderful friends that way.

One of those friends was a photographer in Philadelphia named Kyle Cassidy, a classic couch-patron who had been enthusiastically letting bands crash in his home for years. We sometimes shared space at Kyle's with other bands passing through town, trading stories over group breakfasts. That house became a dependable haven after our Philly gigs and, since he loved capturing the band and we trusted him, Kyle also became our default official band photographer. If I knew a band was touring through Philly, I'd send them to Kyle and he'd take them in without question.

I started a computer list of our few dozen dependable couchsurfing hosts, organized by city. Kyle in Philly. Brian's dad in New Jersey. His aunt in St. Louis. Josh and Alina in New York. Xanna and her girlfriend in Atlanta. Clare and Brian in Montreal. Emily in Brooklyn. My dad in Washington, DC. Kate in Chicago…

. . .

DIY is a tricky term.

I've been called the "Queen of DIY," but if you're really taking the definition of "Do It Yourself" literally, I completely fail. I have no interest in Doing It Myself. I'm much more interested in getting everybody to help me.

I think a better definition might be UWYC: "Use What You Can." It is, unfortunately, not a very catchy term.

Everybody has access to different tools, people, resources, situations, opportunities. If you're privileged enough to have family well-off enough to loan you money for your first recording? TAKE IT.

If you have a friend with a shack on the beach who's offering you a quiet place to write? TAKE IT.

There's really no honor in proving that you can carry the entire load on your own shoulders. And . . . it's lonely.

Maybe we can break DIY mentality into two camps, because "collective" work doesn't actually blow everybody's dress up.

"Minimal DIY" is the kind of DIY where you literally try to *Do It Yourself.* The emphasis is on total self-reliance and individualism.

Don't have the right kind of microphone? *Use a different one.*

Don't have a huge budget for food/can't afford takeout/have no kitchen? *Just buy a box of ramen in bulk and cook it in the coffeemaker you got for $5 at a yard sale.*

Can't afford to hire a full choir of people? *Don't use a choir. Your song doesn't need it and it'll sound pompous and pretentious anyway. Or, if you must, record your own voice fifty times, singing slightly differently at different spots in the room.*

Car runs out of gas on a long stretch of road? *Grab the empty canister out of your trunk and start walking, sucker.*

Then there's "Maximal DIY," which is more about expansion and asking. The emphasis is on collectivism; you throw the problem out to your circles to see what solutions will arise.

Don't have the right kind of microphone in your studio? *Use Twitter, shouting towards the musicians and studios; some kind person may lend you the right one.*

Don't have a huge budget for studio food? *Ask if anyone local feels like helping/cooking/bringing you leftover food from their job at the bakery.*

Can't afford to hire a full choir of people? *Send out a blog and have your fans come in and sing with you. They may sound amateur, but it'll be fun, and people love being on a record.*
Car runs out of gas on a long stretch of road? *Put your thumb out. Someone will eventually give you a lift.*
As you can see, the underlying philosophy is actually the same: Limitations can expand, rather than shrink, the creative flow.
Minimal DIY doesn't rely on trust; it relies on ingenuity.
Maximal DIY relies on trust *and* ingenuity. You have to ask with enough grace and creativity to elicit a response, and you also have to *trust* the people you're asking not to ruin your recording session, not to poison your food, not to bludgeon you with a hammer as you sit in their passenger seat.

• • •

We hung out and signed merchandise after every show in every town, Pink-Dots-style, and a natural outgrowth of our beginnings in which the audience had blurred with our circle of friends. If we wound up getting kicked out of a venue because we'd hit curfew and we hadn't finished signing things, we'd parade the remaining fans outside and finish in the street.

We signed our CDs, of course, and shirts and posters, too— usually with a black or silver Sharpie. But we also signed: phone cases, playing cards, sneakers, reading glasses, Bibles, passports (*You know this is illegal, right?*), purses, faces (*please don't get that tattooed*), armpits, puppets, babies (*please don't get that tattooed, either*), feet, shot glasses, teakettles, security blankets, breasts, and once, a guy's penis (it was not erect). And one time, in Santa Barbara, Brian signed a girl's anus. Everyone was impressed.

I asked him to please throw that particular Sharpie in the trash.

People loved giving us art they'd made. Sometimes the signing line would create art collisions unwittingly, like the time a girl at the front of the line gave me an anatomically correct, life-sized, gorgeously hand-knitted vagina, and a guy at the back of the line gave me a little plastic astronaut toy from the 1980s that nestled perfectly into the vulva. Somebody else in the line had a twist tie and threaded them together more tightly. They live, in harmony, on my kitchen shelf at the Cloud Club and have never been separated since that day.

In the early days, we talked to people for as long as they wanted, about whatever they wanted. Once we started touring internationally, these signings would sometimes last longer than the show itself; we'd sometimes play for two hours and sign for two and a half.

In retrospect, the act of signing was far more significant than I realized in the moment. Especially in the early days, when we were playing in small clubs, I was actually AFRAID of the audience. Not afraid they would hurt me, or throw glass bottles at my head (which DOES happen in some genres of music). I was just afraid of their judgment. We were only just starting to get criticized on the hipster music websites for being too gay, too dramatic, too female, too screamy, too lame, too goth. I would imagine that the strangers out there beyond the footlights were the same entities who were judging us in the snarky corners of the music blogs. I feared the critics. In my head, the critics and the crowd were one and the same.

As I played and looked out into the crowd, I could see clearly that the people in the front rows loved us, since they were mouthing the words to our songs, banging their heads, throwing their fists in the air. But what about the people in the ninth, tenth, and twentieth rows? I couldn't see *them*. I imagined them all standing there with their arms crossed, rolling their eyes at our gay mime antics, waiting to be sufficiently impressed.

Signing fixed that, because we got to meet a pretty decent percentage of the audience every night. They weren't judgmental hipsters. They were just sweet, human, smart, fumbling people like Brian and me, all of whom had kind faces and, usually, their own strange stories to tell. After hundreds of nights of signing, my instinct to fear the audience was worn away, like running water smoothing down a jagged rock.

It was an epiphany: Holy shit. They're not scary at all. They're just…*a bunch of people*.

It just wasn't possible to feel that anxious anymore: I'd MET them. But I never would've known if I hadn't made the effort to stand at the merch table every night; I might have stayed afraid for years. And when you're afraid of someone's judgment, you can't connect with them. You're too preoccupied with the task of impressing them.

. . .

Once we had enough money to be choosy, I turned down the option of using a real grand piano. Too much fuss to transport, rent, and tune, too hard to fit onstage, too hard for Brian to see my exact hand movements when we played. But most importantly, turning my head to the side to address the audience felt alienating. I wanted to look straight at them. I wanted to see them.

The typical electric keyboard stand is pretty ugly, though, so along with the tea, honey, hummus, and juice that our contract required from the ever-larger venues we were playing, I asked for a few bunches of flowers every night, so we could tape them to the keyboard stand to hide the ugliness. We often had flowers left over, though, and it seemed like a waste to leave them in the dressing room where they'd just be thrown away. Some divas get flowers thrown *at* them, but we started a tradition of pitching flowers *at the audience* when we first took the stage; a love assault of foliage. We started requesting that the flowers have absolutely no thorns, for safety. With some effort, we could usually hit people in the balcony.

People started bringing bouquets to the shows and passing them through the crowd up to the lip of the stage for use between songs, or throwing them at our feet, true diva style, at the start of the show. We would rip them up into manageable chunks and throw them back out to the crowd. The crowd would toss them back at the stage.

This game could last all night.

Later, in the signing line, people would take the flowers from behind their ears and hand them to me as a thank-you gesture. Then I'd recycle the same flower to someone down the line who looked lonely or in need of some extra love.

On a good night, you couldn't tell who was giving what to whom.

• • •

Sharing my life on the Internet has meant that everybody knows the immediate score of my existence. Fans in the signing line will ask, *How's Neil? Did he get to his plane on time?* And, *How's your chest infection—have you finished that run of antibiotics?* I'm on the road and they're on home turf. They bring books, herbs, teas, soaps, beers from the bar, organic wines from the region. The edible items are usually shared with the people standing behind them.

The signing line is a cross between a wedding party, a photo booth, and the international arrivals terminal at the airport; a blurry collision of flash intimacies. It's a reunion with those I haven't met yet. There are a lot of tears and a lot of high-fiving and a lot of hugging. There's also a lot of asking, in both directions.

Will you take a picture for us?
Will you take a picture with us?
Do you need a hug?
Can I have a drink?
Do you want a drink?
Will you hold my drink?
Why are you crying?

It's not always the fans crying. I've been held by many fans on nights I needed a random shoulder on which to collapse.

I've observed signing lines at other concerts that are not like this, where it's all business and security officers stand there making sure nobody touches The Talent. I've had to *argue* with security officers appointed to my signing lines, explaining that, unlike other bands, we don't WANT security to hurry people along, or shoo them away, making sure they don't stop to talk. I *need* people to stop and talk and hug me, or else I feel like an automaton.

Listening fast and caring immediately is a skill in itself. People bring me compact stories: the song that got them through high school, the operation they just had, the recent breakup, the death of a parent. The story about the sick friend who wanted to be at the show but couldn't make it.

Or the longer, more complicated story about the friend who was supposed to be at the show, but had just committed suicide.

What do you do with news like that? You stop the signing line, you take that person in your arms, you hold them and let them cry for as long as necessary.

Then you get back to work.

* * *

If I had a dollar for every time somebody gave me a CD, I'd have a lot of dollars. Instead, I have a lot of CDs. Years after my front-porch encounter with Edward Ka-Spel, I found myself empathizing with the mountains of tapes that he'd been given on tour.

Can I give you my CD? I'm in a band.

Can I give you my CD? My girlfriend is a singer-songwriter.

Can I give you my CD? I run a death-metal label here in town. I make beats in my bedroom. I make a cappella music on my phone.

The answer is always yes, yes, yes, and yes. I see those CDs as something more than just some local kid trying to get his band a break. They're like a thank-you letter, a way for one artist to wave a flag to another, like two lighthouses; part of the must-never-stop, ever-circulating gift.

And you do not refuse that gift, ever.

* * *

Whether you're prepared for it or not, part of the job that goes along with being a confessional songwriter is that you become a makeshift therapist by default. Except you don't have a nice, quiet office: you're doing it in loud, dingy nightclubs, in dark alleys outside tour buses, and in backstage bathrooms. I feel simultaneously honored and depressed when someone pulls me close and says, "There's nobody else I can tell this to…" and proceeds to detail a secret abortion, a rape, a diagnosis of a mental illness.

In that instant of intimate exchange, I want to adopt every teenage kid who tells me their parents kicked them out of the house for being gay. I want to follow the story of every recovery, I want to stick around to see every baby get born and every wound heal and every heart evolve. But I don't. I can't. Every night, I drive away.

• • •

You see twenty patients a week. How do you deal with taking in so much pain from strangers? I asked Anthony one night, over the phone as I lay on a pull-out bed in a friend's living room in Montreal. The post-show signing had taken ages and I was exhausted, but I couldn't sleep.

Have you ever heard of a "sin-eater"?

No, I said. *Tell me.*

It's when a local holy man, or a guru, takes on the sins and sufferings of the community by opening to those who are in pain, and filtering the pain and suffering. He takes all the emotional trash and, through his body, through his love and capacity to stay present, clarifies the pain into compassion. Lots of religions have their version of it. Jesus does it for the Christians.

A community confession-booth attendant, basically, I said.

Ha. Basically. There were professional sin-eaters in England. A guy, for money, would come around and eat bread over the corpse of a dead family member to purge the body of sin before it went to heaven. It's also the magic and mystery of what we do—when we nail it—in psychotherapy. We take on the suffering of others, digest it, transform it.

And artists? I asked. *Sounds like art.*

Yeah, good artists do it. You know, the "Artist" and the "Medicine Man" used to be the same guy. "Musician" and "Shaman" used to be the same characters, in a way. Our jobs aren't that different, you and me.

I've seen you at the signing line, I've watched you. Eat the pain. Send it back to the void as love.

Can I ask you a question?

Ask, he said.

Do you ever have days where you can't take it all in, and it just makes you too sad?

Yeah, beauty. It happens all the time.

. . .

Sometimes the signing line keeps me from having to be alone.

Sometimes the signing line reminds me that this job isn't about me, it's about everybody.

Mostly the signing line makes me feel connected to the people around the fire.

I need to see their faces.

Sometimes I feel like I need the signing line more than they do.

I notice a difference if I don't sign after a show. It can feel deeply lonely.

Not signing or hanging out after a show is like taking someone home for a one-night stand, having passionate sex with them, and then watching them, from the bed, as they get dressed and leave right after the orgasm. I need the postcoital cuddle, the bit where you spend the night spooning, looking into each other's eyes with a confirmation that, yes, that happened. And now let's at least get breakfast and talk about the mundane details of our lives even if we're probably never going to see each other again.

I hate it when people don't spend the night.

. . .

Michael Pope and I decided to make a music video—he was a filmmaker, my housemate, and one of my best friends; it made sense—so we picked one of the band's most popular live songs, "Girl Anachronism," and co-wrote a treatment sitting at my kitchen table, then spent a week transforming our home into a production house. We asked Ron, the photographer friend of Anthony's and all-around art enthusiast, to front us the money for film stock (real film stock!). We asked Lee to help decorate the top floor, we asked our housemate Zea to do the costumes, and we asked our fans to volunteer behind the scenes. We fed everybody pizza and beer, and shot for twelve straight hours (we couldn't afford to rent the equipment for longer than a day), using almost every room of the Cloud Club, along with the back garden and the roof, as our film set. When the video was edited and we put it up on our website (these were pre-YouTube days), everybody in our immediate community had taken part in one way or another. And Lee was ecstatic: this was how he always imagined the space being used. We went on to shoot full-scale music videos in the house, and at my parents' house, and at Ron's house, and at my old high school, using the drama students. Through the act of asking, we created our community. That's how it worked.

• • •

Our audience was growing. We sent hundreds of packages to hundreds of labels. Nobody wanted us. We finally decided that we should stop running a CD-toasting business out of my kitchen and make our own legitimate studio record. On our own, no label. If we printed a few thousand copies, the whole undertaking would cost us about $20,000, including the studio time, and then we'd have a high-quality CD with all of our songs to sell at shows, and make the money back.

But we didn't have that kind of money. We were making a few hundred dollars here and there from gigging, but even when combined with our incomes from stripping, statue-ing, and scooping ice cream, that didn't leave us with more than a few thousand dollars at a time, and we still had to get around, pay rent, buy food.

We did have a growing fanbase and a hardcore work ethic, though, and I figured that was decent enough collateral to guarantee a few personal loans. I made a short list of people, and then one by one, I asked them: Ron Nordin, Anthony's best friend, a photographer and local arts enthusiast; my parents; our New York couchsurfing hosts Josh and Alina; a generous uncle who lived in Los Angeles. And we asked Tom and Steve, a gay couple who came to almost all of our gigs, lived in a house, and appeared to have real jobs. I asked everyone if they would pitch in up to $5,000 for the recording and printing of the record, with the promise that we would pay the money back within a year, sooner if possible.

They all said yes, and sent checks. I mailed them all printed letters so that they would have some sort of a legal record, even though they knew we weren't going to run off to Mexico with the money. They trusted us.

I thanked them all profusely.

We spent a couple of harebrained months driving back and forth from Boston to Brooklyn, where we slaved over the record, and we hired two of my Cloud Club housemates (Zea, the painter, and Thom, the graphic designer) to create the album artwork. Then we sold the CD (which we titled, simply, *The Dresden Dolls*) straight to the fans at the shows for $10 a pop. We quickly sold out of the first batch of 5,000 and ordered another. My kitchen became a wonderland workshop of envelopes and packaging as we started mailing them out to fans in more and more distant states and countries, and to labels, radio stations, publicists, and managers, hoping someone would help us run our business—answer the phones, mail the T-shirts, handle the bookings. We couldn't cope with all the work. We were getting overloaded.

After two years of constant gigging with no manager, no booking agent, and a growing pile of rejection letters from every indie label on the planet saying "we don't sign goth bands" (we weren't a goth band, dammit!), I started to get desperate. We were drawing five hundred people a night by then in a handful of cities, and though I was enjoying our Bohemian Traveling Circus Fantasy, our time between shows had become completely consumed by emails and phone calls, trying to organize our schedule while trying to get signed. I couldn't keep up with being the touring act and the office manager. We got bigger and bigger, but nobody would sign us. We were too strange. We didn't sound like any other band currently becoming famous.

Then a promising email came in from a guy named Dave. He wanted to talk to us. I'd never heard of his label, and when I googled it, I found bands with names like 3 Inches of Blood, Baptized in Blood, Make Them Suffer, Mutiny Within, and Satan. A METAL label? I'd been hoping to get signed by Matador. Or Mute. Somewhere we could stand alongside Belle and Sebastian, Neutral Milk Hotel, The Magnetic Fields, The Pixies, and other arty indie bands with harmless names. I found a music lawyer and showed him the contract.

They basically want to give you fifty grand to sign away your firstborn, he told me. *They'd take a cut of everything you ever earn, now and forever, including your merchandise and the rights to every song you ever write. Are you sure you want to sign with them even if I sweeten up the deal and let you keep your firstborn?*

I wasn't sure, but we were working as hard as we could and nobody else wanted us. We were desperate.

Let's de-firstborn it, I said. *I'm game to try.*

We played a show around that time with Karen Mantler, an off-the-wall jazz singer who, after releasing three CDs on an indie, was picked up by a major label (*bloodsucking scum*, is how I believe she referred to them) only to learn that the major considered her, as Karen put it, a "tax write-off." She told us that after her album, of which she was incredibly proud, had been released, they'd mailed her ten copies, fired the guy who'd signed her, and did absolutely nothing else to sell or promote it—you literally couldn't find or buy it in any stores. She was completely disillusioned, but fighting back, in her own way. At the merchandise table after the show, she was selling hand-burned copies of the CDs that the label wouldn't put into circulation; she even designed a new cover that declared,

"KAREN MANTLER'S PET PROJECT—BOOTLEG EDI-TION," with a message on the back explaining how her label had screwed her.

I think we should sign, I said to Brian. *I mean . . . we'll always have a CD burner. We can always go all Karen Mantler on their asses.*

After a few more go-rounds with the lawyers, we signed the con-tract in blood. (Actual blood. It was a metal label; we figured that was appropriate.) They paid us $100,000 for the eternal rights to the album that we'd recorded for $20,000 (territory: "the universe," just in case our albums started selling big on Mars). Thanks to the lawyer, I kept my firstborn—my publishing and merchandising rights.

First, we paid our lawyer.

Then I wrote checks to pay back all the loans, which I mailed back with thank-you letters. Then Brian and I took all of our parents out to a celebration dinner in a restaurant fifty feet from my main Bride spot in Harvard Square.

And then we quit our ice cream, statue, and stripping jobs once and for all.

.   .   .

I introduced Neil to Anthony in an Italian restaurant in the North End of Boston. Neil and I had been dating for a few months. If they didn't like each other, I was going to die.

We ate and drank wine, discussing all manner of things, and I couldn't help feeling that they were tactically sizing each other up, like two dogs in a park.

Neil seemed to like Anthony just fine.

So? So? What did you think? I asked Anthony the next morning, over the phone.

Anthony said: *I don't know, beauty. He's smart, that's for sure. But he seems nervous. You know? Like, freaked out.*

*That's because he **was** nervous and freaked out, clown-head. I've* been talking about you since I met him. He was terrified you wouldn't like him. So...do you like him?

Anthony made a *hmmmmmmm* sound.

WHAT DOES THAT MEAN??

Why's it so important to you what I think?

I dunno. Because you're you. Just help me out here, okay? You know me better than anyone. And you've saved me from like, what—five fatal relationships?

I have not, said Anthony.

You have so. Remember Mike? Remember how I thought it would be hilarious to get married in college because NOBODY would BELIEVE IT ha ha ha?

Well, yeah. That's true.

And Oliver? The one who OD'd?

Well...okay.

• • •

We got a lot of fan mail. Some of it was hate mail, and we built a special page on our website to feature the worst of it. I hand-selected some choice excerpts for the website back in the day:

> *You are the worst act I have ever heard. Avril Lavigne is WAY better than you. BUT so are The Backstreet Boys. And THEY FUCKING BLOW. You ugly-looking fuck and the hairy French lookin' Chinese chick* [sic].

> *I'm not usually into violent imagery, but when I'm forced to listen to your album I start channeling violent thoughts.*

> *This shithead in my work (where we have an employee playlist on all the time) keeps putting "Coin-Operated Boy" on the playlist. I hate you, and I hate her. The female in the band looks like German Gestapo unshaven monkey shit. The dude in the band is a coin-operated child molester. Please eat shit and die.*

The hate mail page included, as the centerpiece, this letter to the editor in a Boston music zine:

It always amazes me how easily impressed Boston audiences are. Especially when it comes to an act like The Dresden Dolls, who are not only mediocre as a duo, but totally unoriginal as well. Amanda can't get through a show without trying to shock people... and her piano playing is atrocious. It's obvious that the real brains and the real musician in that band is Brian (stellar drummer by the way, too bad his playing is totally mocked by Miss Palmer). I can't help but wonder... if Amanda didn't act like a total ass, or rather, an attention-starved daddy's girl, flaunting her flabby, hairy body to everyone and playing herself off to be "a performance artist"... would anyone care?

The hate-mail page became the most heavily trafficked spot on our website.

People started writing to thank me for being brave enough to display the nastiness. But it didn't feel brave; it felt like the only option, the only way I could deal with the pain. I still practice this same style of Internet jiujitsu to this day: I grab the hate and air it out, try to laugh at it, and share it back out into the world, so it doesn't eat me alive. Around the same time that we built the hate-mail page, I started blogging regularly, sharing the good press, the bad press, and my emotional struggles riding the *I AM LOVED! I AM HATED!* yo-yo of praise and criticism as I tried to simultaneously balance touring, recording, managing the band, and whatever shreds were left of my local social life.

I was beginning to learn about online abuse, but, as people started to follow my blog by the hundreds, then the thousands, I also had my first taste of crowd power, and how double-edged the sword was.

We had just gotten our giant label check, paid off our loans, and had enough left over to buy a top-of-the-line drum kit for Brian and, my heart slamming with pride (I was Signed! I was Legitimate!), I started to shop for my first real piano, with a budget of about $20,000, to replace the dilapidated, untuneable piano on which I was currently composing in my apartment (someone had been about to throw it away; I'd paid the moving costs). I wanted something bright sounding and rugged, since I had a tendency to break strings. I went into every single used and new showroom in Boston, fingering the keys and nooks and crannies of every piano for sale with a kind of erotic disbelief that I was in a position to actually buy one. It felt so incredibly *real*.

One day I walked into a little piano shop in a converted old house in the deep suburbs. There were only a few other customers poking around; a lone nice-looking guy in a cardigan was minding the floor. I sat down at one of the baby grands and started test-driving it with some loud Beethoven, then with one of my own songs. I closed my eyes and listened, feeling the weight of the keys, hammering away like a maniac.

The guy approached me politely. I stopped playing.

Miss? Hello. I'm sorry but I'm going to have to... ask you to leave.

Holding my breath, I stood up, picked up my bag, walked out of the store and back to my car, and before I could process what had happened, I broke down crying. *He thinks I'm a fraud.*

I drove home and, still weepy, took to my blog. I poured out the whole story for my small readership, how ashamed and angry I felt, how devastating and embarrassing it was. I included the name of the shop, and the address, and encouraged my fans to write the guy a letter if they felt so inclined.

It wasn't until the next day, as I read a few emails from fans who told me they had proudly written letters to the shop in protest, that I felt the gravity, the stupidity—the *meanness*—of what I had done.

I imagined scolding, scalding hate letters piling up on that poor guy's desk as he tried to eke out a living running a little piano shop.

Sure, he was a dick for throwing me out of his store, but wasn't I a bigger dick to torment him like that? And wasn't it even more dickish to use my own fans as weapons of destruction? Ashamed by my realization, I went back to my blog, removed the store name and address, and wrote a follow-up post, telling my fans that I'd been an idiot diva, that it was the insecure teenager talking. Then I prayed that the poor guy would be left in peace. I was afraid to drive down that street for a while.

I had sampled the power of cruelty. And it tasted awful.

. . .

Still, most of the early fan mail was love mail, not hate mail, and I started exchanging emails and letters with hundreds of fans. It was like having an infinite number of pen pals, and I eventually despaired when, after a few years, the number of emails coming in was more than I could keep up with. It made me feel like a bad friend.

Sometimes I'd dip into the fan mail just to cheer myself up, to feel useful to the world when I was depressed. Writing songs offered no instant gratification, but reading and answering a letter somehow did. There were recurring themes in the letters: unhappiness, rape, identity crises, self-abuse, suicidal thoughts. I answered as honestly as I could. *I hope your parents eventually understand. Stay strong. I know how that feels, I've been there. It gets better. Yes, I'm happy to recommend some books on Buddhism. No, I haven't always been this fearless... I was afraid to play my music for years.*

During one of these answering sprees, I answered a note from a poetic, eccentric-sounding eighteen-year-old named Casey who had written to me from a hospital in Boston. She had ovarian cancer and they had put her in the children's ward, where she was the oldest patient and having a hard time watching so many of the other children suffer. Getting to know all the parents was the worst thing, she told me. She would meet them and make friends with them and then watch them watch their kids die. After exchanging a handful of emails, I came back to Boston from a West Coast tour and, with my suitcases still unpacked, found myself staring at one of her emails on the screen.

She'd never asked me to visit. But I got in my car, happy to put off unpacking and facing my real life for an afternoon. I found her room number at the front desk, walked up, and rapped on the door. Her mother opened it, and her eyes blinked with a dawning recognition; she knew my face from The Dresden Dolls gig flyers Casey had taped to the wall of her unit. *Hold on*, she whispered. She scuttled back behind the curtain and I heard a yelp.

That was Casey. She was wearing a wig, because of the chemo. I stayed in her room for an hour, picking up where we'd left off over email. She showed me how she'd been taping up hopeful paintings she'd made in her windows, so the children in the ward across the courtyard could see them.

She didn't die. We kept emailing. And gradually, she became my close friend. After she recovered, she came to Dolls shows and created beautiful chalk drawings on the sidewalks outside the clubs. Then she went to art college. Then I asked her if she needed a place to live.

She's twenty-seven now, a painter with one ovary, the right one, and she's been my Cloud Club housemate for five years. Lee brings her more reams of paper than she needs. She had a fish for a while named Left Ovary. Then Left Ovary died, and she named her new fish Everything.

I'd text her from the road to ask,

How's everything?

And she'd text back,

Everything's really good. He just pooped.

When things were particularly bad and she was going through boy trouble or something, I'd text,

Everything's going to be okay. Everything exists.

One day, while I was on tour in Europe, I got a text from Casey saying,

Everything is gone.

. . .

The politician Tip O'Neill once said something along these lines: If you want to make someone your real friend, ask them for a favor.

As we forged along, the band made an art out of asking for help—from our housemates, from our friends, from our fans, from our family, from anybody who'd give it.

We'd done a good job of thoroughly angering and confusing the hell out of the local Boston nightclubs by showing up for gigs with our volunteer artist friends and fans, whom we'd dubbed "The Brigade." Busker friends of mine stood outside the gigs playing accordions and posing as statues. Burlesque dancers roved around the venue in costume, handing out flowers and ripped-out pages from poetry books. Painter friends set up easels and worked, doing portraits. Volunteers decorated the sidewalks outside the venue, festooning the nooks and crannies of the lobbies and bathrooms with glitter, garlands of flowers, fortune cookies, Barbie doll heads.

We tried to set up an arm of The Brigade in every city; you just had to volunteer over email—to do basically anything—and I'd grant you a guest-list space. We paid with the usual currency we had on hand: T-shirts, CDs, backstage beer, shout-outs from stage, tickets, love. I announced any local shows or art openings from stage if a member of The Brigade had something coming up.

In my free time, I tried to hunt down potentially interesting local performers, which was becoming easier now that Google existed and you could search for "insane cabaret performers detroit." If an extra performer we'd reached out to wanted to get paid for the gig, those decisions were random and made on the fly:

We'd love to come, but we're all professionally trained ballerinas, so we need backstage space to warm up, a voice said over the phone as we barreled down the highway to our next stop. *Then we set ourselves on fire to songs by Led Zeppelin and AC/DC, mostly all classic rock... but all the dancers live at least an hour outside Detroit and we each need fifty dollars for gas and there will be at least five or six of us.*

I put my hand over the mouthpiece of my phone and turned to Brian, who was driving.

They're ballerinas who set themselves on fire to AC/DC but they need money for gas, I whispered.

For gas to set themselves on fire? Brian asked.

No, gas for the car.

HIRED! Brian said, banging the steering wheel.

We're totally down, I said into the phone. *You sound amazing. We can do like two hundred bucks—however many ballerinas that buys us. Just grab the cash from me after the show. And for god's sake, talk to the club about the local fire laws. Do you have a website I can post?*

Yes, it's Tutu Inferno dot org. Spelled T-u-t...

I got it, I got it. See you Sunday.

In the streets of Edinburgh one year, I ran into a busking duo called Bang On! who played percussion on junk and household objects. Our UK tour was already packed with opening stage acts, but I asked if they'd like to try a new experiment: to set up and play on the theater floor as people were filing in before the show, then pass the hat. They said they'd give it a shot. I came out half-dressed and half-made-up for the show, watched and applauded them, and then made a personal plea to the crowd, letting them know that these people had come to entertain out of the goodness of their own hearts and weren't getting otherwise paid. The money poured in, and something about *asking* everybody—on the spot—to reach into their pockets to help these two artists changed the energy of the room. It turned the random crowd into a real community. It also meant that nobody ever came late to our concerts—the preshow entertainment started being too interesting to miss.

Other bands pissed off clubs because they would trash the dressing room and steal liquor from the stockroom. We pissed off clubs because the half-naked marching band outside the venue would elicit noise complaints, or because someone would leave a glittery cage of trained mynah birds in the hallway, thus blocking the barbacks' path to the ice machine.

. . .

Neil didn't dance. He wasn't much of a drinker. He didn't like hanging out in loud bars unless he had a book.

These things worried me.

But I was infatuated with his accent.

Say it again! I'd plead. *Say tomato!*

ToMAHto, he would deadpan, as if not enjoying this game at all.

I would squeal with glee. *Say it again!*

ToMAHto.

Shivers. It also worked with "schedule" and "banana," and my very favorite: "wastepaperbasket." One night I asked him to say it fifteen times. It didn't get old.

Late in bed that same night, when I wasn't expecting it, he surprised me.

ToMAHto. He whispered into my ear. *SHEdule.*

I half opened my eyes and whimpered with pleasure. And then, sounding very pleased with himself, he murmured:

BaNAHna.

. . .

The label helped us a lot in the early days. They went right to work making the band better known around the world, especially in Europe and Australia. What we'd been doing at a grassroots level had been effective, but it was slow. They worked fast. They got our music into stores, onto the radio and television. Soon we were flying everywhere, hopping on and off tour buses, doing interviews with bigger and bigger magazines.

We'd heard that they had a reputation for squeezing bands dry and only caring about the bottom line, but that wasn't what we noticed, not at first. What quickly became apparent to us was that they didn't understand how to treat—or rather, *not* treat—our fans. It seemed simple enough to me: you work hard, you play for your crowd, you talk to, communicate with, hug, and connect with them in every possible way, and in turn, they support you and convert their friends into the fold. That's when music works best, when people use it to commune and connect with one another. Simple.

However, the label thought that we could somehow be mega-launched into the echelon of indie bands that were blowing up and selling tons of records out of the gate around that time: The Hives, The Shins, The Vines, The Strokes. We couldn't: we were too cult-y, our name wasn't short enough, and we didn't actually feel hip or destined for hipness. We functioned best as part of a tight community that grew slowly, fan by fan. If it grew too fast, it wouldn't work. It'd be like suddenly pouring too many new unfamiliar fish into an aquarium and screwing up the ecosystem.

The label and the band had different ideas about what "enough" meant.

What *was* enough to make the band "successful"? We weren't starving. We could pay our rent. What did we actually... *need*? To live? To be happy?

* * *

If you're looking for help, it stands to reason that you're going to start looking among the people most able to give you the help you need. When your house is on fire, you don't call the fire department from seven towns over—you call the outfit down the street. They're the most equipped to help you.

One of the strategies the label employed that always baffled me was wanting us to focus all the energy on casting the net elsewhere, to attract strangers, while ignoring our established fanbase. I loved new people. Of course. But it seemed insane to jeopardize the current relationships to find them.

The label's theory probably followed some kind of cutthroat marketing maxim: once you've got a customer, you've got 'em. Move on to the next victim. Except that our driving motivation was to hang out with and bond with our small group of existing customers, whom we'd worked so hard to find in the first place. We knew from experience that our evolving friendship was slowly but surely bringing new people into the fray. Making fans that way—in person, one by one, as they were won over at our shows by our harder-core fans—seemed more effective than going out there and hollering on the radio to a group of unknowns, hoping to be heard by someone who might like us. Our way felt more like getting introduced to a person by a mutual friend, personally, at a bar over drinks. It felt real.

When I reflect on the last fifteen years of my life in music—all the touring, talking, late-night signing, blogging, twittering, couchsurfing, and crowdsurfing, and all other variety of eye-to-eye, soul-to-soul, hand-to-hand connection I've shared with the members of my crowd—I see it as a net.

It has to start with the art. The songs had to touch people initially, and mean something, for anything to work at all. The art, not the artist, is what fundamentally draws the net into being. The net was then tightened and strengthened by a collection of interactions and exchanges I've had, personally, whether in live venues or online, with members of my community.

I couldn't outsource it. I could hire help, but not to do the fundamental things that create emotional connections: the making of the art, the feeling-with-other-people at a human level. Nobody can do that work for me—no Internet marketing company, no manager, no assistants. It had to be me.

That's what I do all day on Twitter, Facebook, Tumblr, Instagram, and my blog. The platform is irrelevant. I'll go wherever the people are. What's important is that I absorb, listen, talk, connect, help, and share. Constantly. The net gets so strong at a certain point that I can let it go for a few days—maybe weeks—and it keeps weaving and bolstering itself. But I can't leave for very long.

The net tightens every time I pick up my phone and check in on Twitter, every time I share my own story, every time I ask a fan how their project is coming or promote somebody's book or tour.

The net tightens when someone in the community loses her

houseboat in a fire and tweets me for help, and I throw the information out to the fanbase, who go to work offering money, shelter, cat-sitting, and words of kindness.

It tightens when two people meet in line at one of my shows, fall in love, and come to a signing line after a concert three years later, asking me to Sharpie a swelling, pregnant belly.

I feel pride when I see that magic happening: the fans helping one another out, giving one another places to stay, driving one another around, helping one another with comforting words and links in the middle of the night, breaking the boundaries of "stranger" etiquette because they feel a trust and familiarity with one another under our common roof.

And I feel it at my shows, when I see people standing aside to allow a short person to see the stage, or carving a path for a person in a wheelchair, or just sharing a bottle of water. We're all helping each other. Here. Now.

. . .

The label didn't understand why they should pay for the band to maintain a website year-round. They thought it was something that only needed to be "up" when we had a new record to promote, and wouldn't pay to keep the site active the rest of the time. I was baffled.

I don't think you guys get it. Our website is like...a Real Place. It needs to exist all the time. You don't shut it down and then come back later.

The whole point of being an artist, I thought, was to be connected to people. To make a family. A family you were with all the time, like it or not. This was the way we'd been doing it for years, whether or not we had an album or a tour to "promote."

I knew the way to keep the fans happy was by staying present—through the forums, through sharing people's art and music back out through the Internet channels, through keeping everybody connected. That's just how a relationship works. And when the time came to ask them to buy a record, to buy a ticket, whatever...if I'd been there for them, they'd be there for me. It went beyond the emotional; it also seemed like smart business. The label disagreed. They wanted to expand. Immediately.

Tightening the net is not the same thing as expanding it. If you spread your net too far, too fast, it stretches too thin and it breaks; or it stretches too wide to be able to catch anything. The label didn't seem to understand that we didn't work like a pop band. We were far more interested in serving our slowly growing, tight-knit community of weirdos than we were in topping the charts.

So we threw up our hands and paid for everything ourselves: our web designers, our forum, our emailing list costs. The label asked for access to the mailing list, but I said no. I didn't trust them with my fans' email addresses. They were more than addresses; they were relationships.

I didn't ask them for any more help in the Internet department.

The relationship with the label was doomed from the start, when I think about it.

They got the sex part. But they didn't understand the cuddle.

. . .

I shot the video for my song "Leeds United" in London, casting hundreds of volunteer fans we'd enlisted through the blog and the email list. They came, from all over the UK, dressed to the nines in everything from Victorian formal wear to tongue-in-cheek soccer hooligan garb, and dutifully engaged in a pie-throwing brawl while I lip-synched and danced around onstage. While the video was being edited, one of the label higher-ups called me in for a meeting at their offices in New York.

Just wanted to chat with you about the new video. The director just sent us the first cut.

Yes! Isn't it great? She killed it!

Yeah. It's a great video. So, Amanda. Here's the thing. We think some of the shots of you aren't that... flattering.

He told me how they were concerned about my image and how they hoped I could edit out the shots that made me look fat.

Now, my relationship with my body is pretty healthy. I've never been massively overweight or underweight. I've never had an eating disorder or any kind of body dysmorphia. I'm pretty comfortable with myself. I don't shave my armpits or legs very often (though sometimes I will, just to feel my legs slide around on fresh sheets like slippery eels; it's delightful), and I've learned to accept that people sometimes stare. I shave my eyebrows and paint them back on.[4] I like to think I've managed to attain a decent level of corporeal self-acceptance over the years. That being said: I'm still vain. I still cringe when I see my belly after a monthlong muffin-and-beer binge, spilling over a waistline that's too tight. No lie: I wanted to look hot in this video. But try as I might, I just couldn't agree with the label's assessment. The shots the label objected to didn't seem unflattering to me. They just seemed...real. I thought I looked fine.

So I refused to make the edits.

The video went up, "unflattering" belly and all, and I told the whole story to the blog. The label considered this an act of war, and in a way, it was. It was the first time I'd publicly complained about our relationship.

Then something unexpected happened. A few people posted pictures of their own bellies—some fat, some thin, some hairy, some with Caesarean scars—on the band discussion forum. A few bellies bore messages aimed at the label (*LOVE THY BELLY! BELLY PRIDE! THIS IS WHAT A BELLY LOOKS LIKE!*) in paint and marker. I watched, in happy amazement, as more people followed suit. This was in the days before I was on Twitter and Facebook, but

---

4. That started as a temporary solution after shaving my face for a Marlene Dietrich look-alike contest that Brian and I attended shortly after forming the band. I lost the contest. I kept the eyebrows—I found, to my delight, that it had the unintended side effect of causing people to look me in the eye. When you have creatively painted eyebrows, people will assume you're approachable and affable, and talk to you. It's like having a funny mustache.

a few days later, hundreds of pictures had been uploaded, and one fan took it upon himself to bind them into a book. The fans had even given the viral movement a title: the ReBellyon.

It was the first time my fanbase had created something like this on their own at this scale, and I watched from a distance like a proud parent.

The irony wasn't lost on me. *These* were the people I was making the video for. In my opinion, *they* were the ones who were supposed to love it, and thereby feel encouraged to buy more music and drive the sales up. *They* were the target audience, as far as I was concerned, not some ephemeral, theoretical audience—dreamed up by the record label—who would rush to Walmart demanding my music upon seeing my svelte figure in a video. My crowd was making it very clear to me that not only were they *fine* with seeing my non-anorexic belly, they were also locked in solidarity with my decision to look like an average person instead of a Photoshopped supermodel.

I figured, if my fans were okay with it, I could be okay with it. Because really, who was trying to impress whom?

I'd thought that I already had a relatively healthy body image, but this moment shifted things for me. I started to take a sense of pride in my own "flaws." I blogged about the wrinkly crease on my forehead, challenging myself to accept it, I twittered a picture of my thigh stretch marks. Every piece of sharing opened a floodgate of shared insecurities and relieved "it's not just me" comments and photos from men and women alike.

And bit by bit, I started judging myself a little less harshly every time I looked in the mirror. The fans gave me that gift, very directly. They weren't some imaginary enemy, sizing me up and judging my weight, my skin, my tits, my ability to look perfect. They didn't care how the package delivering the music—me—looked as long as we were all making one another happy, and taking care of one another.

They were all just a bunch of people.

The imaginary enemy had been in my head.

If I had an enemy at all, it was the label.

. . .

Anthony never really asked me for anything—certainly never for money, I didn't have any. He hated lateness, so he would ask me to be punctual for our groks.[5] He also asked, usually joking, that I love him unconditionally, and without judgment, which was easy. That was love, or so I was learning. It was what he was teaching me.

But one time he asked me for something specific, and big. I was in my midtwenties, in the midst of making the first Dresden Dolls record. It was Christmastime, so I was kicking around closer to Boston for a few days, off tour, to be with my family and spend time on the couch in Anthony's study, recuperating and grokking.

We'd been talking on the phone almost every day that month, and I knew that Anthony's wife, Laura, had been going through a rough time, and he'd been worried about her. He'd been going through a pretty hefty depression himself. I'd take breaks from the studio and from cranking out vocals and fiddling with piano levels to check in and see how he was doing.

Laura and I hadn't been very close when I was a teenager; she'd wondered, like everyone else in the neighborhood, what this angsty teenage girl was doing hanging out with her husband all the time. And she just looked to me like...an adult. But once I hit my twenties and created my own life, while deepening my friendship with Anthony, we started to understand and even love each other. We never got as close as Anthony and I had, but we became warmer friends. Allies.

They never had kids. I was sort of the closest thing.

Anthony was older than Laura. He started morbidly musing one

---

5. "to grok": from Robert Heinlein's made-up word from *Stranger in a Strange Land*, meaning to communicate and understand deeply, empathetically, completely.

night about how he hoped she would die first, just so she wouldn't ever have to be alone without him.

But if I do die, look after her, okay? he said. *It's been haunting me lately. I can't handle the idea of her being alone. I can't stand the idea of her falling down the stairs, and being hurt... any of that. Just promise me you'll check in if I check out.*

A few nights later, I wrote him a letter. On Christmas Eve, I walked across my folks' lawn to his study. I knocked the snow off my boots and collapsed onto the couch.

Here, I wrote you something.

It was a pretty simple letter. He poured me a glass of wine from a bottle in his little study fridge, and sat down to read it.

I promise I'll take care of Laura if you die, the letter said.

I'll watch out for her, I'll check in, I'll make sure she isn't too alone.

And I'll do it not because you asked me.

Not because you love me.

I'll do it because I love her, even though she barely knows it.

I'll do it because you've taught me what love is, and how easily you can give it.

I'll take care of what you love.

I'll be there for Laura when you're gone and you're not around to do it.

I promise.

He put the letter down and looked at me.

That was the first time I saw Anthony cry.

·   ·   ·

My blog readership grew steadily as I started to dump more of my inner self onto the page. I shared the backstage stories, I promoted the shows, I asked for volunteers, I posted digital postcards from every visual and emotional vantage. I publicly thanked anyone who helped us. I was punch-drunk from the instant gratification of sharing life in real time, the random closeness, the feeling that I wasn't going through my struggles alone. When things went well, I blogged. When they went badly, I blogged. I tried not to sugarcoat. Sometimes I would post a short blog and get back over a thousand comments in which people would share their own stories, their own experiences. Sometimes I'd post a lengthy commentary about something I found fascinating, and get little or no response. I learned to love that about my fans: they weren't sheep, they were people. I never knew what to expect, or how they'd react.

People started using me to help one another. I wrote blogs about body image and watched discussions and confessions explode in the comments, because people (of all genders) felt safe talking to one another. I took a poll on Twitter about health insurance. I asked people to provide: *1) COUNTRY?! 2) profession? 3) insured? 4) if not, why not, if so, at what cost per month (or covered by job)?* Thousands responded. I posted the poll results on my blog and watched teenagers from the UK and the US now discussing health care, amazed by the fact that their systems were so different. They hadn't known.

The dots kept connecting. One day, I stumbled across the story of Amanda Todd, a Canadian teenager who had committed suicide after being bullied, online and off, by some cruel kids in her school. A few months before her death, she'd posted a plea for help on You-Tube, in which she simply held up written signs telling her story of loneliness, suicide attempts, and fear.

I posted the story and her video to the blog. It had hit a nerve for me. I've become adept at fielding Internet hate bombs: people hated my band, my lyrics, my eyebrows, my videos, my feminist politics, my armpit hair. I'd gotten used to waking up to a daily assault of love and hate coming at me over the Internet, and dealing with all those emotional landmines was becoming a skill in itself. I was a thirty-five-year-old who had grown a thick skin, and it was *still* a daily struggle. Amanda Todd was a kid. Fifteen. I couldn't imagine being the target of an Internet hate campaign at fifteen. I wrote about all of this, and a young woman named Shannon Eck commented on the blog:

Story time. I am fat. I'm not a fan of being fat and have, in fact, struggled with it my entire life...

She told us about a boy named Austin who used to torment her in gym class, calling her a cow, making up songs about how she was a fat bitch, and about how much she struggled to deal with his constant onslaught of cruelty. And about how a few months into that school year, Austin killed himself. And about how she wept the day he died.

Most bullies are the way they are because of how they have been treated, she wrote. *They just don't know any different. They don't know how to deal with their emotions, so they lash out. Austin's death broke my heart, but it made me open my eyes. What if I had tried to just talk to him? Would it have made any difference? Probably not. But at the end of the day, we're all human. We're all broken in a way, and we're just trying to feel whole. I try to understand where people are coming from, even if they are being horrible to me. When I would get mean messages online, I would instantly retaliate with something equally terrible and soul-crushing. After Austin, I didn't do that.*

Her story set off a rash of sharing and other stories, and the readers deepened the conversation in the blog comments, sharing confessions from both sides of the bullying fence. One young teenage girl blogged about her suicidal thoughts, and a few fans rushed in to support her, comfort her, send her their own phone numbers. The net tightened.

That blog (which I titled "On Internet Hatred: Please Inquire Within") still lives online and now has more than two thousand comments. Every time someone reads it and adds in their own story, the net continues to tighten. We were and are creating our own space, our own history. The blog started feeding my songwriting.

But since The Media (*Rolling Stone*, the *New York Times*, MTV) wasn't reporting on any of these sorts of things at the time—the blog discussions and the Twitter exchanges involving thousands of people—it didn't seem important to the label. They were busy bemoaning the fact that *SPIN* still didn't want to review our latest record. This was happening before anyone was paying much attention to Twitter: these sorts of new social media happenings—which had yet to be defined—were something the label missed completely. None of it seemed to have anything to do with how many records they could sell. It wasn't in the marketing plan, so it didn't exist.

I was learning, slowly but surely, that The Media—the traditional one, at any rate—mattered less and less. The ability to connect directly, under our own umbrella, was making one thing very clear:

We were The Media.

. . .

From the dawn of The Dresden Dolls, I saw our fans making art inspired by our music, and I loved it. Anything that was band-inspired was uploaded to the website and celebrated, and as video came to the Internet and YouTube exploded, the fans started to make their own unofficial music videos using our tracks. Some artists pulled and punished content like that, since the fans didn't own rights to the music.

We not only allowed it, we encouraged it. One year, while opening up for another band, we booked a string of sideshows in arthouse cinemas and ran a film festival with content made by our friends *and* the fanbase, including fan-made Dresden Dolls videos and the fans' own original animations and shorts. We called it "Fuck The Back Row."

To this day, some of the fans' unofficial videos surpass the view counts of our official videos on YouTube. We not only don't mind it—we openly celebrate it.

. . .

I was in a meeting at the label's New York office with my manager at the time, Emily, who was young and sharp and understood the concept of pay-what-you-want. I was trying to figure out how to leverage all my digital power for the release of a new album. It seemed like a good idea, given the spirit of generosity and trust we shared with the fanbase.

Three weeks before, Radiohead had put out *In Rainbows*, the first pay-what-you-want album release from a well-known band, and we had been jumping up and down, saying, "Yes! Yes! *That!*" The story was all over the music and tech news and was a vital, breathtaking moment in the industry: for better or worse, it was obvious that the Internet had already changed *everything* and was going to make it possible for bands and fans to start doing business directly. Emily and I stood by a window in one of the corner offices, with the owner, the president, the in-house label lawyer, and a handful of other people, to talk about The Future.

The president said to the owner:

Have you heard about this whole "Radiohead" thing?

Emily and I looked at each other and were about to say *Yes! Yes! The Thing! The Thing!* before we were interrupted by the owner, who asked, suspiciously:

What is this "Radiohead"?

Our jaws dropped. We stayed silent.

Radiohead, said the president to the owner. *You know, the British band.*

The owner frowned.

They're big, they're big. Anyway, they just released an album on THE INTERNET, for NOTHING, they let the fans decide the price of the album, in a little box where you can choose your price.

The owner shook his head in disgust. The president shook his head in disgust. The lawyer shook his head in disgust. And Emily and I shook our heads in a totally different kind of disgust.

I didn't know what was worse: that the owner of my label didn't know who Radiohead was, or that he didn't know that Radiohead had released a free record THREE WEEKS AGO in a move that had the ENTIRE MUSIC INDUSTRY talking. I figured he must at LEAST be like the president of the United States, getting little briefings at his desk every morning from some interior secretary of music industry information. Who *was* this guy?

• • •

When The Dresden Dolls recorded our second studio album in collaboration with the label, things went from okay to bad to toxic. We'd made our first record totally on our own, with no outside input, using all those loans from friends, fans, and family, and then simply sold it to the label. For this second record, the label fronted the money and the costs for the studio and producers, and told us that

THIS RECORD WAS GOING TO BE THE ONE THAT MADE US BIG!

We still had piles of songs that we hadn't recorded yet, and I was writing all the time, so we went from touring to promote our first album straight into the studio for the second. With the label's financial resources and a small army of engineers and producers, we recorded *Yes, Virginia*.

The record took about a month to finish and sounded magnificent; every song was an emotional nuclear bomb and it was a perfect sonic snapshot of the band at our live, bombastic best. The first week it hit the stores, we played a new city every single night and signed in record stores every day. The album hit the *Billboard* charts and sold twenty-five thousand copies. Brian and I were elated and danced around like kids on crack.

TWENTY-FIVE THOUSAND PEOPLE BOUGHT OUR RECORD!!!

The label was not so quick to celebrate. When the second week of sales didn't surpass the first week, they phoned to say they were cutting the entire promotional budget of the record. All the videos we'd planned wouldn't be shot; any tour support they'd promised was pulled immediately: any marketing ideas on the table were scrapped. They were very sorry, they said, but they didn't see any point in continuing to push it given that the initial sales were so bad. The album was considered a failure.

I could not wrap my head around the idea that selling twenty-five thousand records was *bad*—especially when our fans hadn't even had the chance to really hear it yet, talk about it, spread the word, tell their friends, and so forth. People were still just finding out about us. We knew these songs. We knew our fans. We'd seen how it worked on the first record, which continued to sell consistently after every show and online, as people fell, one by one, slowly in love with the band. I knew how this worked. It would be gradual. But it would happen.

The label didn't want to discuss it. Their decision sent us up shit's creek financially, because we'd laid out tens of thousands of dollars from our own pockets for tour costs that the label had promised to repay, and now they were reneging. I couldn't believe it.

You're leaving?

No CUDDLE?

I tried to argue. When they finally stooped so low as to use the H word—*We've also sent the album to people who specialize in radio play, Amanda, and to be honest . . . they just don't hear a Hit*—I gave up completely.

We didn't need a fucking Hit. We were a punk-cabaret duo specializing in tear-jerking seven-minute songs with *drum solos*. We were not radio friendly. Our audience loved us precisely for all the weird, radio-unfriendly shit we did. We weren't in the hit business, or anywhere near it; we were in the community-art-cult-poetry-family-love business. Even the music itself was only a part of it.

The recorded songs, the tangible CDs, were only the tip of the iceberg: the perfect, frozen, beautiful soundtrack for something far bigger, and far deeper.

The connection underneath was everything.

• • •

A 2010 Princeton University study conducted by two economists concluded that money DOES buy happiness, but only up to the point (which turns out to be an individual annual income of about

$75,000) where you have your basic needs met along with a few extra comforts. After that, the ability to buy happiness with money nosedives.

Right: it's not rocket science. We need to eat, we need shelter, a meal in a restaurant is nice. But there's a satiation level, a happiness threshold you hit when you have *enough*.

I don't know of any such formal studies of working musicians, but I see the same patterns in artistic success. The happiest artists I know are generally the ones who can manage to make a reasonable living from their art without having to worry too much about the next paycheck. Not to say that every artist who sits around the campfire, or plays in tiny bars, is "happier" than those singing in stadiums—but more isn't always better. If feeling the connection between yourself and others is the ultimate goal, it can actually be harder when you are separated from your crowd by a thirty-foot barrier. The ideal sweet spot is the one in which the artist can freely share their talents and directly feel the reverberations of their artistic gifts to their community, and make a living doing that. In other words, it works best when everybody feels seen.

As artists, and as humans: if your fear is scarcity, the solution isn't necessarily abundance. To quote Brené Brown again:

Abundance and scarcity are two sides of the same coin. The opposite of "never enough" isn't abundance or "more than you could ever imagine."

Which is to say, the opposite of "never enough" is simply:
Enough.

. . .

We had to get off the label. But they wouldn't let us go.

At first, I asked nicely. During a tour in Europe, I went out to dinner with the owner, and requested to be dropped.

Amanda, Amanda, he said. *You are a very talented girl. Very charismatic and you write very good songs. But you get in your own way wasting your time on all this fans-this and fans-that and the Internet-this and the Internet-that. One of these days you are going to focus and write some hit songs that are going to make a lot of money. I have faith in you. We are not dropping you.*

Then he winked at me.

I blasted them in my blog. I complained about them openly in the press. I wrote them a letter-song called "Please Drop Me" to the tune of "Moon River," performed it live, and asked the fans to video and upload to YouTube (they obliged). The label ignored it.

Meanwhile, the age of burning and downloading was in full flourish.

Because I was blogging so openly about wanting to be dropped from the label, and also explaining transparently that we, the band, were seeing absolutely no profit from the records people were buying in stores (it was obvious, at that point, that we would never recoup our advance) an interesting phenomenon sprang up at the signing table. People started handing us money.

I know it's illegal, but I burned your CD from a friend. I know you hate your label and stuff…I just wanted to give you this ten dollars. I love the record.

I've been downloading your stuff for a few months and there's no way to pay you. So here's a twenty. I read on your blog that you wouldn't get the money even if I went into a store and bought the CD, so here.

I feel really guilty, I've been listening to burned copies of both of your CDs. Here's five dollars. I know it isn't much but I can't stand the feeling that I've never paid for them.

A few people even took their checkbooks out and wrote us checks for the money they thought they "owed" us.

I was happily astonished, and I also took every single dollar. I'd been a stripper and a silent street performer; I was used to taking people's dollar bills with grace. I never refused, I just took the money given to us, feeling grateful that I had a voice, literally, to thank the patrons personally.

Thank you.

Thank you.

Thank you.

. . .

The label still wouldn't drop us.

Asking wasn't working.

Finally, I decided to lie.

I don't like lying.

I had a tour stop in Los Angeles, and Freddie, my A&R guy (Dave, the guy who signed us, had long since been fired), was also in town. I called him up and we arranged to meet for dinner.

Ten minutes before he showed up, I drank a shot of whiskey. I poured another shot down my shirt. As he was pulling up in his car outside my cousins' house where I was staying, I gargled. With whiskey. *In vino veritas*; I figured if he thought I was drunk, he'd never think I was lying. I got in his car, hugged him, and told him I'd been feeling really bad about all the tension and crazy label stuff. I was sorry. I hiccupped.

Over dinner, I asked Freddie about parenthood. He had kids, and happily told me his child-rearing stories. I listened, getting misty-eyed.

Finally, over dessert, I burst into what I hoped were uncontrollable-looking tears. Freddie sat there uncomfortably as I told him that all I wanted was a family. How I was tired of touring, tired of the fans, tired of the grind. I worried aloud that if I got pregnant, the label would think of me as a failure. I sniveled through my martini, swayed a little, and blew my nose on the sleeve of my dress.

No, no. Oh . . . Amanda, Freddie assured me, putting his hand on my arm. *So you know, that would never happen. We've put all this time* *and energy into you because we BELIEVE in you. Okay? And in your whole career. It may be bumpy now but we're in this for the long haul. That's exactly why we **won't** drop you. And if you want to have children, you should. And that would never hurt your standing with the label. Never. Ever.*

Really? Truly? I said, sniffling.

Really. Truly, Fred said, kindly.

Okay. Please, please promise me that this stays between you and me, okay? Please don't tell anybody at the label. Promise?

He promised, and drove me back to my cousins' house. I called Neil.

I just pretended to be drunk and lied to my label guy all night about being brood-y and it felt really, really, really gross.

I love you, fake-drunk girlfriend, he said. *Did it work? Were you a good liar?*

I want a fucking Oscar. I cried real tears. Meryl-Streep-level shit, I told him.

A month later, I got a letter from my lawyer.

The label had dropped me.

DO YOU SWEAR TO TELL THE TRUTH THE WHOLE TRUTH & NOTHING BUT THE TRUTH SO HELP YOUR BLACK ASS

(with thanks to N.W.A)

When I was six years old my
   sister Alyson
Asked for a stove for her
   birthday
A miniature one you could
   actually cook with
And my mom was nice and she
   bought one
Alyson needed a reason to
   bake something
Barged in my room and she
   grabbed me
She said:
"I made a cake and we're
   going next door
To Sam Weinstein's and you're
   getting married"

The cake was burned
It tasted gross
She made me kiss him
On the mouth

Now I am thirty-three
Unmarried happily
No plans in life and I'm
   planning to keep it that
   way
I do kissing with only one
   mission:
Do you like to kiss? Then you
   have my permission

And I have already spent
   too much time
Doing things I didn't want to
So if I just want to make out
   all the time
You can bet your black ass
   that I'm going to.

When I was nine I was kind
   of a loser
The kids in my class didn't
   like me
Melanie Chow was the meanest
   of all
And my mom made me go to
   her party

Nobody talked to me, I sat
   there quietly
Drawing with crayons on a
   napkin
A picture of Melanie skewered
   with a pitchfork
Her legs getting eaten by
   lions

The cake was good
I took some home
I had a party
In my room

Now I have friends and I'm
   not such a loser
But I go to bars all the time
   and I sit there
And order red wine and
   I write and I like
   being alone around
   people
Yes that's how I like it

And I've already spent too
   much time
Doing things I didn't
   want to
So if I wanna sit here and
   write and drink wine
You can bet your black ass
   that I'm going to

Yes I come here often
Sure I'll have another one
Yes I come here often
Sure I'll have another one.
(But I don't have to talk
  to you)

When I was seventeen I was
  a blowjob queen
Picking up tips from the
  masters
I was so busy perfecting my
  art I was clueless to what
  they were after
Now I'm still a blowjob queen
  (far more selectively)
I don't make love now to make
  people love me
But I don't mind sharing my
  gift with the planet
We're all gonna die and a
  blowjob's fantastic

And when I was twenty-five I
  was a rock star
But it didn't pay too well,
  I had to strip on the side
Of the road to get ready
  for shows and the cars
  driving by
Baby, they'd never know

What a bargain they'd
  gotten
And if I'm forgotten
I'm perfectly happy with all
  that has happened
And I still get laughed at but
  it doesn't bother me
I'm just so glad to hear
  laughter around me

And I've already spent too
  much time
Doing things I didn't
  want to

So if I want to drink alone
  dressed like a pirate
Or look like a dyke
Or wear high heels and
  lipstick
Or hide in a convent
Or try to be mayor
Or marry a writer
Smoke crack and slash tires
Make jokes you don't like
Or paint ducks and retire

You can bet your black ass
  that I'm going to.

—from *An Evening With Neil
Gaiman & Amanda Palmer*, 2013

You remember what Joe said, about the horse? Anthony once asked me.

Joe was Anthony's dad, who would show up as a recurring character in Anthony's stories. I loved the stories from when he was little.

Okay, Anthony, Joe would ask. *You wanna be smart? Or you wanna be stupid?*

I wanna be smart, Anthony-the-kid would answer.

Okay, I'll tell ya. You wanna be stupid? Then you do what you want. If you wanna be smart? You listen to me. And with that, Joe would dispense his advice.

Joe's saying about the horse was one of Anthony's favorites.

It's one thing to want a horse to win, Joe would tell him. *And it's another thing to buy the ticket.*

•   •   •

All artists connect the dots differently. We all start off with all these live, fresh ingredients that are recognizable from the reality of our experiences (a heartbreak, a finger, a parent, an eyeball, a glass of wine) and we throw them in the Art Blender.

My songs are personal and intimate; a lot of them chronicle my inner life. I mine the depths of my own experience and lay it on the page, sometimes naked, sometimes in costume. I fictionalize to protect myself and my targets (though I've still had to organize several apology dinners with ex-lovers in order to ask forgiveness). I tend to only let things mix and blur very slightly, which is to say, I usually keep my blender on a low setting. On a scale from one to ten, it's at level three. If you look, you can still recognize the component parts: in the final art gazpacho, the finger might be severed and mangled, but you can still peer into the bowl and see it floating there.

Neil writes fiction about very non-real things: a book about a boy raised by ghosts in a graveyard; an America in which old gods and new battle over humanity's fate; graphic novels in which a star that falls from the sky turns out to be a girl with a broken leg. Neil sets his Art Blender at eleven. The reader usually has no idea where the experiences of his life have settled in the superfine purée of the final product. You may taste a finger, but it's not recognizable as a human one.

Since I've met him, he's dialed his blender down a bit for certain projects, and I've dialed mine up. Neil and I have wound up as human ingredients in each other's work. During my previous breakup, and before I'd started the slow descent into loving him, Neil and I went to a trout farm, and found ourselves witnessing our dinner being clubbed and gutted by the fishmonger. One of the tiny trout hearts laying on the metal counter didn't stop beating for several minutes. It was tragic, and beyond symbolic, given the relationship from which I was currently struggling to extricate my own heart.

The image gave birth to a poem by Neil ("Conjunctions"—blender level: 8) and one of the best songs on my then-forthcoming Kickstarter record ("Trout Heart Replica"—blender level: 5). Neil told me an anecdote about a relationship where the beds and the emotional distance got bigger and bigger, and I turned it into a song. We started to blend with each other, the only way we knew how. Using art. Collecting and connecting the dots of each other's lives. All art, no matter what shape it is, has to come from somewhere.

We can only connect the dots that we can collect.

. . .

As soon as the label dropped me, I posted a celebration blog, thanking everyone at the various international offices of the label for all the work they'd done (the thanks were sincere; many of them had done wonderful, helpful things for us, and I was sad to lose the relationships), and thanking the fans for supporting me. I also raced into a studio and recorded a song I'd just written, which stole its title from lyrics from "Fuck Tha Police" by N.W.A: It was called "Do You Swear To Tell The Truth, The Whole Truth and Nothing But The Truth So Help Your Black Ass" and it was, appropriately, about how I hate being told what to do.

I uploaded the song, for free download, along with my jubilant blog, and, for the first time, I put out my virtual hat. I asked the fans to pay whatever they wanted for the song. Some took it for free, some paid a dollar, some paid a hundred dollars in a gesture of symbolic congratulations. It worked.

I decided, at that moment—unlike other bands who were aligning with the RIAA (who was shutting down Napster and arresting teenagers for "pirating" music)—that I would try to make things as freely available as I could: I would encourage sharing, burning, torrenting, and downloading. But I would leave my hat out, I would ask, and I would work from a place of gratitude if people stepped up to help. I wanted it to be like the street.

I didn't want to force people to help me. I wanted to let them.

. . .

They say: *What's the harm in asking?*

But asking can hurt.

When I was just breaking ground on this book, I was on tour and found myself staying with Duncan, one of my very distant European relatives, one night while everybody else camped in the tour bus. We were enjoying a late breakfast on his sunny back porch, and he asked what I was scribbling in my journal. I told him that I was thinking about the difference between "asking" and "begging."

Asking... Duncan said. *Asking. Hm. That's interesting. I'm a person who really doesn't like to ask for things. And the funny thing is, the less you like asking, the worse off you can be when you finally do.*

What do you mean?

I'll tell you a story. My mother and my aunt were in this awful feud, he began, pouring milk into his second cup of coffee. *When my grandmother died, she left an antique rosary to my mother, who felt she deserved it because she'd converted to Catholicism when she married. But my aunt was an antiques dealer and apparently had expressed an interest in it, and my grandmother had promised it to her, and blah blah blah...you get the picture. Fury on both sides. They didn't speak for three years. Can you imagine? And when my mother started battling cancer, I suffered watching them not talk for another year, while my mother got weaker, until I finally found the nerve to call my aunt and say, "Listen. I've never asked for anything from you, but now I am, with everything I've got. Call my mother. Please, just pick up the phone and smooth it over, apologize even if you feel you're lying. She's dying and this is helping kill her. You don't even have to do it for her. I'm asking you to do it for me."*

And do you know what she said?

I shook my head.

She said **no**.

I let out a sigh.

It was so hard to ask, Duncan said. *I never ask anyone for anything. And I'd finally asked.*

He was quiet for a second.

That answer, Amanda...it crushed me.

. . .

Around the time the label freed me, I was still skeptical about Twitter, which I thought of as the social media tool that people used to share what they'd had for breakfast.

A few months later, I was in Austin for the SXSW music conference when Neil and Zoë Keating, my touring cellist, dragged me onto the Twitter wagon and gave me a quick lesson, showing me the little box into which you could input your 140 characters of text.

I set up the account and told the fans. I twittered a few pictures. Then I dipped my toe in more experimental water, announcing that I would be hosting a pillow fight.

ANYONE IN AUSTIN!?! TODAY. 3:17 PM!!! PILLOW FIGHT. Corner of red river & 6th. TELL EVERYBODY. Bring pillow!

I only had a few thousand followers, but I guessed at least a few dozen of them were at SXSW. I wasn't giving them a whole lot of warning, though, and I had no idea what to expect. Ten people? Twenty?

At 3:15 p.m. I showed up at the corner of Red River and Sixth Streets with a pillow to find a crowd of around a hundred people—all armed with pillows—milling around. As soon as they saw me, with no words exchanged, we all attacked each other. (Nobody was injured.)

It was AN AMAZING PILLOW FIGHT, I said to Neil, showing him the photos later that night. *I wonder if they enjoyed it as much as I did.*

Have you checked Twitter? Neil asked.

What do you mean, "checked Twitter"?

Neil started laughing. I hadn't realized that Twitter allows you to see the people talking to or about you. I'd thought it was simply a one-way communication device. I had been shouting into my Twitter megaphone without realizing, for three weeks, that thousands of people had been responding.

STOP LAUGHING AND SHOW ME HOW TO DO IT, I said.

Neil introduced me to the "mentions" function, and my phone filled up with a list of hundreds of comments, pictures, short videos of pillow fights, thank-yous, and general buzz about the event that had just occurred. After that, I was convinced. I haven't left Twitter since.

Explaining how I use Twitter to those who've never used it is difficult. It's a blurry Möbius strip of love, help, information, and social-art-life exchange.

Only now does it occur to me that my first official "twittered" flash gig—The Epic SXSW Pillow Fight At Sixth And River—featured no actual music. I just twittered, hit my fans with pillows, hugged them, and took off. But I didn't bother to play any songs, and nobody seemed to mind much. They just seemed deliriously happy to be part of something so sudden and surprising. Plus, how could I play music spontaneously in the street? I'm a pianist.

I started playing the piano when I was three—because there it was, in the house—and since then I've been a generally monogamous instrumentalist. Occasional fantasies of learning how to play the cello, the guitar, and the acoustic bass have all been left unrealized.

Around the time I discovered the joys of Twitter, I bought a twenty-dollar wooden red ukulele with a plastic fretboard—the world's smallest, cutest, easiest instrument—as a gag for a friend's benefit at a small nightclub. In one short evening, I taught myself to play "Creep" by Radiohead, looking up the chords on the Internet. Instead of playing on the nightclub stage, I hopped up onto the bar, and then hopped down to weave through the crowd, playing my ukulele—truth be told—pretty badly. I thought my affair with the instrument would end there, but during that five-minute performance, I was amazed at the power that one little mini-guitar could wield.

Playing the song that night felt like a gimmick, but that summer, I toted the ukulele around with me, for kicks. Cyndi Lauper—my childhood hero (eight-year-old me was beside herself)—invited The Dresden Dolls to open for her on a summer package tour called True Colors, the proceeds of which would benefit the Matthew Shepard Foundation. Almost every night of the tour, I did a quick busking experiment and played "Creep" by Radiohead, still the only song I knew, in the parking lot or the lobby of the venue, with a hat at my feet. I liked surprising people, and they laughed, applauded, and threw in dollars and change. The collected take from the hat went to the foundation, and there it was again, that feeling:

I can play this instrument for people ANYWHERE, as long as it's not raining!

In a field! In an alleyway! On the bus!! On a beach!!! In a closet!!!

People will listen to me sing, and I don't need a stage!

I will never have to be enslaved behind a piano again!

I hadn't realized how limiting the piano had been, but now that I knew, I'd had it. I decided to start dating other instruments.

This combination of Ukulele Freedom and Twitter Freedom led to the birth of the Ninja Gig, which was the name I gave the flash events I started creating once I realized how easy it was to whip a crowd up to any place at any time. Before and after official gigs, on off days when I was in the mood, or when I was visiting cities where I didn't have any official gigs planned, I could summon a crowd using Twitter on only a few hours' notice.

There's something uniquely thrilling about conjuring up a crowd of five hundred people and watching an instant free festival sprout up before your very eyes in a public place, but it took me a few years of bouncing between official gigs and ninja ones to realize what really drew me to the latter: I felt like I was in control of my life again. I had missed the freedom of the street.

The "freedom" of ninja gigs didn't actually translate to more free time. Adding them last-minute to a tour made my schedule more hectic on paper, but I didn't really notice that I was taking my off days to play spontaneously any more than you would have seen complaints from a high-security prisoner who was given the option to spend their recreational yard time out at the local bar. I loved waking up and thinking, *MAYBE I'LL PLAY IN A PARK TODAY!*

Sometimes I'd go to bed thinking I'd do an afternoon ninja gig the next day, then wake up, feel tired, and cancel on myself. Canceling an official show is never an option. Not really. A canceled show wreaks havoc on the schedules and pocketbooks of the ticketholders, the venues, and the promoters, to say nothing of the work of rescheduling and the black mark on your reputation. It's almost always easier to take the "show must go on" approach; take the stage sick and barrel through. During the long winter tours of The Dresden Dolls, Brian and I would sometimes get the flu simultaneously and still play the gig, both battling fevers, boxes of tissues beside our instruments transforming into foot-high snot-covered mountains by the end of each night. The crowd would sympathize.

But ninja gigs aren't at all pre-organized, so they aren't hard to un-organize.

All the intimacy, none of the commitment. So nice.

I also realized that ninja gigging solved an irritating problem that I'd been battling for years: the dearth of all-ages venues. I'd battled many promoters and agents to ensure that my gigs would be all-ages at all costs, because a good handful of my fans are teenagers. The ninja gigs are always free, always all-ages, and generally never announced more than a day in advance. There is no advertising: only Internet posts and word of mouth. People are encouraged to bring instruments, cameras, children, pets, or whatever else they think of, and there's no official end time or shape to the event. I usually throw the attention to another musician for a while if I have songwriter friends in town or on tour with me who can show up with an acoustic instrument. It feels a little like an old-school folk hootenanny.

I once paraded a group of two hundred people in Brisbane from a corset shop to a modern art museum and played gigs at either end. I've done ninja gigs on the steps of the Sydney Opera House to a crowd of seven hundred in the rain (we paraded to shelter). I played a string of Occupy sites up and down the West Coast when I was on tour there during the height of the movement. I did a silent ninja gig inside Powell's bookstore in Portland, Oregon, where I wordlessly recommended and signed books of poetry for hundreds of people.

I found out that the people of Byron Bay, Australia, don't really do Twitter. They don't even really do the Internet. I morning-twittered an evening ninja gig on the beach, expecting one to two hundred people. Seven people came. I played on the beach and then we all went for ice cream.

I did a ninja gig in Canberra, the Australian capital. All of my fans showed up on bikes, or were loaned bikes, at the headquarters of Rat Patrol, a "freak bike community" of men, women, and children who ride through the city regularly on tall bikes, choppers, and other creatively Frankensteined cycles, wearing flamboyant helmets. We all rode, a pack of a hundred people, to the strains of a battery-powered boom box, passing beers back and forth, through the center of town and to the National Carillon, the five-story bell tower to which someone had a key. I was given a tour of the tower and allowed to play one of my songs on the bells for the crowd gathered down below. A local band played acoustically as thunder roared in the distance. Someone showed up with a surprise upright piano, which they offloaded from their flatbed truck. We wheeled the piano under the bell tower, and I played an all-request concert as the rain pelted us. Everyone was soaked and freezing, we covered the precious piano with jackets, and it was one of the best gigs of my life.

Exactly one year after my TED talk, I arrived in Vancouver for a guest performance at the conference and twittered:

THINKING OF A NINJA GIG AT TED! WHO'S GOT IDEAS?

Three days later, the Vogue Theatre had volunteered their space, and about a dozen TED speakers and performers showed up and shared whatever they felt like. It was like a 1,500-capacity living room. Chris Hadfield, the astronaut and songwriter, played "Space Oddity" on guitar while everybody sang along. A local punk marching band showed up and hung out onstage. The Vancouver food bank, who'd recruited volunteers through my Twitter feed, passed buckets through the crowd and raised almost $10,000.

The most miraculous part of this gig, though, was Sarah Shandl, a girl who raised her hand on Twitter the night I announced the gig, volunteering her services as a last-minute stage manager. I hired her over Twitter, and we spent the next eighteen hours emailing and texting back and forth at least ninety times. She created order in the chaos, helping arrange food and booze, liaising with the food bank, emailing all the performers updated info. She even brought along a friend to manage the guest list of TED people and guest artists for whom we had agreed to save seats. I'd barely met her and she'd saved my ass.

When I took her out to lunch the following day to thank her and get to know her better, I learned that she'd never heard of me, or my music, before the moment she'd volunteered. She'd just seen that someone with a bunch of Twitter followers was throwing a free gig in Vancouver, and thought that that person might need a hand.

.   .   .

Neil got to know me better. I had a bad habit of wanting to disappear completely for a few full days after freshly separating. When we first got together, I couldn't stand that he wanted to send back-and-forth texts as soon as we separated. Like, five minutes after saying good-bye at the airport.

He learned to adjust to my *Run Away! Run Away!* approach every time we parted company, and I was learning to resist emotionally vanishing once we weren't in the same space together.

I started learning how Neil worked. I figured out how to reassure him that I wasn't actually leaving him; I was just thrilled to be alone and able to work, to make art, to think, and to email by my lonesome. We pissed each other off, royally, frequently, in those early days. But we were getting better, bit by bit. I stopped thinking he was going to cage me, and he stopped thinking I was trying to flee. The poetry wasn't lost on us: He had abandonment issues, and I had commitment issues. Go figure.

Also, the sex, which had been fumbling and awkward at the beginning of our relationship, got really hot. We figured that was a promising sign of general relationship progress.

Mostly we realized it was about leaving the doors and windows of the relationship wide-open enough. That way, he could see in, and I could see out.

. . .

I was backstage talking with a friend I knew from the road, the lead singer of a pretty big indie band, after their show at a club in Boston. I'd come to visit, since I was off tour.

Our shows are selling like shit, he said, tossing his sweaty shirt onto the couch and putting on a fresh one.

You sounded great, I said. *And the new album is amazing. But you know—it couldn't hurt if you would actually talk to your fans from stage. They're there. They're crowdsurfing. They're screaming and yelling. But most of the time you acted like the audience wasn't even in the room. You barely talked to them.*

He opened a beer for himself. *Easy for you to say. I remember when you stopped in the middle of your set in Seattle and asked them all to text people they knew in Portland for the next night, because it wasn't sold out. My whole band was backstage, like, in PAIN because it was so awkward. I mean…it's kind of genius. But we could never do that. You're such a freak.*

Why? Because I talk to my fans?

But, like, who DOES that? I mean, YOU can get away with it because you're Amanda Palmer Queen Of The Internet "it's all one big happy family" and whatever. But that is NOT us. Do you know how fucking CRUCIFIED we'd get if we even so much as mentioned that we had a mailing list? We don't even announce that we have merchandise for sale…it just seems so tacky.

Well, dude, you've got nothing to lose. Your tour is tanking. And it might not be so bad. In fact, if you ask your fans for help, they might surprise you.

How?

They might be really flattered that you trusted them enough to look uncool.

Crowdsurfing is like couchsurfing is like crowdsourcing.

You're falling into the audience—you're asking them to help you. By asking, you're building.

Crowdsurfing is where this moment of trust is at its physical paragon, and best of all, it's set to the climactic soundtrack of the art itself: the music.

You stand at the lip of the stage, you trust, and you dive.

There is nothing in the world like being held aloft in the cloud of loudness by a sea of random, sweaty arms, every single one of them like a tree in a huge, storm-blustered forest of trust, being floated along by hundreds of fingers and palms. I also feel a sympathetic rush when I look out into the crowd during shows and see the audience hoisting each other up, holding one another in the air, carefully but impulsively pushing each other over the crowd with the cooperative, fevered camaraderie of a barn raising set to a rock-and-roll score. You're a human-sized symbol of trust, and if you don't stay in circulation, you not only cease being a gift... you become a liability. Falling to the ground from a crowdsurf isn't pretty. But you survive. And, usually, people grab your arm and pull you back up. That's also a wonderful feeling.

Side note: If you ever get a chance to crowdsurf, do it. It's a blast. Stash your wallet somewhere you won't lose it, don't wear loose jewelry, and for god's sake, no sharp heels, you wanna kill someone?

. . .

After almost four years of nonstop touring and recording side by side, Brian and I experienced classic band burnout. Even though we'd graduated from The Vulva to a van (named Ludwig) to a rented tour bus, we were driving each other mad. We took a break and I started working on my first solo record, *Who Killed Amanda Palmer*, the one with the dead/naked-Amanda photo book I'd asked

Neil to help me caption. Touring on my own sounded liberating and lonely at the same time—so I hired Zoë Keating, who plays intricate, electronically looped solo cello music, to open for me and play on a handful of my new songs during the stage show. Then I called my friend Steven Mitchell Wright, an Australian theater director whose work draws on the Japanese Butoh tradition, in which performers paint themselves white and writhe in joyously painful existential ecstasy.

Want to figure out a way to add some theater to my tour? I asked him. *There's almost no budget. But we'll create something magnificent with some actors, I'll pay for their flights and make sure everybody has a place to stay and food to eat. We'll need to pass the hat for your salaries. You may also have to help me find couches for us to sleep on.*

Steven, who is crazy in the very best ways, said yes and selected three equally crazed and committed Australian performers, and threw in Lyndon, his classical violinist friend, as a bonus. Steven named this company The Danger Ensemble, and they became my touring art family for the next year.

We drove around America, Canada, Europe, and Australia in various cheap tour buses and vans, relying heavily on crowdsourced generosity. Zoë and my sound and light crew were paid a regular support wage, but Steven and The Danger Ensemble relied on the generosity of the crowd throughout the entire tour. Each night onstage, I would introduce them all towards the end of the show and announce that these performers had come on tour with me for no fixed salary and were relying on the audience. The five of them would rove through the crowd during the next song, holding their boots to collect donations. Some nights, they made less than a few hundred dollars. Other nights, they'd make over a thousand. It balanced out. I was relieved, but I wasn't surprised that the crowd liked helping.

While my busking, bohemian circus friends had no problem passing the hat, not everybody was quite so comfortable. I once brought an opening band on tour with me: five guys in dapper suits who played cabaret music for half an hour before I hit the stage. As the tour progressed, they got into the spirit of all-hands-on-deck and backed me up for five or six of my own songs—learning a new song each night during our soundcheck. I suggested we ask the audience to directly reward their extra effort, and so they went into the crowd, each night, hats in hand, where the fans happily gave them an extra few hundred dollars. It all worked splendidly, but there was one musician in the band who hung back in the dressing room and refused to take part. I asked him one night why he didn't join the others.

I just... can't, he said. *It's embarrassing, Amanda. It feels too much like... begging.*

But the fans didn't seem to mind being asked. On the contrary, it made them feel included at a new level.

We also crowdsourced our nightly meals, which was a new test for my professional crew, who were accustomed to a tour diet of ordinary takeout pizza, falafel, and pad thai. I wasn't certain they'd be thrilled about trading consistency for adventure. Towards the beginning of the tour, I had a conversation in Dublin with one of my sound guys who was somewhat suspicious.

*Are you sure about this? Some of your fans are pretty intense and I mean... doesn't it sort of creep you out? They could put, like, **anything** in our food.*

But I trust these people, I said. *I trust them more than I trust, I dunno, random line cooks in restaurants who might piss in my food because they hate their jobs. These people like me. Why would they hurt me?*

I'm just saying... watch yourself, Amanda. You trust people too much.

Sometimes a supreme feast would arrive: In Philly and Seattle we were treated to five-course dinners created by chefs who spent two days in preparation for the meal and arrived backstage with burners, sauces, and flambées. In Chicago, a restaurant owner who was dating a fan supplied us with twenty-five varieties of sushi rolls. There was also a flip side. In one Austrian city, a girl arrived with a single red plastic beach pail filled with undercooked pasta. We supplemented that night's dinner with takeout falafel.

. . .

Neil and I were in a giant drugstore, in a hurry, and all we needed to buy were condoms and tampons. I approached a woman who worked there who seemed to be in her late seventies, and asked her. Then I proudly called out to Neil, who was in another aisle, loud enough that he, and everyone else in the drugstore, could hear me:

HONEY, I FOUND OUT WHERE THE CONDOMS AND THE TAMPONS ARE. THEY'RE BOTH HERE IN AISLE FIVE.

Neil came around the corner into the aisle I was in, looked at me, and began to laugh.

Darling, he said, *you're human after all. You're blushing. You're embarrassable.*

I could feel my cheeks burning. He was right. I'd been trying to prove how fearless I was, but truthfully, I had embarrassed myself.

He loves telling people the story of the time that he learned I was not quite as shameless as he had believed: the time he saw Amanda blush, when she asked for a tampon.

. . .

I had a manager who couldn't understand why I was upset that his assistant had booked me a hotel with no wireless during a three-day press trip in London.

I NEED A NEW HOTEL WITH INTERNET, I tried to explain over the phone. *I NEED THE INTERNET TO LIVE.*

You're on a three-day press trip doing ten hours of interviews a day. What do you need the Internet for?

Another manager didn't understand why I thought it was so important that she read my Twitter feed to understand what was actually happening. To see what the fanbase was feeling, saying, sharing, complaining about, and how they were responding to the shows.

It was a massive leap of faith for these people to believe that "just connecting with people," in an authentic, non-promotional, non-monetary way, is so *valuable*.

But it is. It's *in*valuable.

Those managers seemed really reluctant to believe that if you just trusted and listened to, talked to, and connected with the fanbase, the money and the profits would come—when the time came.

Managers kept telling me to stop twittering and get back to work.

I broke up with a lot of managers.

They didn't understand. That *was* the work.

* * *

As we barreled along, crowdsourcing food and passing the hat, I continued crashing with fans, and when I left the Dolls and brought along my merry, motley crew of Australian performance artists, things became even more challenging: there were seven of us. We offered our typical exchange of tickets, merch, and gratitude—and with Steven at the helm, we sorted through hundreds of email offers of crash pads. My traditional road crew—sound person, light person, tour manager, and merchandise vendor—were all on full salary, and I paid for their hotels. But nobody bitched about a double standard. The road crew weren't taking a job with me for an exercise in humanity-trusting. They were taking a job with me to tour in a bus, get their off days in hotels, get paid, and do their jobs. I could afford to put them up. The rest of the performers and I tried our luck on the couches of the universe.

One summer in Melbourne, where we did a run of shows at a

venue called The Famous Spiegeltent, we all slept in a single room, on a compilation of mattresses and futons loaned by various people. It was like a weeklong slumber party, or like a bunch of artistic bears hibernating in a very hot cave, all piled up next to each other with no particular boundaries. Mostly, we were staying in places like the ones we lived in ourselves: share houses full of grad students; giant messy lofts inhabited by musicians and painters. But sometimes we stayed in the more grown-up homes of working professionals who were happy to leave us behind with the Wi-Fi password, instructions for the espresso machine, and the keys, because they had to split for work early in the morning. It was a testament to the generosity of my fans that on several occasions, our hosts couldn't even come to the shows, but still welcomed us into their homes.

Couchsurfing is about more than saving on hotel costs. It's a gift exchange between the surfer and the host that offers an intimate gaze into somebody's home, and the feeling of being held and comforted by their personal space. It's also a reminder that we're floating along due to a strong bond of trust, just like when I surf the crowd at a show, safely suspended on a sea of ever-changing hands. It can feel almost holy, looking at somebody else's broken shower nozzle, smelling the smells of a real kitchen, feeling the fray of a real blanket and hearing the crackle of an old steam radiator.

Sometimes we'd have the energy to burn the midnight oil with our hosts over tour stories and wine, but usually we were all so exhausted from the show itself that we were more likely to collapse as soon as we were assigned our sleeping spots. Mornings were often more social, though we usually had a strict deadline to get out the door to the next city. Off days were even more fun—we could hang out with our hosts and spend more human time petting cats and learning about who these people truly were.

Staying in your own home can be corrosive and stifling, especially for creative work. The surroundings can smother you with the baggage of your past and the History of You. Staying in a hotel can be a blissful blank slate. There's no baggage, just an empty space onto which you can project anything. But staying in a stranger's home can inspire like nothing else. You get to immerse yourself in the baggage of someone *else's* past, and regard someone *else's* mess of unsorted books piled up in the corner of the living room.

It's not always all rainbows and unicorn bedsheets, though. Couches come with people who own couches. Sometimes people just aren't good at the dance, and can't tell when the performers need to stop socializing. In those awkward situations, you smile wearily, edge politely towards your toothbrush, and make the best of it, hoping the hint will be taken. I will hug you. I will love you. I will genuinely admire your kitchen cow collection. But when it is time, please let me go the fuck to sleep.

There's an inherent, unspoken trust that happens when you walk through the door of your host's home. Everybody implicitly trusts everybody else not to steal anything. We leave our phones, our wallets, our laptops, our journals, and our instruments lying scattered around our various mini-couchsurfing campsites. To my knowledge, I've never had anything go missing.

I'm often asked: *How can you trust people so much?*

Because that's the only way it works.

When you accept somebody's offer for help, whether it's in the form of food, crash space, money, or love, you have to trust the help offered. You can't accept things halfway and walk through the door with your guard up.

When you openly, radically trust people, they not only take care of you, they become your allies, your family.

Sometimes people will prove themselves untrustworthy.

When that happens, the correct response is not:

Fuck! I knew I couldn't trust anybody!

The correct response is:

Some people just suck.

Moving right along.

. . .

Shortly after my tour with The Danger Ensemble ended, I went on a solo tour of the American South with a sister duo called Vermillion Lies opening up for me, plus a merch girl and a sound guy, which made us a small, cramped van of five. We were staying with fans wherever people had volunteered, and in cheap motels when they hadn't.

The morning of our Miami show, we navigated our van through a rough-looking neighborhood towards the house where we were staying, eager to unload our stuff, say hello to our hosts, and take a nap after the long drive from Texas. As we approached the address, we exchanged worried glances as we passed desolate, boarded-up houses, cars broken down on lawns, and the subtle signals that crystal meth was probably easy to score. Arriving at the house, we were welcomed by Jacky, our eighteen-year-old host, into a small but warm and inviting home.

Jacky's family were undocumented immigrants from Honduras, her mother barely spoke English, and they made an absolute fuss over us. Jacky, who was beside herself that we were staying, brought out the medical-lab jackets that she and her friends had bedazzled and paint-splattered to wear to the show the next night, before showing us to our beds. There were only three beds in the house, but I had already met Jacky, her mother, and her brother.

I'm confused, I said.

No confusion! In our family, the guests always sleep in the beds. We're all sleeping outside and on the couches... We've been planning this for weeks. You should have seen our shopping adventure for vegan food for you! She looked so happy. *We're going to give you tortilla lessons at breakfast tomorrow!*

I lay awake that night in Jacky's comfy little bed with the purple quilt, staring at her moonlit dressing table covered in tiny perfume jars and books and the necklaces she'd hung on the mirror.

How is this fair? I thought. *These people have so little. I'm being treated like royalty by a family living in poverty.*

It wasn't guilt that I felt; that would have been an insult to their generosity. It was an overwhelming gratitude, more than I knew what to do with. I thought about how I used to feel as The Bride, when people would throw in a ten- or twenty-dollar bill. Or when a homeless person would give me a dollar, and all I had to give them in return was my gesture of thanks, my gratitude, my stupid token flower. And sometimes it would feel so small.

We woke up the next morning, and tortilla lessons were under way. They tried their best to teach us, Jacky's mother gesticulating helpfully in Spanish. My tortillas were terrible and fell apart immediately. Jacky's and her mother's were perfect. My tortillas, even after many tries, did not improve. Everybody laughed. Breakfast was delicious.

We hung around the kitchen for a little while, and Jacky told me the complicated story of her dad—who was stuck in Honduras—and how everybody was living on a knife-edge of worry that he wouldn't be able to get back to Florida because of immigration issues. Jacky's mother called out from the living room.

Ooh! My mother wants to give you a present, said Jacky. *She's all excited.*

Jacky's mother took me aside and pressed a teeny little Bible, the size of a pack of cards, into my hand. Then she said,

For you. Thank you, for stay here. Your music, helps Jacky. You make her so happy, you help her. Thank you, thank you.

I felt my insides cringe.

How is this fair?

This is fair, I realized.

*This **is** fair.*

The music is the flower.

. . .

Things you get when you couchsurf that you don't get in a hotel:

The rattling sound of pots and silverware in the morning. Bathrooms with ratty, beloved mismatched towels. Leftover birthday cake. Dark hallways humid with the smells of baking. Looking at the weird shit people keep in their medicine cabinets. Cats to pat, who are at first standoffish then decide they love you at four a.m., when you're finally asleep. Walls of Elvis plates. The recaptured feeling of having a sleepover party. Dodgy electric blankets. A chance to try on hats. Morning coffee in a wineglass for lack of enough cups. Children of all ages and temperaments who draw pictures for you. The ability to make your own toast. Record players. Wet grass in the backyard sunrise, where the chickens are roosting. Out-of-tune pianos and other strange instruments to fondle. Candles stuck to mantelpieces. The beautiful vision of strangers in their pajamas. Weird teas from around the world. Pinball machines. Pet spiders. Latches that don't quite work. Glow-in-the-dark things on the ceiling.

Late-night and early-morning stories about love, death, hardship, and heartbreak.

The collision of life. Art for the blender.

The dots connecting.

* * *

I assumed that because Neil had poured out so many details of his life the second time we met, he must be, like me, a chronic self-sharer. In fact, he was the opposite. Shy and guarded about his real feelings most of the time, he had a lot of friends, but hadn't told many people about his past and his own personal stories. That surprised me.

You tricked me, I said. *Why did you tell me so much about yourself when I first met you?*

Because you asked me, he said.

Asked you . . . what?

How I was doing. About my life. Nobody else had ever asked me before, he said.

That's totally ridiculous, I said. *You've been surrounded by people all your life who love and worship you. You have friends. You've had a million girlfriends. I'm sure you've been asked relentlessly. Like, to the point of being annoyed.*

No, said Neil.

Nobody ever poured you a Scotch and said, "So, hey, Neil, how the hell are you really doing?" No girlfriends ever asked what was truly going on? That's utterly impossible. I'm sure they were asking but you weren't hearing them.

Maybe, said Neil.

Maybe you just weren't ready to be asked, I said.

Or maybe, he said, *I found the person I could answer.*

• • •

Back in music-release-land, I decided to stay totally independent. I'd had it with labels. I decided to see what would happen if I released everything direct to the fanbase, posting digital downloads using pay-what-you-want and sending CDs and vinyl straight to their mailboxes. I recorded two experimental little records: *Amanda Palmer Goes Down Under*, a mishmash of live recordings from Australia and New Zealand (including a song about how much I detest Vegemite), and *Amanda Palmer Performs the Popular Hits of Radiohead on Her Magical Ukulele* (featuring "Creep" by Radiohead, of course, and four more songs I'd proudly added to my burgeoning Radiohead-ukulele repertoire). I hired a publicist so that the newspapers wouldn't forget I existed, but other than that, I flew under the radar and went straight to the fanbase, using the golden email list, my blog, and my Twitter feed to spread the news of every release. As I'd do later on Kickstarter, I released both of these records along with Bundles of Extra Things: $15 for the CD, $25 for the CD plus a personalized Polaroid sent from the Australian tour, $35 for the vinyl + T-shirt + button, $100 for the CD + the pillowcase + screen-printed tie + poster + pilsner beer glass + neoprene beer cozy + T-shirt + orchestra patch + three stickers + two buttons. (That's not made up. That was an actual package.)

It was also my first experiment selling house parties. When I released *Amanda Palmer Goes Down Under*, $3,000 bought you All The Things plus a show in your own home; I sold half a dozen of these, and had a blast delivering them throughout my next Australian tour. I took these preorders well in advance of manufacturing the goods so that we didn't over- or under-order and wind up with an excess of neoprene beer cozies (the realities of price breaks meant, unfortunately, that I am STILL the proud owner of about 500 neoprene Amanda Palmer beer cozies—these are the joys of small-business entrepreneurship).

I coped with the gargantuan task of manufacturing and shipping all of these releases with the help of my office staff of three or four people, some part-time, some full-time, all working in different parts of the world, on the Internet, from their own kitchens.

Neil and I also did a quick tour together, recording a bunch of live songs and stories we released as *An Evening with Neil Gaiman & Amanda Palmer*. I was very proud: Neil sang onstage for the first time since getting a full beer can thrown at his face (requiring stitches) during his very brief tenure as a punk singer in the 1970s.

Instead of selling that record straight from one of our websites, we decided to try using Kickstarter, which indie artists were just starting to use as a way to finance and ship records. I chatted constantly online, and listened to input and feedback from the fans. If they wanted high-end lithograph posters, I made high-end lithograph posters. If they wanted 180-gram vinyl, I made 180-gram vinyl. If they wanted Things—pillowcases with hand-drawn art on them, T-shirts that came in gray in size XXXL—I made the Things. The only department where I wasn't open to input was the writing, the music itself. That's my job, not theirs, but I tried to involve them in every other facet of the new world of independent artist-hood. They were now officially along for the ride.

* * *

Right around the same time, I was with Jason Webley in New York doing a weeklong run of shows in a small theater in the West

Village. We were performing in character as the conjoined-twin Evelyn Evelyn sisters, wearing a custom dress lovingly hand-sewn for two people of considerably different heights by our seamstress friend Kambriel. I was the right Evelyn, Jason was the left Evelyn, and we each used a single hand to play one side of each instrument—guitar, piano, and accordion. We wore matching wigs, Jason shaved his beard and wore lipstick, and the result was absurdly unconvincing. Our friend Sxip played the role of our sleazy Svengalian stage manager, and our *actual* tour manager, Eric, pulled double duty playing the role of the silent, oppressed, and worrisome stagehand. The twins were reluctant performers. The shows were shambolic and perfect.

As usual, I was crashing with Josh and Alina across the river in Brooklyn. One day I realized that our show and signing wouldn't be over until eleven thirty, and I had a meeting next door to the theater at ten the next morning. It seemed pointless to spend an hour getting to Brooklyn just to sleep, get up, and turn around again, but it also seemed ridiculous to splurge on a hotel. Without giving it much thought, I twittered:

Who's got a couch/decent bed anywhere in/near West Village? Need crashspace. Will be low-maintenance, in and out. Will trade tickets for the @EvelynEvelyn show

Which is how I arrived, six hours later, at the doorstep of Felix and Michelle. In the moment my finger touched the buzzer, I started to worry that perhaps I was taking this whole Twitter-crowdsourcing thing too far. I'd only ever couchsurfed with Brian, or with the Australians, or with Jason by my side. What if these people were axe murderers?

Axe murderers don't follow me on Twitter, I reassured myself.

But think about what the neighbors say about certain killers, I argued back, *as they're being interviewed by the local news. "They seemed so normal."*

They said in the email that their names were FELIX AND

MICHELLE. How could a nice-sounding couple like FELIX AND MICHELLE be axe murderers?

Bonnie and Clyde, I argued. *Bonnie and Clyde. Plus—*

The door opened and there was Michelle.

Hi, Amanda! She threw the door open and ushered me into the kitchen of the apartment. *Jesus, you must be exhausted. How many shows have you done in a row? Five? Sorry we couldn't take you up on the ticket offer, we had some stupid museum benefit to go to. Let me show you the guest room...I've just changed the sheets for you and... wait, before anything...WINE. Red or white? Or Scotch? Felix just brought back a special bottle from Scotland...*

And she bustled me into the guest room, where fresh towels were folded on the bed.

I stood there in awe, wondering how I ever could have doubted the universe.

• • •

In 2011, I was on tour in New Zealand, an hour from boarding a small plane bound for Christchurch, when the giant earthquake hit. My flight was canceled. All the flights were canceled. My show, which was scheduled that night in central Christchurch, was also canceled. The venue no longer existed.

I spent that entire day—and most of the next few days—on Twitter, talking nonstop with my Christchurch fans. All of them were okay, but a lot of them were freaked out, and everybody knew someone who knew someone who'd been killed, since it's a small community. Some people had traveled there for the show and were trapped with no place to stay. And everybody shared their stories, and I shared the stories back out to the worldwide crowd. We tightened.

One of the New Zealanders, Diana, had suffered an unbelievable loss. Her entire family—mom, dad, and two brothers—had been killed in the earthquake. I reached out to her online and asked for her address and phone number. She was staying with cousins in Australia, and in too much turmoil to talk, but I told her to stay in touch, to call if she needed me, to use me, to use the whole community.

A few days later, I played a show in Melbourne, and over a thousand fans decorated, kissed, and markered love-wishes for Diana on a bedsheet-sized blank poster I arranged to have hung in the lobby. I mailed it off to her. A few days later, she did call and we spoke for about an hour while I paced around a friend's backyard in Melbourne.

What could I say? She'd lost everything. Her family. Her home. Her whole life. Her Australian cousins were being kind, but she was having difficulties sorting out her head, and I asked her gentle questions, comforted her, tried to distract her and make her laugh. I assured her that she was loved, that she had a whole human family around her that would not let her fall or feel alone. She sounded strange, despondent, distant, confused, which wasn't surprising.

A day later a friendly newspaper journalist called me from Auckland. He was a fan as well, and had done some research because he wanted to do a story about this phenomenon: the girl, the fans, me, the net. He had just talked to the Christchurch Red Cross, asking for the details of the teenage girl who had lost both her parents and siblings.

No such girl existed.

. . .

All of the people in Melbourne who'd turned the lobby into a group art-therapy project had felt something real. They'd been deceived. I'd been deceived. I didn't tell them that the tragedy was fictional. (They'll know now, though, and I wonder if that girl will read this book. I hope she is okay.)

The saddest thing about Earthquake Girl was that either way—

truth or fiction—the story was tragic. Anyone who was unhappy and unhinged enough to pull a stunt like that clearly needed love.

Oddly enough, her lie had pulled us all together. She was like a broken thread in the net, hanging down.

A lot like art, I thought, *like any work of fiction.*

The story was fake, but the impact was real.

TROUT HEART REPLICA

They've been circling
They've been circling
Since the day they were born

It's disturbing
How they're circling
Fifty feet from the pond

Pretty often
Pretty often
I don't want to be told

It's a problem
It's a problem
It's a problem I know
And I won't keep what I
    can't catch
In my bare hands
    without a net
It's hard enough to walk on
    grass
So conscious of the
    consequences

They've been jerking
They've been jerking
In a pail by the dock

I know that oxygen might
Make them blossom and die
But I'm not going to talk

Feed them details
Feed them emails
They'll eventually grow

But it's not working
It's not working
Not as far as I know

And killing things is not
    so hard
It's hurting that's the
    hardest part
And when the wizard gets to me
I'm asking for a smaller heart

And I got you
I thought that I got you
Now I'll ruin it all

Feeling helpless
Acting selfish
Being human and all

And they're jumping
And they're jumping
But they'll never get out

Just keep touring
Just keep on ignoring
Be a good little trout

And the butcher stops and
    winds his watch
And lays their lives down on
    the block
He raises up his hatchet
And the big hand strikes a
    compromise

Wait, we'll trade you
Wait

Please just one more day
And then we'll go with
No complaining...
No complaining...
No complaining...
Stop
Come...

And they're cutting
And they're cutting
And I think that I know
And they're gutting
And they're gutting
And I think that I know
And it's beating
Look, it's beating
And I don't want to know
And it's beating

Look, it's still beating
God, I don't want to know

And killing things is not
   so hard
It's hurting that's the
   hardest part
And when the wizard gets
   to me
I'm asking for a smaller heart
And if he tells me no
I'll hold my breath until I
   hit the floor
Eventually I know I'm doomed
To get what I am asking for

Now my heart is exactly the
   size
Of a six-sided die cut in half

Made of ruby red stained
   glass

Can I knock you unconscious
   as long as I promise
I'll love you and I'll make
   you laugh?
Now my heart is exactly the
   size
Of a six-sided die cut in half
Made of ruby red stained
   glass
Can I knock you unconscious
   as long as I promise
I'll love you and I'll make
   you laugh?

—from *Theatre Is Evil*, 2012

For most of human history, musicians and artists have been *part* of the village, accessing one another freely. They've been healers, listeners, mind-openers—in touch with the community, not untouchable stars on screens and behind barricades. I grew up believing that the distance of "real" stardom was glamorous. But in truth, feeling love from a distance is just lonely. Maybe even worse than no love at all, because it feels so unnatural.

The Internet has shaken things up in this regard and brought us, in some ways, full circle: we're back around the fireside, albeit sometimes using our smartphones. The sorts of connections I make with people on Twitter and on my blog are real, honest, and loving. I'm able to reach safely into people's heads and hearts, allow them to reach back into mine, and—most importantly—give them a place to reach into each other.

. . .

This morning, as I was getting ready to sit down and write this book, I popped onto Twitter and:

- I shared a news link about nine people who had been killed by a nineteen-year-old college student in Santa Barbara.
- I posted a live clip of one of my friend Mali's songs and gave a shout-out to the West Coast fanbase to see if anybody could couch-host her or help her fill in some tour dates.
- I sent an old blog link to a fan who'd asked about some controversial lyrics I'd written years before.
- I told Neil, who was in Europe for his mother's birthday, that I loved him.

- I encouraged anybody in the New York area to go see my friend Andrew O'Neill doing standup in Brooklyn.
- I looked at and shared a beautiful calligraphy-based painting by a kid in Brazil that was based on some Dresden Dolls lyrics.
- I reposted a link to the piece that Neil wrote about the trip he took last week to a refugee camp in Jordan.
- I shared the link to a school-project video some girls from Thailand had made about my Kickstarter.
- I asked for some book help as I tried to conjure up a good two-way megaphone metaphor (lots of people suggested cans and string, which was perfect). I eventually edited that section out of the book, but whatever. I used it here. Hooray!
- I pointed out that my last record producer, John Congleton, just joined Twitter. He twittered back and posted a photo of boobs.
- I asked for everybody to wish me luck as I started my ten-hour writing day. Ksenia, a Russian author I know on Twitter, offered me an encouraging bowl of virtual borscht. It's a daily joke.

and

- I told two people I loved them and gave them each a Twitter hug ((((((()))))))). Just because they asked.

This all happened in fifteen minutes, the time it took me to order and drink my morning espresso and eat a croissant in the corner café. It's not my job. It's my life. It's me.

I have over one million Twitter followers. As I ate my croissant, I chatted in real-time 140-character chunks, and a few hundred people posted responses to the things I'd just shared. I scanned all their messages and publicly discussed a few issues—personal, emotional, and political—with a few friends and strangers. I probably twittered about twenty times. I walked back to my apartment. By the time I got there, a few hundred more tweets had flowed in. I looked them over before I settled down to write, and was pleased to see a wave of thankful messages from the people whose artwork and photos I'd shared, a few 140-character pom-pom waves wishing me luck with the upcoming writing day, and a variety of other conversations and connections bobbing along in the wake of my fifteen-minute Twitter flurry.

This is a normal morning.

*   *   *

I asked my blog readers a question.

WHAT DO YOU WISH YOU'D ASKED FOR?

There were thousands of responses, and the overwhelming majority were variations on this:

I wish I'd asked for help.

One girl wrote:

I was born legally blind to a rural family that didn't know how to deal with disability, but wasn't going to give up on me either. I was raised with the best of intentions, but ultimately I grew up as a mixture between a cherished porcelain doll for display and a feral dog let to run wild. I'm twenty-four and I've spent all of my late adolescence and early adulthood reteaching myself simple day-to-day life skills (using an oven, cleaning a toilet)…I wish I'd asked for independence.

She wishes she'd asked people to help her by *not* helping.

It's the same thing, isn't it?

I was comparing notes with my older sister Alyson one night, over wine, right around the time I was also struggling with a marriage-and-money freak-attack. She's a scientist, and I've never totally been able to grasp what she does. Stuff with genetics, gene sequencing, finding cures for rare forms of cancer, and other simple things like that. She experiments on fish in her work, and I usually lose the plot a few seconds after she starts explaining what she does. I can't stop worrying about the fish.

She and her new husband, like me and Neil, had been keeping their finances more or less separate since getting together. But also, like me and Neil, some things had merged; she'd ditched her apartment and moved into his flat. She had her upstanding position at the university, he had his freelancing tech job, and life was good—but she was about to come up for tenure. She wasn't confident she was going to get it, and her husband had offered to support her so she could take time off to look for a new job, go back to school, or even spend a few months communing with nature and finding herself. She couldn't stand the thought of it, the shame of it. She hadn't taken more than a few days' vacation in twenty years.

All my friends think I'm crazy, she said.

All MY friends think I'M crazy! I said.

What the fuck happened to us? I asked. *Why are we so weird?*

I don't know, she said. *Our self-sufficient, breadwinning mother? Our New England upbringing? Hangover from the witch-burning Puritans? Society as a whole?*

I blame society, I said.

Well, we're not alone, Alyson said. *I have a couple of friends with this same problem. They make a ton of money, but not as much as their husbands, and they can't stand feeling inadequate. I don't think we're crazy.*

I thought about the men in my life, the ones who'd let me into their heads and hearts. Most of them didn't have a hard time in certain departments of asking, but when it came to their emotional needs, it was a mess. They could ask for a raise, but they couldn't ask for a hug.

I thought about Anthony. He was a professional therapist, listening to people, asking them about their deepest fears and problems all week long, and even *he* would clam up when things got rough. He likes being in control, he loves having answers, he loves fixing and helping people. But he has a really hard time letting people help *him*. Sometimes, when he gets depressed, he shuts down and doesn't like to talk. When that happens, I figure it's time for me to step up, ask him questions, help him through, talk about the problems. But he clams up and doesn't like talking to anyone about his own problems. He calls it Going Into The Box.

When we ask for anything, we're almost always asking for help in some form: help with money, permission, acceptance, advancement, help with our hearts.

Brené Brown has found through her research that women tend to feel shame around the idea of being "never enough": at home, at work, in bed. Never pretty enough, never smart enough, never thin enough, never good enough. Men tend to feel shame around the fear of being "perceived as weak," or more academically: *fear of being called a pussy.*

Both sexes get trapped in the same box, for different reasons.

If I ask for help, *I am not enough.*

If I ask for help, *I am weak.*

It's no wonder so many of us just don't bother to ask.

It's too painful.

. . .

Sometimes it was like Neil was from an alien planet, where people never asked for or shared anything emotional without deeply apologizing first. He assured me that he was simply British. And that we Americans, with all of our loud oversharing and need for random hugs and free admissions to people we've just met of deep, traumatic childhood wounds looks just as alien to them.

When he started to trust me, he told me that he'd believed for a long time, deep down, that people didn't actually fall in love. That they were all faking it.

But that's impossible. You're a professional writer, I said, and you've seen a thousand films and read a thousand books and memoirs and know real people authentically in love. What about John and Judith? Peter and Clare? Did you think they're just lying? And you've written whole books, stories, scenes where people are deeply in love. I mean...I just don't believe you. How could you write about love if you didn't believe it existed?

That's the whole point, darling, he said. *Writers make things up.*

. . .

While I was working on the first draft of this book (which I did over a few thousand coffees in various cafés in Melbourne), I shared a coffee with Samantha Buckingham, an Australian indie guitarist/ singer-songwriter, during which I picked her brain about her process and her relationship with her own fanbase.

Sam is typical of a lot of indie musicians eking out a living. She's not on a label, she crowdfunds and releases music directly to the Internet, she plays house parties in her fans' living rooms. We were comparing notes about the pros and cons of Patreon.com, a new subscription service Sam was using, which allows fans to automatically deposit money into a musician's account every time the musician releases a song, kind of like a book-of-the-month club for artists putting out content, so they can rely on a somewhat predictable income instead of praying that their Kickstarter will get funded every time they have something to release. (At the time of this writing, she's got forty-four patrons—including nineteen $1 backers and one backer at $50—and is paid about $200 every time she releases a song. Patrons can choose how much they pay per song, and they can cap their monthly bill so she doesn't all of a sudden dump one thousand songs on people and run off to Mexico. Although running off to Mexico when you're Australian seems weird, so I'm thinking she would more, like, run off to Papua New Guinea.)

Sam was, in fact, about to travel to Asia with her boyfriend, and she was fretting about what her backers would think if she released some of her new songs to Patreon while she was "on vacation." She was worried that posting pictures of herself sipping a mai tai was going to make her look like an asshole.

What does it matter where you are or whether you're drinking a coffee, a mai tai, or a bottle of water? I asked. *Aren't they paying for your songs so you can... live? Doesn't living include wandering and col-lecting emotions and drinking a mai tai—not just sitting in a room and writing songs without ever leaving the house?*

I told Sam about another songwriter friend of mine, Kim Boek-binder, who runs her own direct-support website through which her fans pay her monthly, at levels from $5 to $1,000. She also has a running online wish list of musical gear and costumes, like a wed-ding registry, to which her fans can contribute money anytime. Kim had told me a few days before that she doesn't mind charging her backers during what she calls her "staring-at-the-wall time," which she thinks is essential before she can write a new batch of songs. Her fans don't complain; they trust her process.

These are new forms of patronage, and it's messy; the artists, and the patrons, are making up the rules as they go along. But whether these artists are using crowdfunding ("front me some money so that I can Make A Thing!"), subscription services ("pay me some money every month so I can Make Things!"), or pay-per-piece-of-content pledge services ("pay me some money every time I Make A Thing!"), the fundamental building block of all these relationships boils down to the same, simple thing: trust.

If you're asking your fans to support you, the artist, it shouldn't matter what your choices are as long as you're delivering your side of the bargain. You may be spending the money on guitar picks, mai tais, baby formula, college loans, gas for cars, or coffee to fuel your all-night writing sessions. As long as art is coming out the other side and making your patrons happy, the money you need to live—and "need to live" is hard to define—is almost indistinguishable from the money you need to make art.

Like me, Sam, and thousands of new-school online artists, Kim is in daily communication with her fans. Her ongoing arrangement with her two hundred supporters functions because she shares her songwriting process, along with her bad days and heartaches. They trust her decisions. When she posts a photo of herself in a vintage dress she just bought, nobody scolds her for spending money on something other than effects pedals. It's not like her fans' money is an "allowance," with nosy and critical strings attached. It's a gift, in the form of money, in exchange for her gift, in the form of music.

The relative values are messy, but if we accept the messiness, we're all okay. If Beck needs to moisturize his cuticles with truffle oil in order to play guitar tracks on his crowdfunded record, I don't care that the money I've fronted him isn't going towards two turntables *or* a microphone. Just as long as the art gets made, I get the album, and Beck doesn't die in the process.

But that doesn't mean observers are going to stop criticizing artists and their process anytime soon. No less than Henry David Thoreau has been called a poseur.

Thoreau wrote in painstaking detail about how he chose to remove himself from society to live by his own means in a little ten-by-fifteen-foot hand-hewn cabin on the side of a pond. What he left out of *Walden*, though, was the fact that the land he built on was borrowed from his wealthy neighbor, that his pal Ralph Waldo Emerson had him over for dinner all the time, and that every Sunday, Thoreau's mother and sister brought him a basket of freshly baked goods for him, including *donuts*.[6]

The idea of Thoreau gazing thoughtfully over the expanse of transcendental Walden Pond, a bluebird alighting onto his threadbare shoe, all the while *eating donuts that his mom brought him* just doesn't jibe with most people's picture of him as a self-reliant, noble, marrow-sucking back-to-the-woods folk hero. In the book *An Underground Education*, Richard Zacks declares: *Let it be known that Nature Boy went home on weekends to raid the family cookie jar.*

Thoreau also lived at Walden for a total of two or three years, but he condensed the book down to a single year, the four seasons, to make the book flow better, to work as a piece of art, and to best reflect his emotional experience.

---

6. As I learned from a marvelous talk given by Maciej Ceglowski, awesome founder of the "social bookmarking" site Pinboard, at the 2013 XOXO Festival.

I told this story to Sam over our coffees.

Poor Thoreau, said Sam, shaking her head. *The donuts are totally the mai tai.*

. . .

Taking the donuts is hard for a lot of people.

It's not the act of taking that's so difficult, it's more the fear of what other people are going to *think* when they see us slaving away at our manuscript about the pure transcendence of nature and the importance of self-reliance and simplicity. While munching on someone else's donut.

Maybe it comes back to that same old issue: we just can't see what we do as important enough to merit the help, the love. Try to picture getting angry at Einstein devouring a donut brought to him by his assistant while *he* sat slaving on the theory of relativity. Try to picture getting angry at Florence Nightingale for snacking on a donut while taking a break from tirelessly helping the sick. It's difficult.

. . .

So, a plea.

To the artists, creators, scientists, nonprofit-runners, librarians, strange-thinkers, start-uppers, and inventors, to all people everywhere who are afraid to accept the help, in whatever form it's appearing:

Please, take the donuts.

To the guy in my opening band who was too ashamed to go out into the crowd and accept money for his band:

Take the donuts.

To the girl who spent her twenties as a street performer and stripper living on less than $700 a month, who went on to marry a best-selling author whom she loves, unquestioningly, but even that massive love can't break her unwillingness to accept his financial help, please...

Everybody.

Please.

Just take the fucking donuts.

. . .

You can never give people what they want, Anthony said.

What do you mean?

We were lying by the side of Walden Pond in Concord, two towns over from Lexington, where we'd created a ritual of ambling around the circumference of the water, then lazing under the trees with a picnic for a nice long grok.

People always want something from you, he said. *Your time. Your love. Your money. For you to agree with them and their politics, their point of view. And you can't ever give them what they want. But you—*

That's a dreary worldview.

Let me finish, clown. You can't ever give people what they want. But you can give them something else. You can give them empathy. You can give them understanding. And that's a lot, and enough to give.

. . .

As Sam and I sat in the café, pondering the donut and mai tai dilemmas of all artists, we were joined by Xanthea, who had first introduced us to each other. Xanthea and I had met a few months before, bonding at a wonderful Kickstarter house party she'd organized in her parents' backyard in Perth.

Xanthea was twenty-two, worked at a bookstore, didn't want to finish college, organized indie rock shows in laundromats, wrote songs on various instruments, and was a living statue on the side, clad all in white, wearing an old-fashioned sundress, handing out flowers. I'd gone to see her a few days before, where she was performing on Flinders Street, and watched from a distance as she was ignored, loved, ignored, loved again. When I finally dropped some money in her hat, we shared a conspiratorial gaze—the secret statue society. I was proud of her. At the house party, we had shared tales of living-statue hardships, and she'd told me about being harassed by perv-y drunks, and about the time a girl poked her hard in the ribs with a flute. She toughed it out. My kind of girl.

She sat down next to Sam and ordered a coffee, and we explained Thoreau and the donut kerfuffle. Xanthea said she could totally relate. She was just starting to play small gigs and didn't know how to handle the business side.

I'm getting offered all these gigs in Perth, they're offering me actual MONEY to play my stupid songs, not a LOT, but I don't feel like I should take any money... not yet. I think I'm not ready. And it's even less fair because I'm not, like, a BAND yet. I'm just a person.

I got what Xanthea was saying about the Band Thing. Taking money on behalf of a group, a band, a company—any entity larger than yourself—feels very different from taking money on behalf of YOU.

When I took the step from playing my few-and-far-between solo shows to playing in The Dresden Dolls with Brian, I felt a huge difference between asking people to listen to ME and MY songs and help ME ME ME, versus helping our BAND. It felt very different to hand someone tapes whose front cover proclaimed *AMANDA PALMER* as opposed to saying: *I'm in a band, here's our CD.*

One felt selfish, the other felt legitimate.

Right before I met Brian, I'd started putting "Amanda Palmer and the Void" on my gig flyers. I figured nobody could argue with that on technical grounds. I had a backup band of approximately no people. (I'm not the only one who's done it. See: Marina and the Diamonds, Tracy and the Plastics.)

I discovered more recently that this experience has been studied, and not surprisingly, it's a particularly female problem.

In 2010, Emily Amanatullah, a graduate student in management, did a research simulation in which men and women had to negotiate starting salaries in different scenarios.

When the women negotiated for themselves, they asked for an average of $7,000 less than the men did. But when they negotiated on behalf of a friend, they asked for just as much money as the men did. Amanatullah found that women were concerned about "managing their reputation," worried that pushing for more money would "damage their image." And other research shows it's a justified fear, that both male and female managers are less likely to want to work with women who negotiate during a job interview.

On the other hand, when they had to negotiate on behalf of someone else, they presented far higher counteroffers. The upshot? Women were in fact excellent negotiators. They didn't feel comfortable using their negotiating skills *for themselves,* but they felt fine asking *on behalf of others.*

And the other thing, said Xanthea, sighing. *I have friends who've played like a gajillion more open mics than me, who are taking it more seriously and gigging every single weekend. I mean, I get what you're saying. But it doesn't feel fair.*

What do you mean it's not fair? I said. *They're offering you the money because they like you . . . and your music, right?*

I just mean . . . like, there's an ORDER of things—a progression, she said miserably, looking guiltily at me, and then at Sam. *And I'm not at that place where I feel like I'm allowed, you know, to get paid.*

We both just looked at her and said, in unison:

Xanthea. **TAKE THE DONUTS.**

.   .   .

In the early days, The Fraud Police seemed to keep pace with my career. Despite write-ups in bigger magazines, airplay on radio and TV, and playing larger venues, the growing fame and all the outside eyes just made me feel more insecure, like I was pulling a bigger one over on everybody. On a bad day, the success did the opposite of reassuring me. Instead, it compounded my fears of not being real.

The volume of those voices in my head blaring *you're a total phony* weren't diminished by compliments from other artists, or by congratulations from my mentors, or even when my parents stopped asking me what I was *really* doing with my life (due, I feel sure, to the first time I had a show listed in the *New Yorker*, a press outlet that they actually KNEW).

What at last began to quiet the voices and dismiss the deep-rooted psyche-bashing work of The Fraud Police was simply this: after hundreds of signings, after talking to thousands of fans, I started to believe that what I did was just as useful as what they did.

They spoke to me directly. In the signing line. Over Twitter. A lawyer loved listening to my music on her long commute to work. An ecologist said my first album got him through final exams. A young doctor had a psychotic break during med school, and said that listening to my song "Half Jack" over and over again in the hospital had helped get him through. A professor had met his wife years before at a Dresden Dolls concert, and now she was in a coma following a car crash; he sent me a necklace of hers as a keepsake.

These were "real" people with "real" jobs, making society work. And there were a lot of them.

I would take in all these stories, and one by one, ten, a hundred, a thousand stories later...I had to believe it. I would hold these people in my arms and I would feel the whole synchronicity of life and death and music envelop us.

And one day I turned around and it had just happened without my realizing it.

I believed I was real.

. . .

I had just finished a gig in Perth and was driving to a fan's house, to crash with the Australian crew, when Neil called me from New York.

He said, *My dad just died.*

What?

He died. My dad just died. He was in a business meeting, something happened with his heart, and he fell over, and he's dead.

Oh my god, Neil.

What could I do? I was about as physically far away from him as I could possibly be. We had only been dating for about three months, but it was long enough to have started falling in love.

Do you want me to come to you right now? I'll get the first flight out, I offered. *I'll just get on a plane and come be with you.*

No, darling. He sounded like a zombie. *Stay there. Finish your tour. Go to Tasmania.*

No. I'll come. Really. I want to.

No, don't. I'm asking you not to. Stay there. Go make the people in Tasmania happy.

I felt so incredibly helpless. He was in New York City, literally about to start a signing for his new children's book. It was midnight in Australia and eleven in the morning there.

I talked to him for a while longer, then hung up, feeling useless.

I was given our host's master bedroom that night—I was feeling disoriented, and I slept with the phone clutched in my hand. Neil had as deep a connection to his fanbase as I did. I could just imagine him there, those first people coming up with their books in hand, and I imagined him losing himself in their stories, their faces, their details.

I imagined him signing every book very deliberately, focusing on the task at hand, thinking every once in a while, as the ink touched the page and he got lost in a millisecond of space: *My dad is dead.* I called him the minute I woke the next morning, but I got his voicemail.

I called Cat, Neil's old friend, who was helping him out with the signing.

How is he? I asked. *How was the signing? Is he okay?*

You're not going to believe this . . . but he's still at it.

He'd been signing for seven hours straight, for 1,500 people.

I didn't know what to do. Write him a long, heartfelt email? Send flowers? Both seemed ridiculous.

So I called my assistant at the time—wonderful, helpful Beth, who was also in New York—told her about Neil's dad, and gave her instructions. She raced around the city to accomplish several tasks, and stepped up just as Neil was dedicating the very last book to the very last person, after eight solid hours of signing.

She placed a tomato, a schedule, and a banana on the table in front of him.

From Amanda, she told him.

Cat, who was standing off to the side, texted me:

You did it. I don't know HOW you did it.

But he just actually smiled for the first time.

AMPERSAND

I walk down my street at
night
The city lights are cold and
violent
I am comforted by the
approaching sound of trucks
and sirens
Even though the world's so bad
These men rush out to help
the dying
And though I am no use to
them
I do my part by simply
smiling

The ghetto boys are
catcalling me
As I pull my keys from my
pocket
I wonder if this method of
courtship
Has ever been effective
Has any girl in history said
"Sure! You seem so nice! Let's
get it on!"
Still, I always shock them
when I answer
"Hi, my name's Amanda"

And I'm not gonna live my
life on one side of an
ampersand
And even if I went with you,
I'm not the girl you think
I am
And I'm not gonna match you
Cause I'll lose my voice
completely
No, I'm not gonna watch you
Cause I'm not the one that's
crazy . . .

I have wasted years of my life
Agonizing about the fires

I started when I thought that
to be strong you must be
flame-retardant
And now to dress the wounds
goes into question
How authentic they are
There is always someone
criticizing me
She just likes playing
hospital

Lying in my bed
I remember what you said
There's no such thing as
accidents

But you've got the
headstones all ready
All carved up and pretty
Your sick satisfaction
Those his and hers matching
The daisies all push up in
pairs to the horizon
Your eyes full of ketchup
(It's nice that you're trying)

But I'm not gonna live my life
on one side of an ampersand
And even if I went with you,
I'm not the girl you think
I am
And I'm not gonna match you
Cause I'll lose my voice
completely
No, I'm not gonna watch you
Cause I'm not the one that's
crazy
I'm not the one that's crazy,
yeah . . .

As I wake up—two o'clock
The fire burned the block
But ironically stopped at my
apartment

And my housemates are all
   sleeping soundly
And nobody deserves to die
But you were awful adamant
That if I didn't love you
Then you have just one
   alternative . . .

And I may be romantic
And I may risk my life for it
But I ain't gonna die for you
(You know I ain't no Juliet)

And I'm not gonna watch you
   while you burn yourself
   out, baby . . .
No, I'm not gonna stop you
Cause I'm not the one that's
   crazy, yeah
I'm not the one that's crazy,
   yeah
I'M NOT THE ONE'S THAT'S CRAZY

—from *Who Killed Amanda
   Palmer*, 2008

We'd been together for a year, and Neil started asking me to marry him.

The idea of marrying Neil terrified me.

He asked and asked. We'd wake up in the morning and he'd ask. We'd bed down at night and he'd ask. We'd get ready to hang up after a long phone call and he'd ask. It was a running joke, but he also meant it.

I felt my hard insides, my desperation to stay independent, and the irony of it all: the girl who'd stood on the box for five years, falling in love and merging with a million passing strangers, yet remained staunchly resistant to an actual human merger. My inner feminist was also rolling her eyes. *Just date, for chrissake. Maybe move in together. What is this, the fifties?*

But he wanted to get married. There was a practical level (he was dating a rock musician sixteen years his junior, and introducing me as "wife" instead of "girlfriend" meant that—as annoying as it was—people would take me seriously). And the fact that we were both constantly traveling meant we couldn't take the halfway step of moving in together.

And apart from the practical reasons, he simply wanted to get married. He said I made him feel safe.

I didn't care as much about being taken seriously. But I figured we could make a deal.

I asked him a battery of questions.

I want to live and work alone. If we get married, do I have to live with you?

No, he said. *Will you marry me?*

Do I have to act like a wife? I don't really want to be a wife.

No, you don't need to be a wife, he said. *Will you marry me?*

If we get married, will we be able to sleep with other people?
Yep, he said. *Will you marry me?*
Can I maintain total control of my life? I need total control of my life.
Yes, darling. I'm not trying to control you. At all. Will you marry me?
I probably don't want kids.
That's fine. I already have three. They're great. Will you marry me?
If I marry you and it doesn't work, can we just get divorced?
Sure, he said brightly.

. . .

I've yet to ask the Internet for tampons, but I've asked for just about everything else.

Twitter is the ultimate crowdsourcing tool for the traveling musician; it's like having a Swiss Army knife made up of a million people in your pocket.

Back when I had only a few thousand followers, I could ask anything, or ask *for* anything, in 140 characters at a time. The responses poured in. I answered. I thanked people loudly and publicly. Waving my gratitude like a flag is part of what keeps the gift in motion.

Sharing the broadcasting power is part of the fun, and also part of what makes it work. When people—anyone, really—twitters at me asking if I can share their need for a crash pad, I share, and I feel like a magical switchboard operator. I watch the fanbase surf on the waves we've collectively created. I watch them jump, I watch them fall, I watch them trust, I watch them catch one another. I watch the story unfold. I applaud.

A list of things I've asked for on Twitter:

Advice. I was on an Australian tour, in a small coastal town, and found a growing red spot on my thigh that I assumed was an infected bug bite. I snapped and posted a picture and several people, including one EMT from Canada, warned me that it looked more like a staph infection than a bug bite. I got myself to a doctor. They were right. Staph infections, if untreated, can lead to amputated limbs and death.

Song lyrics. I'll ask things like, What's a three-syllable word for something naughty that you're not allowed to take to work? Stress on the first syllable. Please be as creative and surreal as possible. (I needed only two things to fit in the lyrics, but so many answers were so perfect that I changed the nature of that entire song, "The Ukulele Anthem," to accommodate twenty-three of them.)

Pianos everywhere. I've practiced and written songs in people's houses and apartments, and borrowed at least fifty digital keyboards for ninja gigs and practice. (Also crowdsourced: guitars, basses, violins, wah pedals.)

Car rides to the airport. (I call it "twitch-hiking.")

A neti pot. I asked where I could buy one in Melbourne, and a nurse who worked at a local hospital grabbed one from the supply closet and drove it over to the café that I was twittering from. I bought her a smoothie and we had a wonderful chat about nursing, colds, and death.

I once crowdsourced a wedding gown for an impromptu music video I shot while on tour in Texas. I'd come up with the idea to walk into the ocean dressed as a bride, so I twittered to see if anyone knew a good thrift shop I could hit. Instead, a woman who'd just gotten divorced volunteered to drive three hours to deliver her own wedding gown. I invited her to the shoot itself, and hitched a ride with her to Galveston instead of with my film friends. Along the way we went hunting to find a veil. The only one we managed to find was in a roadside novelty shop that sold bachelorette items. It was covered with little glued-on plastic penises. I peeled them off.[7] Driving to the beach, my new friend told me about her divorce (long story, short: *he was a dick*). She watched the video shoot from the pier above the beach, and I felt her eyes on me as I traipsed her long,

---

7. That night, before the doors opened for the show in Houston, I hid all the penises in different locations around the venue—the bathrooms, the bar, the lobby— and twittered photo clues as to their whereabouts. Every few minutes, from my dressing room backstage, I could hear a giant cheer coming from the house as one by one, each penis was discovered.

flowing gown into the waves, where it got covered with sand and sea scum.

That was pretty fucking liberating, she said when the shoot was over and we were wringing out the dress in the parking lot. *Thank you.*

No, thank YOU for the dress. It was perfect. I think we should find a plastic bag for it... it's pretty gross. What are you going to do with it?

I was thinking about that, she said. *I think I'm going to dye it blue and cut the train off. Recycle it into something I can dance in.*

EXACTLY, I said.

. . .

I was still trying to figure out if marrying Neil Gaiman The Writer was a good idea.

I was in love with him, that much was clear to everybody around us, even if it wasn't always clear to me. I kept coming up with reasons that it just Wasn't A Good Idea. Our lives were too different. I would slowly drive him crazy. He was too old. The list went on.

Luke was a musician I'd met at the Edinburgh fringe festival two years before. We'd fallen in fast friend love, a fall made only slightly awkward by the fact that the night we met I'd convinced him to make out with me (and, somewhat confusingly, succeeded) not knowing he was inarguably, 100 percent gay. He still claims I am the only woman he's ever snogged. I'm proud of that.

How long have you and Todd been together? I asked. We were sharing a late breakfast in Sydney, where we both happened to be touring at the time. I was grilling him about his long-term relationship, hoping I could find my own clarity.

About five years, give or take.

And how much older is he?

Ten years, about.

What's the difference in your incomes? I said. *If you don't mind me asking.*

It's not massive... but it varies. We've agreed to split certain things and float each other when we need help. I spent almost half a year out of work last year when Todd took that huge gig in Vegas and I followed him there. It hasn't been easy, but we've found a balance.

It doesn't worry you, I said, *that he might, I don't know, always be ahead of you? Not older... or richer, per se... but just, like, ahead of you in terms of aging, and life experience? It's morbid, but don't you think about the fact that he might DIE on you? And then do you feel like an asshole for thinking it?*

Well... you know that Todd is HIV positive, right?

But I hadn't known. I looked at my tofu scramble, feeling like an idiot.

Jesus. Luke. Nobody ever told me.

No, no, I'm sorry. I thought you knew. I figured someone would have told you. And I'm still negative, in case you were wondering.

I asked nervously, gently, because I wasn't sure if you were supposed to pry about this stuff:

When did you guys find out?

Oh, he said offhandedly. *Todd was HIV positive when I met him.*

What?

Todd was HIV positive when I met him, he repeated.

And it wasn't... a deal-breaker? I felt ashamed even as I said it.

Amanda... it wasn't a question of deal-breaking. I was in love with him.

. . .

And then Anthony got sick.

Really sick. And nobody could figure out what was wrong. He was losing his balance, he was having trouble hearing, he was losing his vision in one eye. The doctors didn't know what to tell him. His calves hurt. His arms hurt. Anthony looked about twenty years younger than his age, and had always been the picture of health; walking everywhere, kayaking, doing yoga. I called him from the road every day, and every day there was a new mystery ailment, a new pain alien that had landed somewhere in his body to launch a fresh attack.

I felt bad bringing him my own stupid problems, but I knew he loved helping, so I continued to lay my life at his feet. My business was an unwieldy mess as usual, and as my fanbase had grown I'd tried out several hotshot managers who worked in big offices running the careers of the famous, but finally gave up on that idea: I pared things back down to me and a dedicated staff of three people who understood me. My income was neither huge nor predictable, but I was getting along fine and able to pay everyone, mostly because I performed relentlessly: it had become a running joke among my Cloud Club housemates that for six years I'd been announcing my impending break from touring, during which I would finally clean up my apartment. I was off the label but unsure of my next step; I had accumulated a pile of great songs but wasn't certain how I was going to release them. Neil was waiting for his youngest daughter to graduate from high school in Wisconsin (where he had raised his kids with his first wife), so that we could move nearer to each other...probably in New York. Every time I came home to Boston for a break it seemed I was battling the flu, a post-tour depression, or a bout of existentially harrowing PMS.

But while my problems felt mundane compared to the frightening and undiagnosed pain my friend was in, he listened patiently, laughed with me, and advised wisely, as usual. For a few months, Anthony went to every doctor, every specialist. The eye doctors treated his eyes, the hearing doctors puzzled over his ears. Nobody could figure it out. We were all getting more scared. One day, his eyes and head started to pound so badly that Laura rushed him to the hospital. I raced back from a show in New York.

They took a biopsy from his temple and they told him that he had giant cell arteritis, a whole-body inflammation of the arteries that strikes people at random.

He was pumped with a giant bag of steroids, taking in enough prednisone in one day to supply a bodybuilder for an entire year.

Watching Anthony in the hospital that night was hard. He likes being in control of any given situation and gets anxious when things don't go according to plan. I'd always viewed him as a worldly, jet-setting adult when I was younger, but as I circled the globe and kept boomeranging back to him, it was becoming more clear to me: he'd built himself a little office in a little town surrounded by things he had known all his life, things he could trust. He was strong on the outside—he had his black belt in karate—but he was fragile and sensitive to sudden change on the inside. Anthony had been abused physically and emotionally as a kid, and he'd told me the stories, a few here, a few there, and had even started writing some down. They were frightening. But whether he was writing or chatting, I was always impressed and struck by his sense of humor about the abuse and its aftershocks.

It hurt to see him there, hooked up to strange machines, vulnerable in a blue hospital gown as the doctors and nurses came and went, poked and prodded. Laura spent the night, curled up next to him in the adjustable bed. Friends took turns bringing food.

It wasn't fatal, thank god. His vision and hearing were damaged, but he'd live. I exhaled. I didn't think I could handle it if something truly bad happened to him.

I used to play a game with myself in high school and college, my own self-taught version of method acting, and it came in handy for a few theater productions.

If I ever needed to cry on command, I had a trick.

I would just think about Anthony dying.

It never failed. I'd burst into tears no matter what.

* * *

I don't really have stalkers.

In order to have a stalker, you need to be a decent stalk-ee, and I'm terrible. I don't think you can stalk somebody who's available after every show, and who announces which café she's writing in and tweets pictures of her coffee, telling you to drop by and say yo. It's not really interesting to go through someone's trash when they've already twittered pictures of it.

Don't get me wrong. I don't *want* stalkers.

I've had fans follow me, and occasionally bug me. If I feel stalked, I deal with it in the most direct way I can: *I* go to *them*. I tell them what I'm up to at the moment, ask what they're up to, humanize myself, and then ask them respectfully...could they please stop sneaking covert photos from across the café, and just come over and say hi, give me a hug, and then leave me to work?

. . .

Anthony called me this morning, Neil said.

I hadn't talked to Anthony in a few days—I was on the road. In my absence, and because of the sickness scare, he and Neil were becoming closer—texting, connecting.

I knew that Anthony was doling out relationship advice when Neil needed it—the same way he'd been doling it out to me for years. We were both relying on him for under-the-table, nonstop marriage counseling. We started referring to him as "The Godfather."

He'd even given Neil a phone therapy session on How To Deal With Amanda And PMS, and talked Neil off the ledge a couple of times when our relationship would hit an impasse and we'd march off to our separate corners, unable to cope with each other. My PMS can be brutal: I transform from a pretty reasonable person into a black hole of doubt, despair, and existentially flailing Muppet arms. To be safe, I bought Neil a book about the chemical workings of hormones and the feminine brain, which he studied like a set of stereo instructions, hoping that he might be able to understand the finer settings of this Monthly Irrational Icequeen. Miraculously, it worked. He downloaded an app to his phone that indicated when my period was due to arrive, and around that time he stopped taking things so personally.

How's he feeling? I asked. *I haven't talked to him since Monday.*

Anthony had been recovering, but in and out of doctors' offices and hospitals for the past month. I tried to call him at least every other day, to get the sick-friend weather report.

He gets more test results back next week, said Neil. *He's annoyed with the steroids they're making him take, and he's angry about everything. I can relate. I once had to take the same steroids for a week, and I just remember thinking everybody around me was incredibly stupid and irritating. And we talked about you. He told me a funny story about you and one of your ex-boyfriends.*

Oh NO. Which one?

Aaron, said Neil. *He told me about the time that you and Aaron were having some kind of problem, and Aaron went to him for advice. Anthony told him, "Whatever you do, just give her some space. Leave her alone. And for god's sake, don't throw yourself at her feet or bring her flowers or anything." And how the next day Aaron showed up at your house with a giant bouquet of flowers.*

Ha. Yeah, I said. *Aaron wasn't a very good listener in general.*

He also said something very wise. He said: "Once she hits 'em, they stay hit."

I laughed. *Yeah, that's a thing he's been saying for years.*

He also said: "You've got a tiger by the tail, Neil-i-o."

Ha. That's such an Anthony thing to say. He actually called you Neil-i-o?

Yes, Neil said somewhat proudly, setting me off into a giggle fit.

Darling, I really like Anthony. I was worried in the beginning that he didn't like me. I think he wants to be my real friend. Do you think so?

I stopped laughing. Neil was being so serious about it.

Yeah, I think so, honey. I think he does want to be your real friend. I think he loves you.

What? Why? Neil sounded amazed.

*Well, first of all, because you love me. But more . . . because you keep offering to help. You're buying the ticket. That's what makes you a real friend, to him. But even more . . . because **you** ask him to help with our relationship stuff. He loves to help his friends with their problems— that's his thing, it's his gift. And if he wants to help you, and you let him help, it seals the deal.*

Really? said Neil. *I was worried about being a bother.* Then, puzzled, *Buying what ticket?*

. . .

As I was really hitting my couchsurfing and crowdsourcing Twitter stride, I booked a ticket to London on Icelandair at the start of a long tour. The catch was that you had to connect through Reykjavik, where they hoped you might stay a day or two to pump some money into the Icelandic economy.

We landed in the tiny Reykjavik airport and my connecting flight was delayed, so I went, like you do, in search of a power outlet and a sandwich. The sole airport café was out of sandwiches. I sat on the airport floor emailing for about an hour, and when they still hadn't posted a new departure time, I approached the information counter.

As I stood in line, I looked up and, cartoonlike, one by one every single flight switched its status to CANCELED.

The volcano had just erupted.

We were on the opposite side of the island, so there was no imminent danger, but there was no saying when planes would be flying again. A day? A week? They didn't know. I was supposed to be in London that night, doing press for the BBC, and then flying to Glasgow the day after to start the tour. I emailed my crew, who were scheduled to meet me in Glasgow. They were all grounded in America. All air traffic to Europe had been canceled. Things did not look good.

Everybody stranded at the Reykjavik airport was given a hotel voucher, and the airline started organizing shuttle buses.

I was stuck in Iceland, a place I'd never been and where I didn't know a single person. Standing at the baggage carousel, somewhat stunned, I twittered the situation. BAM: someone volunteered their bar for a ninja gig that night, the fans in Iceland made themselves known, and a folk songwriter who'd once opened up for me in New Zealand saw my tweet and introduced me via text to her childhood friend Indiana, who screeched up to the airport terminal wearing a cowboy hat and blasting classic rock from her car stereo.

As everybody else glumly queued for the shuttle bus, I felt like some kind of lottery winner when Indiana jumped out of the car, hugged me, threw my luggage in the back, and whisked me away me into the lunar Nordic landscape.

You're a friend of Hera's! she shouted over the Jethro Tull. *So I love you! Where do you wanna go?? You're in Iceland! You have never been?? You make music?? I'll take you anywhere!!!*

Let's go to those thermal baths! I shouted.

Yes! To the Blue Lagoon!!! she shouted.

Who are you!? I yelled back. *And what are you supposed to be doing today instead of babysitting an American stranded by a volcano erupting on your island?!*

I'm a grad student!!! My thesis is late! Fuck my thesis!!!! she replied, and proceeded to host me for the entire day, asking me about the music I made, taking me to the thermal baths, and enlightening me with stories—over a dinner she let me buy her in a local restaurant—about how everybody our age in Iceland was fleeing to mainland Europe due to the current economic climate.

After dinner, Indiana drove me to my ninja gig, which I'd been twittering and texting into existence for four hours straight: I'd twittered back then texted the guy who knew the bar owner who was keen to host the gig, I'd twittered then texted the person who was willing to loan a keyboard, and I'd twittered everybody in the world to please tell Iceland that I was playing a free, all-ages volcano-inspired show that night at Kaffibarinn at nine p.m.

That night was one for the books—or at least for this book. When we pulled up to the bar, the piano and speakers were already set up, the whole room cheered, and the place was so jam-packed that I had to crowdsurf over the crowd from the front door to get to the piano in the corner. I went straight at it, pounding out songs by request and trying every variety of vodka that was being passed from the bar to the piano, and twittered pictures from this glorious accidental moment all night (#StrandedInIceland #SoAwesome). The audience was made up of a few dozen hardcore fans who couldn't believe I had suddenly materialized in this country I'd never toured in, a few dozen people who'd never heard of me, and a handful of Americans, Europeans, and Australians also stuck in Reykjavik who had twittered their situations and been flagged down by fans who told them about my spontaneous gig.

It all happened on just half a day's notice, and it had the camaraderie of an international outpost bar, like a fleeting whiff of Rick's Café in *Casablanca*. I enjoyed enough Icelandic vodka that evening that I didn't even bother to make a mailing list. The country is small. If I came back, it seemed a single tweet would probably suffice to gather all of Iceland on a moment's notice.

• • •

I finally told Neil I'd marry him on New Year's Day of 2010, as we took a pause from a long late-morning walk. I was nursing a brutal hangover, having played a New Year's Eve show the night before with the Boston Pops at Symphony Hall and consumed two bottles of champagne over the course of the evening: the first out of nervousness, the second out of triumph. We'd had brunch with my dad, his wife, and my half brother—they'd all come to town for the show—and I was now staggering down Newbury Street in Boston, trying not to project my breakfast smoothie onto the sidewalk.

Neil was holding my hand, casting no judgment.

No patronizing *you shouldn't have drunk so much, darling.*

No chiding *well, this is what you get for not having any dinner last night.*

My head was plenty busy casting those judgments upon itself. He was just being sweet and helpful, holding my arm as I lurched towards a lamppost to get my balance and resist puking.

I realized, in that moment, that I wasn't afraid to, quite literally, lean on him.

As if

perhaps

maybe
possibly
I wasn't afraid to ask for his help.

He went down on one knee, in the snow. He didn't have a ring, so he took out a Sharpie from his jacket and drew one on my finger.

At least I'd never lose it.

. . .

I loved being the center of attention when I was a kid, and I still do.

Sometimes it made wonderful things happen, like when I convinced the neighborhood girls to enact an a cappella production of *Fiddler on the Roof* on my back porch. (I played Tevye, obviously.) Sometimes it made terrible things happen, like when I wore a bra to school, Madonna-style, on the outside of my dress and got sent to the principal's office. (The principal delivered a lecture that I would absolutely kill to have a recording of, just to be able to use the line *you think you're so special, Amanda, but you are not special* in my techno-remix of "Creep" by Radiohead.)

As I moved through my life as a statue and later as a musician, I started to understand.

There's a difference between wanting to be looked at and wanting to be seen.

When you are looked at, your eyes can stay blissfully closed. You suck energy, you steal the spotlight. When you are seen, your eyes must be open, as you are seeing and recognizing your witness. You accept energy and you generate energy. You create light.

One is exhibitionism, the other is connection.

Not everybody wants to be looked at.

Everybody wants to be seen.

. . .

Following the success of my TED talk, Microsoft called. They were offering to fly me to Seattle to speak to a group of women who worked there (apparently a whopping 16 percent of the employees at Microsoft were female).

I asked the speaker coordinator what I would be speaking about.

Whatever you want, she said.

I started to panic—I had no idea what I'd talk about. Crowd-sourcing? Music? Surely I could wax poetic for a half hour about *something*. But these women were *smart*.

The Fraud Police were paying me a call.

For two months, I avoided coming up with an idea worth Microsoft-ing.

The night before the talk, I was pacing frantically around Jason Webley's Seattle houseboat, still having written nothing, when it occurred to me: my *mother*. She'd been retired for a decade, but she'd worked as a freelancer for almost forty years, applying her math-whiz brain to the emerging field of computer programming.

Growing up, I had no idea what she actually *did* all day after she threw her heels in a bag and drove her car into rush-hour traffic. Whenever she started to explain to me what her job entailed, the words blurred into a wall of noise.

I hadn't called my mother in a while. But now I had something to ask her. I needed her.

She talked for two hours straight while I furiously scribbled notes about what it was like for her to be one of the only female computer programmers at various companies around Boston in the sixties and seventies. I poured myself a glass of wine. On the other end of the phone, on the opposite side of the country, so did my mom. For the first time, in earnest, it was like we were drinking together. I listened to her stories about the sexism, the judgment, the weird harassment.

She told me a story about the guy she programmed with who got fired for looking at too much porn on his office computer.

In nineteen seventy??

Oh no no no. This was way later, when we were working on a Y2K conversion. There was Internet porn by then.

I couldn't believe my mother had just said the words "Internet porn."

I wanted more stories.

Well, you had to work harder than the men just to keep the job, she said matter-of-factly. *And,* she said, *you know... you had to be perfect.*

The way she said it hit a nerve.

Perfect? What kind of perfect?

Well, if a guy messed up a project, there was always another job waiting for him. But a woman? Forget it! You'd never get a job in that town again. And Boston was a small town. There were only a few of us. The men all stuck together.

She told me the story of the accountant, Jerry, who paid all the male freelancers on time but kept withholding her paycheck, claiming offhandedly that she "had a husband" and probably didn't need the money as badly as the men did. She asked nicely for months, persistently, and still it didn't arrive. One day she called him up (*at 6:02,* she said, *when I knew the switchboard operator had gone home for the day and I would get him directly*). She said, *Hi Jerry! Just wondering when you're going to be able to process that check! It's eight weeks late.* And when Jerry made some grumblings about how they would send it out as soon as possible, my mother said, *What are you having for dinner tonight, Jerry?* Jerry said, *Excuse me?* My mother said, *I need that money to buy groceries to feed my family. If you don't cut my check, I'm coming to your house for dinner tonight. And I don't like salmon. And I don't like peas.* The check was on her desk the next day.

I'd never known any of this stuff. But then again, I'd never asked. As we were wrapping up our two-hour conversation and were well into our second (third?) glasses of wine, she said, *You know, Amanda, one thing always bothered me. Something you said when you were a teenager.*

Oh, no. Whatever it was, it couldn't be good. I was a *terrible* teenager, an explosion of hormones and nihilism.

Um... what?

She can do this imitation of me as a teenager that makes me want to crawl under a table. She did it now.

You said: "MOM, I'm a REAL ARTIST. You're NOT."

Oh, god.

Then she added, more kindly, *You know you, Amanda, you were being a typical teenager.*

I winced, and felt my neck tighten and my teeth grit down into mother-fight-or-flight mode.

She continued, *But you know. You would say, "I'm an ARTIST... fuck you, Mom! What do you know?! You're just a computer programmer."*

I had to admit... I could *totally* imagine myself saying that as a teenager. Maybe not the "fuck you, Mom" part. But still.

And then my mother said something that absolutely demolished my defensiveness. I don't think, in all the years I've known her, that I've ever heard her sound more vulnerable.

*You know, Amanda, it always bothered me. You can't **see** my art, but... I'm one of the best artists I know. It's just... nobody could ever see the beautiful things I made. Because you couldn't hang them in a gallery.*

Then there was a pause.

I took in a deep breath.

God, Mom. Sorry.

And she laughed and her voice turned cheerful again.

Oh, don't worry, sweetie. You were thirteen.

As I related this story the next morning to a small theater filled with two hundred Women Of Microsoft, I added a confession. In all my rock-and-roll years of running around, supporting people, advocating for women, giving all these strangers and fans permission to "embrace their inner fucking artist," to express themselves fully, to look at their work and lives as beautiful, unique creative acts, I'd somehow excluded my own mother.

And maybe, by extension, a lot of other people. I looked out at the Women Of Microsoft, seeing present-day versions of my 1970s programmer mother. Maybe they all felt thoroughly misunderstood by their own bitchy, teenage wannabe-poet daughters. Who knew?

So I thought about all the things she'd told me over the phone, I said to the room, *and I thought about her work that I couldn't possibly comprehend, about the actual creative work she had done. All that delicate, handmade programming she did into the dead of night to switch one platform to another on some critical company deadline, how outside of the box she would venture to fix a problem . . . and how insanely proud she felt when it worked, and the true . . . beauty of that. And the sadness, too, because nobody ever, you know, clapped for her at the end of the night.*

As I looked up into the audience, I saw that three or four women were sniffling and dabbing their eyes. My own throat tightened up.

She couldn't hang her work on a wall. I can. I do my art in public. People applaud. My mom never really got that . . . and she's retired now.

After the talk, I hugged a handful of the Women Of Microsoft, got back in my rental car, turned the radio up to eleven, and peeled out of the office park.

Take that, Fraud Police.

● ● ●

I called Anthony and told him that Neil and I had gotten engaged.

ENGAGED?

Yeah.

You're not joking? You're going to get married?

Yeah.

He was silent, then said, softly, *You didn't talk about it with me.*

No, I said.

Anthony didn't say anything.

I didn't need to, I said. *You've already told me everything I need to know.*

Ah, that's the perfect answer, beauty. Now go have your life. I'll be here.

I gradually lined up a great band of musicians to help me make my next record: Jherek Bischoff, a bassist and composer/arranger who had toured with Jason Webley; Michael McQuilken, a drummer and theater director who had toured with Jason Webley; and Chad Raines, who'd never heard of Jason Webley—he was sound designer, and a keyboard/guitar-playing friend of Michael's from the Yale School of Drama. (We briefly considered calling the new lineup Amanda Palmer and the Yale School of Drama, while toying around with possible band names one night, but then someone on Twitter suggested Amanda Palmer and the Grand Theft Orchestra. It seemed fitting, given the crowdsourcing and everything. We took it.)

My public song-delivery system, post-label, had been experimental up to this point, and I was deliberately saving my best material until I was ready to go to the fanbase for help with a full-length, brand-new record, to be released with grand fanfare. I didn't want to just release this album into the Internet abyss with a blog post; I wanted it to feel bigger and realer, but without a label, my options were limited. After thinking about it long and hard, and strategizing with my office staff, we decided to use Kickstarter. We'd already used it a few times for smaller projects, and the fans seemed to understand, even love, it. Kickstarter also had its own little ecosystem of supporters, and I'd met and liked the guys who ran the company. My staff and I cooked up a schedule. I decided I would take the band into the studio, record all the songs using the last of my cash, then launch the Kickstarter to pay myself back. If we timed things perfectly, it should work out without a hitch. WHAT COULD POSSIBLY GO WRONG?

. . .

Neil and I eloped in our friends' living room in San Francisco, and used their children as impromptu flower girls and ring bearers. It happened suddenly. We had been trying and failing for months to solve the impossible puzzle of how to throw a Wedding The Right Way. We'd been looking forward to a simple dinner party with our friends, but called ahead to ask if they wouldn't mind hosting a wedding before dinner. I brought three outfit possibilities in a bag, and let the kids pick. They chose the old Eight-Foot Bride dress. I'd made sure to wash it first. Jason Webley came along to officiate the ceremony with a poem, I wrote up some vows sitting in the upstairs bathroom, and everybody got tipsy and ate pie.

Someone had seen on Twitter that we were in San Francisco, and had offered us a free tango lesson. We showed up at her house the morning of our elopement. Neil was panic-stricken, and I wasn't sure whether the panic was brought on by the impromptu wedding plan or the impromptu tango lesson.

I CAN'T DANCE, he kept insisting. *I **DON'T** DANCE.*

We didn't tell our volunteer tango instructor that we were getting married in a few hours.

She gave me a pair of tango shoes. I had never tangoed. She positioned us chest to chest, put on a record, and waved her hands around, examining us from all angles, giving us directions.

*No, no, no, Neil...you need to GRAB her...this is a dance about trust, and control!! It's a whole dance about the difficulty of love!... Good!...Yes!...She needs to **feel** you leading...and Amanda, Jesus, relax...let him lead...trust him...you keep trying to lead and you're messing him up...STOP TRYING TO CONTROL THE DANCE! Foot BACK!!! GOOD! Now...trade!*

I didn't tell her why I was crying.

. . .

The Bride never spoke a word. I learned from her.

There is a difference between simply "being able to ask" and "asking gracefully."

Sometimes asking gracefully means saying less.

Or saying nothing.

You can move your mouth to ask, but what is the rest of your body saying? What is the message behind the words? Everybody knows how it feels to be asked in a way that creates discomfort, whether the asker is a drunk homeless person on a street corner or the naked person in bed beside you.

Can we have sex? It's been a month.

Could you spare any change?

Both can be asked with a sense of trust and graciousness, or with a sense of force and gracelessness.

Anthony once told me: *It isn't what you say to people, it's more important what you do with them. It's less important what you do with them than the way you're with them.*

. . .

You trust people too much, Amanda.

I always figured it was GOOD to trust people too much. Better than the other way around. Right?

One of my favorite ninja gigs of all time was on Hermosa Beach in Los Angeles. I was staying at my cousins Katherine and Robert's cottage-like house a few blocks from the ocean, and I was beside myself to discover that Robert, age eighty-seven, could not only play the ukulele, he could *shred* the ukulele. He was like the HENDRIX of the ukulele, and better yet, he knew kinky songs from the Prohibition era about booze and women.

I twittered the next morning that I would play on the beach that afternoon, joined by my ukulele-shredding cousin, and requested people come dressed for a group photo shoot.

My request was granted, hundreds of Angelenos converged in all sorts of costumes, and after I'd played for about two hours (and cousin Robert slammed out a few songs on his old, splintered ukulele), I tried something new. I told people that the gig was, of course, free of charge, but if they felt moved they could toss money in my ukulele case (a wonderfully shabby antique trumpet case I found in the trash, and that also serves as a really handy purse, which is nice, because I don't *do* purses). I left the case wide-open on the sand, tossed my treasured kimono down next to it, and gave my ukulele to a volunteer guardian. As the evening wore on I chatted, signed random things, hugged people, and took pictures. Out of the corner of my eye I could see the first person drop a few dollars in the ukulele case.

When I finally went back up the beach to the case, the last of the revelers were packing up their blankets. What I saw was shocking.

My ukulele case was filled with offerings—about $400 in rumpled bills (including a few twenties), flowers, love notes, and loose change. But that wasn't what shocked me.

What shocked me was this: in my flakiness, I had left my cell phone, keys, and wallet right in the case, in plain view.

And nobody had taken them.

. . .

So. Right around the time of my insomniac meltdown as the sun rose and the sheep mourned before that Scotland family wedding party, I had also been battling a nasty urinary tract infection. By the day after the party (which went fine, by the way) it had morphed its evil, sneaky way into a full-blown kidney infection. I found an emergency health clinic in the rural Scottish Highlands to treat me.

Before the nurse gave me the extra-high-powered antibiotics I'd been prescribed, she asked, was I allergic to anything?

Nope.

Was I pregnant?

Not a chance.

Taking any other medications?

Well...I wanted to make a joke about how she might want to refer me to a psychiatric professional, because I felt like I was *losing my fucking mind*, but she looked so nice and Scottish and helpful.

She handed the antibiotics over.

They worked. The kidney infection cleared up within a few days, which was good: we'd rented a big place in Edinburgh for a month to accommodate a ton of houseguests, plus Neil's kids, plus my band. I had a string of shows booked, and a bunch of rehearsing to do to start prepping the Kickstarter recording. We'd been looking forward to this monthlong working vacation for a while, anticipating a nonstop parade of dinner parties, theater outings, and spontaneous fringe-festival adventures.

But I wasn't in the mood for fun. My body hurt, my soul hurt, my skin was breaking out, and I'd been listlessly staying in bed. That wasn't like me. That night before the family wedding party had frightened me, and I couldn't shake the crazy-feeling. One afternoon, while Neil was off doing press and all our guests were off at fun fringe activities, I didn't have rehearsal and decided to peel myself out of bed and go for a jog. It was a frigid, foggy day, the type you keep thinking just shouldn't happen in the month of August (no matter how many times you've been to Scotland). I stepped outside, bundled in running gear, a sweater, and a scarf, and started to run. I felt the life force slowly oozing back into me. I looked like shit, I felt like shit, but goddammit, I had left the house. I took a deep breath, looking at the beauty of the old Scottish architecture, and felt my mood finally lifting.

Four blocks later, I slipped on a loose brick of the sidewalk and twisted my ankle. Badly.

I lay there sprawled on the bricks, emitting a small moan, while ready to explode with laughter at the poetry of it all. *Really?*

I couldn't put any weight on my foot. I was going to need to ask a passing stranger for help. I had nothing on me—no phone, no money, just my house keys. It was a quiet street, but a woman about my age wearing a smart raincoat saw me and stopped to help. Then another woman, an older one, stopped as well. My fellow humans were coming to my aid.

You all right there? one of them asked.

No—actually, I'm not, I said, trying to look amiable. *I've twisted my ankle and I can't really walk.*

Oh dear, said the older woman.

A third woman wandered up behind them.

Do you need an ambulance? the first woman asked.

I tried to get up, to put a little weight on my ankle, but it shot back lightning signals of agony.

I don't know, I said, trying not to cry. *I think it's just twisted, I don't think I need a hospital. But I can't walk.*

How can we help?

Yes, is there anything we can do? They huddled around me in a concerned triptych, like a bunch of mother hens.

I grimaced as a new searing pain shot up my leg, but tried to express my gratitude. *Well, thank you....yes, sorry. You're so kind. Can one of you just grab me a cab and hop in it with me? I don't have any cash on me, but my house is literally right around the corner. I'll need someone to just help get me inside so I can pay the cabdriver.*

The three women all looked at one another, then at me, then at one another.

Um....

no,

they said collectively.

But is there anything else *we can do to help?* one of them asked.

I was dumbstruck. And humiliated.

Are you sure you wouldn't like us to call an ambulance? said one of the women.

Did they think I was trying to...scam them? Trick them? I was a thirty-five-year-old woman in jogging clothes with a twisted ankle on a quiet street in Scotland. We weren't in a Dickens novel, for fuck's sake.

One of them was at least kind enough to help me hobble over to a passing cab, and I threw myself at the mercy of the driver, who drove me the four blocks, took my arm, and half carried me up though our front door and into the kitchen, where I thanked him profusely and gave him a twenty-pound tip.

Ya'right, love? he asked, kindly. I knew I looked like hell. *You're sure?*

Yes, I'm fine, really. Fine. I'm great. Thank you so, so very much.
He left, closing the door behind him.

Then I hopped over to the sink, ran some cold water over my leg, and started sobbing uncontrollably. In that moment, I couldn't tell which hurt more, my ankle or my heart.

•　•　•

Brené Brown writes:

> In a 2011 study funded by the National Institute on Drug Abuse, researchers found that, as far as the brain is concerned, physical pain and intense experiences of social rejection hurt in the same way...Neuroscience advances confirm what we've known all along: emotions can hurt and cause pain. And just as we often struggle to define physical pain, describing emotional pain is difficult. Shame is particularly hard because it hates having words wrapped around it. It hates being spoken.

•　•　•

I was walking around Edinburgh on crutches. I was an emotional mess. And to cap it all, my period was really late.

While Neil waited at a table, I peed on a stick in a restaurant bathroom and sat there absolutely stunned, and strangely relieved, by the result.

So that's why I have become a crazy person. I'm a hormonal mess.
I'M PREGNANT.

All of a sudden my flailing worries about whether or not to take a business loan from my husband—or whether or not I was crazy to be grappling with the dilemma in the first place—seemed completely insignificant. What did it matter whether or not I was going to be a few grand short and borrowing money from this guy? *I was carrying his child.* Neil and I left the restaurant, walked home, and cuddled each other in bed for the next twelve hours, in shock.

It wasn't until the next morning that the nurse's question echoed back into my head. I googled the name of the antibiotic I had taken. Pregnant women were very strictly warned to avoid it. Birth defects.

I called our family doctor.

It's not good, Amanda. Very risky. Especially in the first trimester. That antibiotic blocks the effects of folic acid, which is crucial to the fetus at the beginning of pregnancy.

What do you mean risky? I asked. *How risky? HOW not good?*

Really, really not good. He hesitated. *As your doctor, I'm afraid I'd advise you to terminate the pregnancy.*

Neil and I spent a hard few days in bed together, talking, accepting the decision, spooning each other. I cried a lot.

The day of the abortion itself was a nightmare: I don't remember it very clearly. I lay in a hospital bed in Edinburgh, having taken the pill I was prescribed. I threw up and slept, then woke and threw up again, feeling powerless, my whole body and heart in pain. I didn't know what to feel.

Neil sat there beside my bed the whole time, holding my hand and saying nothing.

Then I hid away and spent a few weeks in bed with a hot-water bottle on my abdomen, trudging out for rehearsals and shows and trudging back to bed, staring at the ceiling, feeling like an empty shell of a person.

Neil was just as sad as I was, possibly sadder; he withdrew from talking, he got quiet and distant. My usual life of colorful online back-and-forth became anemic. I told the band, and told a few of the friends who were staying with us. But I didn't want to tell the world. I wasn't ready for that. Keeping it seret made everything feel even lonelier. I wanted to reach out to everybody I knew online, I wanted to blog and tweet the entire, harrowing story to my fans, but there was no way I was going to do that. I just stopped doing anything, feeling more and more broken.

And, as the days wore on, I got more and more upset with Neil. I knew that he was having a hard time, but I was the one stuck in bed, bleeding, nauseated, and weak. He brought me Scottish-style hot-water bottles, and things to eat and to drink, but he was really quiet. I didn't need a selfless faucet of sympathy, but I wanted him to stroke my cheek, ask how I was feeling, give me a good cuddle. He stayed silent. With every passing day, he felt further and further away.

I started wondering if I'd made a horrible mistake, getting married. What had I been thinking? Who was he anyway? Didn't he care? He was physically there, but he felt like a ghost. I knew what I needed, but asking for specific emotional things felt impossible and obnoxious. He was a human being. He should just instinctively know how to take care of an emotionally exhausted, sick, post-abortion wife.

*He ought to just **know***, I thought.

I shouldn't have to fucking *ask*.

• • •

Once, in London, at the very beginning of my relationship with Neil, I had decided to do a ninja gig because my official show at a church had sold out. There was a pub called The World's End near John and Judith's house in Camden where we were staying, and one of the bartenders was a fan. It had a concert space in the basement. Perfect. I asked if they'd be game to host a secret free show, which I was eager to do since my official show had sold out. They giddily agreed to do a lock-in.

I twittered a teaser photo of the secret late-night location the morning of my official show. The ninja gig filled the basement to its capacity of about five hundred, and I showed up with Neil, high from my success at church. (I'd played Bach! On a big pipe organ!) The bar staff all came down and pulled pints for the collected crowd. A violinist friend from Ireland who'd seen the announcement on Twitter joined me onstage, plucking out improvisations for a song or two while the room cheered her on. An artist named Robin hopped on the stage with a terrifying life-sized Amanda-Doll he'd made and gave a puppet lip-syncing dance routine while I played requests. The puppet's head came off. Everybody was riotous and drunk on cider and the magic of being hidden underground, singing, sweating, and making new friends.

It was one of those nights where I felt my heart open and stay stuck open, like it had grown a size bigger. There was a backstage dressing room but no security, given the nature of the night, and the guest musicians, random friends, and puppeteers had left their shit all over the tables and couches. We left at four a.m., tired and happy. As we walked out the door, it dawned on me.

Someone had stolen my red ukulele.

I was crushed. I loved that ukulele. And I loved that ratty trumpet case it lived in. It was the very first ukulele I'd ever bought, and it had traveled the world with me for four years. It had resisted theft on the beach in Los Angeles. I had even started writing songs on it, regularly. It was MAGIC, that ukulele.

The heartbreak wasn't so much in the loss of the object, it was in the fact that someone in Our Crowd had crept off with it. I'd seen and talked to, hugged and kissed, sweated on and toasted every single person who'd been drinking in the dressing room. Who would do such a thing?

I wept a little on our late-night walk home, feeling my flowering faith in humanity wither, and then slither, lifeless and trampled, into the London gutter. I was a fucking fool. People sucked.

Neil soothed me, reminding me that everyone had been very drunk, and that people do stupid shit when they're drunk.

I know, I said. *I've been one of those people. But I still can't believe it. You were there. We were all in love. What the hell? Did someone think it would be funny?*

You'll ask Twitter tomorrow, darling, he said. *I bet it'll turn up.*

I woke up. I twittered.

I AM REALLY SAD. SOMEBODY TOOK MY RED UKULELE AT THE NINJA GIG IN CAMDEN LAST NIGHT. IF YOU KNOW ANYTHING, TELL ME.

A few hours later, someone twittered back. They knew who took it. The thieves were sorry, this person said, and they wanted to give it back. My heart soared. I direct-messaged my phone number to the intercessor via Twitter, and the thieves texted me soon after, to arrange a drop-off. I told them not to be scared; I wasn't angry. I just wanted my ukulele back. I texted the address of the friends' apartment where I was staying, and waited.

A few hours later, the doorbell rang, and there stood two British teenagers, a boy and a girl, looking like the two most frightened people I'd ever seen. They started babbling:

Oh my god oh my god Amanda we're so so so soooooo sorry
We were really drunk
We love you so much you're our favorite musician
We thought it would be funny
We were really REALLY drunk

I shushed them. I hugged them. I told them to come inside for a cup of tea.

We sat down.

I have done some very stupid stuff while drunk, I said. *I have had mean-ingless sex. I have gone to strange people's houses when I shouldn't have. I have drunk dialed ex-boyfriends and ruined perfectly cordial breakups. I have stolen the CDs of my favorite band when I was selling their merchan-dise as a teenager, which took me ten years to confess to them, and they laughed and totally forgave me. And I totally forgive you. Okay?*

They looked at me.

Oh my god. It was so stupid.
We're so so sorry.
We can't believe you're not madder at us. Oh my god.

It wouldn't help anything, I said, *being mad. Now hug me and go home and please. Try not to steal any more ukuleles.*

We won't. It's really cheeky but, um…can we give you our CD? We're in a punk zydeco band.

And I took their CD, and they hugged me and I closed the door behind them, and I looked at my ukulele, and I watched my faith in humanity not only crawl back up from the gutter but blossom a new little flower I'd never seen before.

• • •

For our wedding anniversary, Neil and I decided to spend a low-key, romantic night in New York City. We were both in town for work and staying in a hotel.

It was two nights after New Year's Eve. We walked through the cold, dark streets of SoHo to a little sushi restaurant and lingered there, reflecting on our life, marriage, the abortion, our friends, writing. The summer and fall had been painful and turbulent, and we were just starting to settle down and heal.

I lost my appetite quickly for reasons I couldn't figure out. I love food. I even turned down dessert.

We bundled up and walked out into the freezing winter night, and I'm not sure who puked first, but it doesn't really matter: one of us vomited, *Exorcist*-style, into the street, and a minute and a half later, the other one did. Was it the oysters? The salmon mousse? We'll never know. It was a fifteen-block walk home. One of us would puke in the gutter, or in a trash can, and the other one would feel sorry for the puker. Then, half a block later, the roles would reverse. Neil stayed up until five a.m., throwing up every twenty minutes. I fell asleep and resumed puking the next morning. By noon, Neil had mostly recovered, but I was trembling, couldn't keep down any water, and was starting to get worried. I lay on the bathroom floor next to the toilet, while Neil read a newspaper. I dragged myself back to bed and waited to be patted and soothed. But Neil was acting sort of distant. Silent. It was that *thing* he did. That was worrying me, too.

After I hadn't been able to keep water down for twelve hours, we went to the hospital. Neil sat with me, holding my hand without saying a word. The doctors rehydrated me and I started to feel human again, like a dried-out sponge plopped back into the sea. But my blanked-out husband was scaring me.

We hobbled back to the hotel on foot for the fresh air, just as the sun was starting to set.

Neil drew the curtains and seemed to have returned to normal. I was lying in bed, feeling flattened.

Honey, I said. *I need to ask you something.*

Yes, darling?

Earlier today, when I was puking, you were acting really...strange. You did it in Edinburgh, too, when I was sick, after the abortion. And you just did it again. It's kind of freaking me out. I looked at him. *It's like you couldn't see me.*

What do you mean?

*I don't know. There's just this **thing** I expect my lover or my friend to do when I'm really sick...you know?*

I felt stupid and childish all of a sudden.

*What **thing**?*

I don't know. Cuddles? Talking? Love? Patting my head? Telling me everything will be fine? You stopped talking to me. Why? I said. *I'm not angry. I swear. I'm just...asking.*

He looked confused. Then deep in thought.

Well.... he said slowly. *Maybe it has something to do with what I was taught growing up, about sick people.*

Tell.

The way I was taught to deal with a sick person was to just...be very quiet around them. I was taught that you're not supposed to say anything, or show any sympathy or anything. You're just supposed to be very quiet. He blinked his eyes at me. *Is that wrong?*

My throat clenched and I took a deep breath.

You mean, I said, *that all this time you've just been trying to leave me alone...because you think it's RIGHT? Not touch me because you think it's...good for me? Are you serious?*

He looked at me.

Well...yes. He blinked. *That's how I was raised.*

You didn't get cuddled and talked to and smothered with love when you were hurt or sick?

No, darling… that wasn't really the way it worked.

Oh, baby. I sat up in bed. *Do you know how weird that is?*

No. Is it weird?

Well, no. Well, YES, it's weird for me. Jesus.

I sat there, trying to make sense of this, while Neil stood at the foot of the bed, looking apologetic.

Wait wait WAIT, I said. *Is **this** why I lost my shit in Edinburgh last summer? When I thought maybe I'd made the biggest mistake of my life marrying your ass because you didn't know how to take care of a sick person?*

He looked lost. Then found.

Maybe. Well… probably. I dunno.

Oh god, Neil. I got up and put my arms around him. We stood there at the foot of the bed, silent for a second.

I guess it's a stupid question, I said. *But… did you ever ask?*

Ask for what?

For the THINGS. Did it ever occur to you to ask for… like, a cuddle when you were hurt, when you were a kid?

He stared at me.

Amanda, darling. You can't really ask for what you can't imagine. You can't ask for what you don't know. That was my world. It was what I knew.

I shook my head, tightened my arms around him, and stood there holding him and not wanting to say anything stupid.

I love you, he said.

I love you, too.

We were silent for a while.

I thought about Abortion Month. When I'd needed him so badly, and been so infuriated that he wasn't acting the way I'd expected. I tried to remember if I'd even asked him. I *must* have asked. But maybe I just assumed that my state of being was a ball of asking in itself. I couldn't remember just outright asking him for the things I needed, the simple things. To be held. To be cradled and patted… it seemed ridiculous to ask for that.

Maybe it wasn't ridiculous. Maybe it had just been a communication breakdown. Maybe it had been both of our mistakes. He'd been in pain, too. Had *he* asked me for anything? I couldn't remember.

I think, I said, *I'm going to ask you, from now on. When I need the things.*

He cocked his head and said, tentatively, *Can you show me?*

Show you . . . what?

He sat on the bed. *Can you show me what you mean? For when you ask? For the things?*

I sat down. I closed my eyes, took his hand, and put it softly on my face. I guided his fingers down my cheek, up my cheek, and pressed his palm into my neck, opened his whole hand, lay it on my chest, and held it there. He paid close attention, like a focused child, as if I were teaching him how to spell a word or tie a shoe.

Like that, I whispered, my eyes filling with tears,

. . . like that.

• • •

We have a fucked-up relationship with artists.

While artists are, on one hand, applauded for their awe-inspiring, life-changing works of art, they're simultaneously eyed with suspicion, disdain, and other sentiments of the **GET A JOB** variety. Look at the media: we deify artists one second, demonize them the next. Artists internalize this and perpetuate the cycle; artists do this to each other, and they do it to themselves.

It's no wonder artists have such a difficult time maintaining the romantic standard they try to achieve not just to please others but to hit their own internal bar that was set early on, when they were just starting to grasp their artistic identity. It's no wonder that so many artists crack under the pressure, go crazy, do drugs, kill themselves, or change their names and move into hiding on remote islands.

Artists can get mentally trapped in The Garret, that romantic vortex where painters, writers, and musicians find themselves stuck in a two-dimensional nightmare starring their own image.

You know The Garret. It's a candlelit attic room, where the artist sits with a pen, a paintbrush, slaving away. Alone. Drunk. Chainsmoking. Creating. Agonizing. Probably wearing a scarf.

The artistic workspace is real and necessary, but it takes on every shape imaginable, and it wasn't until I started twittering that I realized I'd created very strict, superstitious rules around my process: *I need to be at home. I need total privacy. I create in silence. I need to look like an artist.*

Then one day I broke my own rules with "The Bed Song," which took me about two hours to write, by leaving my computer open and my phone on. I'd always had a rule about that: no twittering while songwriting. Only *bad* artists do that. This time, though, I announced on Twitter that I was heading into a songwriting session and I updated the feed with in-progress photos and scrawled lyric drafts at the piano. People cheered me on. It wound up being one of the best songs I'd ever written. Who knew?

A balanced artist knows when to hide in The Garret, when to throw the windows open, and when to venture out into the hallway to the kitchen, where society exists. Most important is the understanding that there are no rules—what works on one day, for one song, won't work the next.

Once the art is finished there is a new challenge. Down to the ground floor and out the front door, you have the marketplace. It's loud down there. The stalls of exchange, the sound of bargaining and bartering and clanging cash registers. It's crass and mundane compared to The Garret—no matter what your version of The Garret looks like—where the art gets dreamed up.

Some artists need to create in complete peace, but all artists are now empowered by technology to open the front door and chronicle their backstage and behind-the-scenes working processes. More importantly, they're equipped to distribute the work themselves, sharing their writing, their music, and their digitally reproducible wares infinitely and at their own will—without printing presses, without CD manufacturers, without movie theaters. The art goes from the artists' lips or pen to the audiences' ears and eyes. But in order to share directly, the artist still has to leave The Garret and head down into the bustling marketplace, and that's the catch: the marketplace is where you have to deal with *people*. To many artists, people are scary.

In The Age Of The Social Artist, the question echoes everywhere: what about the introverted or antisocial artists who have no desire to leave The Garret and enter the marketplace? What about the singers who don't want to tweet, the novelists who don't want to blog? What will happen to the reclusive J. D. Salingers of the world?

The marketplace is messy; it's loud and filled with disease and pickpockets and naysayers and critics. For almost any artist, carrying your work through the stalls of exchange can be painful.

But there is another option, which is to yell from your window. You can call down to your potential friends outside, your comrades in art and metaphor and dot-connecting, and invite them to a private party in your garret.

This is the essence of crowdfunding.

It's about finding *your* people, *your* listeners, *your* readers, and making art for and with *them*. Not for the masses, not for the critics, but for your ever-widening circle of friends. It doesn't mean you're protected from criticism. If you lean out that window and shout down to find your friends, you might get an apple chucked at your head. But if your art touches a single heart, strikes a single nerve, you'll see people quietly heading your way and knocking on your door. Let them in. Tell them to bring their friends up. If possible, provide wine.

If you're not social—and a lot of artists aren't—you'll have a harder time. Risk is the core cost of human connection. In most cases, the successfully independent antisocial artist pairs with an advocate to shout the message down to the street. Sometimes it's a record label. Sometimes it's a patron. Sometimes it's a best friend.

Art and commerce have never, ever been easy bedfellows. The

problems inherent in mashing together artistic expression and money don't go away, they just change form. Nowadays a lot of apples get chucked at artists who try to get help through crowdfunding: *Stop self-promoting. It's shameless!* Those words poke at the emotions most artists are already struggling with. That fear of being called *shameless* is what makes us think twice about sharing our work with ANY-BODY in the first place.

No art or artist exists in a vacuum. Although artists may have access to all the latest social media tools, it doesn't necessarily mean they're all eager to use them. At least now there is a choice: you can either leave The Garret, or you can invite everybody in with you, or you can send somebody out on your behalf to round up your crowd and drag them up the stairs.

A warning: With every connection you make online, there's more potential for criticism. For every new bridge you build with your community, there's a new set of trolls who squat underneath it.

· · ·

I was in the study, sharing an evening grok with Anthony, depressed and bitching to him about the Problem Of Neil. My Kickstarter was delayed and I was facing the looming cash shortage. He was offering to help, and I wouldn't bend.

What is it you're so afraid of? Anthony asked. *What do you think is going to happen?*

I don't know. I guess I'm just afraid it's going to bite me in the ass. At some point in our relationship he's going to slam a door and scream, "BUT I LOANED YOU ALL THAT MONEY, YOU UNGRATE-FUL BITCH."

That sounds very unlike Neil, Anthony said.

I know, I said. *I'm not saying my fears aren't totally deluded.*

He isn't the problem, beauty. You are. You preach this whole gospel of asking and accepting help, you make your friends hitchhike with you, you sleep on all these couches, but you're holding out on your own husband, who wants to help you. You somehow don't want to give him the gift.

I sat there, smoldering, then I tried to switch topics.

I just never expected that I'd wind up with a shy, British writer sixteen years older than me. You know?

Well, Anthony said, *you did. You know, I remember asking you, a few years before you met him, what you were looking for in a partner. You said "I want an expert." You got one. He's an expert in making things up.*

But he can't dance, Anthony. Like, not even a little. And when he tries, he kind of goes into a panic, I said.

So what? said Anthony.

*So... I **miss dancing**. And ANOTHER THING*, I said. *He doesn't go to bars. And he can't drink more than a glass or two of wine without getting obnoxious or falling asleep. AND...*

But you drink and dance with everybody else, said Anthony. *What are you trying to accomplish here?*

Why did I marry this guy? I asked.

I don't know, said Anthony. *You tell me. Because from where I'm sitting, you're just not that into him.*

That's not true!!

*So why **did** you marry him?*

I thought hard. Anthony was not going to accept a bullshit answer.

I think I married him because... I love him?

Nice dodge, beauty. Why do you love him?

Because... he sees me?

Does he?

Yeah, I think he actually really does. I think he really, really does.

As I said it, I realized it was true.

And also... I think I see him. It's dark in there, he hides so much. But I see him. And... I don't know, I said with a shrug. *I think that's enough.*

Anthony looked at me. I felt like a disappointment. I didn't expect my vague answer was going to cut it.

Then he smiled.

You're turning out good, my girl. You're getting it.

. . .

Conditional love is:

I will only love you if you love me.

Unconditional love is:

I will love you even if you do not love me.

It's really easy to love passing strangers unconditionally.

They demand nothing of you.

It is really hard to love people unconditionally when they can hurt you.

. . .

It finally got to the point where I couldn't put it off. I was down to the wire, about to launch the Kickstarter, but I needed to make sure everybody got their paychecks on time. I needed a loan to bridge the gap. I weighed my options. I sat paralyzed for a few days, battling the imaginary voices in my head.

Yep. Just as we've always said. She's a bullshit narcissist with a rich husband. She's not a real artist at all.

Next to them, I could hear the feminist bloggers:

Are you kidding? She's no fucking feminist. When it comes down to it, she's an irresponsible wreck who goes running to hubby; she's a hypocritical fraud who falls back on the patriarchy.

I could hear an imaginary version of Neil, a year down the line:

I should have known you were a user. Remember when I loaned you thousands of dollars to cover your ass? I never should have trusted you. I've had it.

I could hear my family:

You always were selfish, little miss attention-getter. You've never thought about anybody but yourself.

I put my hands over my ears.

SHUT UP.
SHUT UP.
SHUT UP.
JUST STOP IT.
And I called Neil.
Hi, darling.
Hi. I love you. Say tomato?
Tomahto.
Okay, I'm ready.
Ready for what? he said.
I'm going to need the loan to cover me for the next few months. I need you to help me.

He sighed as if I'd just said "I love you" for the first time.
Of course I'll help.
I'm not going to go back on the road. I'm going to crowdfund this fucking record instead. I can probably pay you back in three months.
If it takes longer, it's fine, he said.
I really hope it doesn't.
Amanda, I love you. I'm proud of you.
I love you, too.
I paused. Then I added, *That was really fucking hard.*
Listen, love. We're married. We're a team. And I'm glad you're finally over it, he said.
I'm not over it, I said. *I fucking hate this. I hate that I have to ask you for this. I hate it, and I hate myself.*
Is there anything I can do? Neil asked.
No.
And I wasn't over it, not really. I was terrified.

But I'd done it. I'd achieved asking enlightenment. I'd accepted a massive donut. I was on my way to being a fully fledged . . . something.

But it didn't feel fine. It felt terrible. I felt like an asshole.

And I wondered why.

Doesn't hurt enough yet.

. . .

I'd set the Kickstarter goal at $100,000, which felt conservative to me. I'd sold $100,000 worth of vinyl albums with five Radiohead songs directly from my website—and now what I was looking to fund was a full-length record of my own songs. It had to work.

The night we launched, Neil and I were staying in my apartment at the Cloud Club. I was nervous; I had no idea how many people were actually going to hop on board the Kickstarter bandwagon. It launched at midnight—my whole staff stayed awake and we twittered, facebooked, and blogged the link to high heaven. We asked everybody who backed it to share the link. I refreshed the page a few minutes after midnight, and it had about $200 in backing. I checked the site again after an hour: $600. Neil and I went to sleep. I woke up at about four a.m., in a mild panic, staring at the ceiling, certain that I'd asked for too much.

Don't check the computer.

Don't check the computer.

I checked the computer. Four hours later, the Kickstarter had only made about another $500, pulling it over $1,000. I'd asked for a HUNDRED GRAND, for fuck's sake. If you don't make your minimum goal on Kickstarter, you don't get anything.

I shouldn't have checked the computer. I went back to bed.

It's a failure, I thought. *What if this Kickstarter only makes forty thousand dollars? How am I going to pay everybody? How am I going to face society? What the fuck am I going to do?*

By the end of the next day, it had cleared $100,000. The word had spread. I had hit my goal in under twenty-four hours. I wondered how I ever could have doubted the universe.

As the number continued to skyrocket, I was more inseparable than usual from my phone, checking the Kickstarter status and thanking people via Twitter for backing the project, every day, every hour, every minute.

Thank you.
Thank you.
Thank you.

My Twitter feed, blog posts, and backer updates to the new Kickstarter community were a conveyor belt of gratitude. The more people backed the campaign and shared their pride in supporting it, the more people found out about the project, the more the numbers grew, the more I thanked. It ballooned.

About three weeks after launching, the campaign had almost twenty thousand backers, and at the very moment it hit the million-dollar mark, I was—coincidentally—with Anthony.

We were, at that point, three weeks into the monthlong campaign, and I'd been running between Boston and New York, doing press, holding production meetings with my office, getting ready to manufacture the record and all the other Kickstarter rewards.

I knew the million-dollar mark was going to be symbolic. It'd be the first time a musician had raised a seven-figure amount using crowdfunding.

Anthony and I had set up a grok date the week before. We were going to do our usual thing: meet for coffee and then drive to Walden for a grok and a walk around the pond.

My visits with Anthony had grown more intense since his illness and scare at the hospital, and I started looking forward to them with equal parts joy and worry. I wasn't just hanging out with my best friend; I was hanging out with a sick person. His latest blood tests and symptom complaints joined our usual topics: the universe, relationships, zits, how we couldn't *stand* when people offer to massage our feet then don't bother to pay attention while doing it.

But the friendship was still a two-way street. Anthony would sometimes tell me, over the phone, that he didn't *want* to talk about his latest list of ailments and the new side effects of the new medications prescribed to alleviate the side effects of the other new medication.

He'd say, *You talk. I'm done. Distract me, please. Tell me anything.*

And I'd prattle on happily about the new song I'd finished, or how I was hiring my PR team to help distribute the new Kickstarter record in Europe, or about the stupid argument I'd had with Neil... and Anthony would slip back to where he was most comfortable: advising.

Some days, it felt like asking for his help was the best gift I could give him.

I'd been celebrating online every time the Kickstarter hit a new hundred-thousand-dollar marker, or had attained another thousand backers, by scrawling the amount of money or the number of backers somewhere on my body with a Sharpie and posting the photo to Twitter.

Earlier that morning I'd checked the Kickstarter page, which stood at about $990,000 and was ticking along at the rate of a few thousand dollars an hour. It was likely that it would hit a million within the day. I walked up to Lee's apartment, where Michael Pope was editing a film on his laptop in the corner and Lee was cooking an omelet. I announced my news giddily. I wanted to celebrate with more than just a Sharpie design on my hand. Pope, a master body painter, created a piece of calligraphy on my belly proclaiming "ONE FUCKING MILLION," and Lee did the photo shoot up on the top floor of the Cloud Club. I saved the photo on my phone, ready to upload it to Twitter at the magic moment, and drove off to meet Anthony.

He was already waiting patiently at a table at Peet's Coffee & Tea, his cane resting against the wall. He'd started needing one due to his vision loss and balance problems.

GUESS WHAT GUESS WHAT? I said breathlessly as I plopped down next to him and knocked his cane onto the café floor.

Slow down for cry-eye, Rocket Girl. Jesus. He leaned over and picked up his cane, examining its glass knob for damage. *One thing at a time, you. Now, you getting coffee? I already got something,* he said, pointing to his pot of green tea and fishing his plastic Peet's card out of his bag. He still loved paying for me.

I checked the Kickstarter from my phone while I was standing in line for my coffee. It was a thousand dollars short of a million. I refreshed. Eight hundred dollars short. I checked my Twitter feed. People were getting excited. It was going to hit. I ordered an espresso, and a scone for Anthony. He waved his coffee card at me and started to get up to try to pay for us, and I shooed him away, paying in cash, refreshing my phone again, bursting with excitement. I headed back to the table.

Listen, I said, *I know I've been explaining this whole Kickstarter thing to you, and I know you don't totally get it—*

I get it, he said.

*Well, I know you **get it,** but it's about to hit a million dollars in backing, and it's the first time anything like this has ever happened in the music business, so it's kind of a big deal. Not just to me, but it means crowdfunding is working, it means you can put out a record like this and not have to have a label and stuff. It's, like, news. You know what I mean.*

Anthony listened.

When it happens…it's going to be an exact MOMENT, you know, an important one, and it's going to be happening ANY second now… and I don't want to be an asshole sitting here on my phone, but there's a picture I want to upload. I need to acknowledge it. You know?

He said nothing and buttered his scone.

I glared at him.

Don't get pissed at me. I'm just SAYING, I said. *I just need to do a thing.*

He leaned back in his chair, and raised his eyebrows.

Do whatever you gotta do, doll.

I refreshed the Kickstarter page. It was still eight hundred dollars away.

Well…it'll take a second. No biggie. So. Anyway. How are you?

He didn't say anything for a second, as if he didn't trust me to pay attention to the answer, then he settled in and shrugged his shoulders.

I hate the steroids. I've got a crushing headache. And I hate this stick, he said, gesturing at the cane. *I fucking bumped right into a lady with a stroller on the way in here. She came up along my right side, which is the side I'm not seeing well out of, and she—*

My phone buzzed. I glanced down at it. It was my manager Eric, sending a group text to me and the rest of the team, saying, ABOUT TO HIT 1 MILLION, READY FOR THIS FUCKING MADNESS?

Anthony cocked his eyebrows at me.

Sorry, sorry, sorry. I got a text. It's the Kickstarter thing. Sorry. Keep going.

My phone vibrated again. I glanced down. It was Hayley responding to the text saying we were almost there.

Listen, said Anthony, leaning back. *Do your thing.* This was code for: *Don't half pay attention to me, you clown.* He wasn't angry. He was just slightly annoyed and amused.

Then the text came from Eric: WE DID IT. HUZZZZAHHH. $1 MILLION. YAY TEAM!

I texted back gleeful congratulations, posted Lee's painted-tummy photo to my Twitter feed, and said,

Okay, okay. It's over. It's done. My Kickstarter just hit a million dollars. I uploaded a naked photo. I'm all yours.

I settled into my chair and took a sip of my coffee, feeling like the queen of the universe. Now, finally, I could focus on my sick friend.

Anthony just looked at me.

Then he picked up his phone and started to fiddle with it, ignoring me.

I sat waiting for him to finish whatever he was doing, wondering if he was going to torture me for this entire day because I'd been such a distracted asshole.

My phone buzzed with a text.

It was from Anthony. I looked at him. He ignored me.

I read the text. It said:

If you love people enough, they'll give you everything.

IN MY MIND

In my mind
In a future five years from now
I'm a hundred and twenty pounds
And I never get hungover
Because I will be the picture
    of discipline
Never minding what state
    I'm in
And I will be someone I
    admire
And it's funny how I imagined
That I would be that person
    now
But it does not seem to have
    happened
Maybe I've just forgotten how
    to see
That I am not exactly the
    person that I thought I'd be

And in my mind
In the faraway here and now
I've become in control
    somehow
And I never lose my wallet
Because I will be the picture
    of discipline
Never fucking up anything
And I'll be a good defensive
    driver
And it's funny how I imagined
That I would be that person now
But it does not seem to have
    happened
Maybe I've just forgotten how
    to see
That I'll never be the person
    that I thought I'd be

And in my mind
When I'm old I am beautiful
Planting tulips and
    vegetables
Which I will mindfully watch
    over
Not like me now
I'm so busy with everything

That I don't look at anything
But I'm sure I'll look when I
    am older
And it's funny how I imagined
That I could be that person
    now
But that's not what I want
But that's what I wanted
And I'd be giving up somehow
How strange to see
That I don't wanna be the
    person that I want to be

And in my mind
I imagine so many things
Things that aren't really
    happening
And when they put me in the
    ground
I'll start pounding the lid
Saying I haven't finished yet
I still have a tattoo to get
That says I'm living in the
    moment
And it's funny how I imagined
That I could win this winless
    fight
But maybe it isn't all that
    funny
That I've been fighting all my
    life
But maybe I have to think it's
    funny
If I wanna live before I die
And maybe it's funniest of all
To think I'll die before I
    actually see
That I am exactly the person
    that I want to be

Fuck yes

I am exactly the person
    that I want to be

—from *Amanda Palmer Goes
    Down Under*, 2011

O ne of my favorite yoga teachers once told a story during class.
Since ever, in China, bamboo farmers have planted baby bamboo shoots deep into the ground. And then, for three years, nothing happens. But the farmers will work, diligently watering the shoot, spreading hay and manure, waiting patiently, even though nothing is sprouting up. They simply have faith. And then, one day, the bamboo will shoot up and grow up to thirty feet in a month. It just blasts into the sky.

Any small, sustainable artist-fan community works like this. Crowdfunding works like this.

There's years and years of authentic work, tons of nonmonetary exchanges, massive net-tightening, an endless collection of important moments. Good art is made, good art is shared, help is offered, ears are bent, emotions are exchanged, the compost of real, deep connection is sprayed all over the fields.

Then, one day, the artist steps up and asks for something.

And if the ground has been fertilized enough, the audience says, without hesitation:

Of course.

But it isn't magic. That first part can take years. Decades.

A lot of misunderstanding about crowdfunding stems from missing this point: if somebody hasn't been watching you farm, suddenly sees the fruits of the labor, and thinks that maybe it all happened by magic, it can be painful. I got a lot of that after my Kickstarter launched:

*But **I've** never heard of her . . . how can people want to give her that much money? What a lucky bitch.*

This is why some lesser-known people have had such real success with crowdfunding—they've fertilized over time, and diligently—and some better-known people who appear to have massive reach haven't done well at all. Fame doesn't buy trust. Only connection does that.

National Public Radio has been following the connect-connect-connect-then-ask model forever: it's called the annual on-air fund-raiser. They create and transmit nonstop, they give away their reporting, storytelling, and content for free all year.

And then when the time comes: they ask.

And, fundamentally, all asking works like this. You must prepare the ground. If you're going to be asking one day, you need someone to ask who is going to answer the call. So you tend to your relationships on a nonstop basis, you abide by the slow, ongoing task, going out there like a faithful farmer, landing on the unseeable bamboo shoot.

And then, when it is time—whether you're asking a bunch of people to preorder your album, or asking one person to hold back your hair while you're puking—someone will be there for you.

• • •

There's a difference between asking a stranger for a handout, a friend for a favor, or a customer for a down payment on a piece of merchandise. Crowdfunding artists are generally working in the third category, in the spirit of the second.

My Kickstarter had been carefully constructed to allow everyone who wanted to get involved to contribute, no matter how little the amount. The lowest price point was a single dollar, which bought you a simple digital download of the album (which we promised would be out within five months). The CD package cost $25, and the more expensive packages included an art book, a painted portable record player (I spent a whole weekend that summer painting them, with Casey and two artist friends of hers, on my parents' back porch), fancy double-disc vinyl records ($50), limited-attendance art parties in five cities ($250 a ticket), and house parties ($5,000 each).

By the time we closed, after a monthlong campaign that gathered over a million in backing, the most astonishing thing to me wasn't the number of dollars. It was the number of *people*: There were just under twenty-five thousand backers. Almost the exact number of sales that had constituted a failure in the eyes of the label. I had fallen into my crowd, and they'd caught me. The backers were ecstatic about the success of the Kickstarter, and everybody who had helped me to build it was over the moon.

But a backlash started in the press and on the music blogs. Some journalists were suspicious about artists doing business via crowdfunding, calling Kickstarter a form of "online begging." I blogged my position and made my business expenses transparent so that people could understand the nature of this system: crowdfunding wasn't charity, as some people seemed to think; my backers were buying things. It was a means for implementing a business model based on the currency of asking and trusting. I was doing exactly what I had been doing for years, going directly to the fanbase, asking them to buy everything in advance: the records, the tickets, the high-level record players and the intimate house parties. Some journalists didn't understand how crowdfunding worked, and many thought that all the money was donations, rather than advance purchases of actual things that I had to create and deliver.

It shocked me that even some of my smart business friends asked me what I was going to do with a million dollars. I explained that, er, the million dollars was going to be used to pay back my recording debts, and to manufacture thousands of records with high-quality packaging, and to print thousands of art books, and to pay thirty-five fine artists for their work in that book, and to pay for the shipping, and to fly me around to deliver what I'd promised. And after that, there wouldn't be a whole lot left.

Even weirder, a few folks who supported the *concept* of crowdfunding singled me out. They grumbled that I didn't have the right to ask my fans to preorder the album using Kickstarter because I wasn't a "true independent"—I was a refugee from the major-label system who was already known. Therefore, I shouldn't be allowed to use Kickstarter, which was, in their minds, supposed to be reserved for the unknown.

These sorts of critics would write screeds online about how I was equipped to "find some other way" to put an album out. This is what struck me as particularly ironic. I *had* found "some other way" to release music: crowdfunding.

This made me wonder: Who *wasn't* allowed to use crowdfunding? Who *wasn't* allowed to ask for help directly from their fans? Lady Gaga? Madonna? Justin Bieber? The answer is: anyone can. Crowdfunding has to be a democratic tool, and mega pop stars have as much right to use the tool as anyone else—as much right as any unknown garage band with no fanbase or head start.

For a couple of weeks, I had a hard time looking at Twitter because for every thousand congratulations, there were another hundred insults being hurled in my direction. They were hard to read.

I REALLY USED TO LIKE AMANDA PALMER UNTIL SHE STARTED BEGGING HER FANS FOR MONEY.

People were calling me "shameless," but I decided to take that as an unintended compliment. Wasn't shame...bad? Like fear? I mean, nobody uses "fearless" as an insult.

I laughed most of it off, but it was hard in truth not to feel a glimmer of doubt. I knew I'd worked hard for all this, and I had an almost unquestionable faith in my songs, my band, and my ability to create something magnificent to send to my backers. But my ego also withered with the amount of people telling me I was a useless, entitled narcissist, conning my fans out of their money.

There was a distinctly familiar ***GET A JOB*** quality to all of the yelling aimed in my direction.

I recognized the voice.

You're not allowed to ask for that. You don't deserve it. You're not real enough.

It was my own.

• • •

After the Kickstarter campaign succeeded and closed, my life turned into a hurricane of preparation for the upcoming tour, which was scheduled to last almost a year and hit dozens of countries. I wanted the stage show to be an unforgettable, rolling, worldwide celebration of the record that the fans themselves had helped me to make, and, to that end, I wanted it to feature as much crowdsourcing, crowdsurfing, and crowd-connecting as humanly possible. I worked together with Michael (McQuilken, the Grand Theft drummer who was also a theater director) on a pile of ideas to take onto the road: we designed a dress with a train the size of a ballroom floor that I wore while crowdsurfing, covering the audience under a giant sheet of translucent blue as they held it aloft and sailed me over their heads; the band dressed from scratch using clothing items the fans brought and tossed up onto the stage; we asked people to upload photos of images that connected to specific song themes—childhood bedrooms, treasured objects, lost loved ones—and we projected them onto a giant scrim above the stage. We communed.

I also thought it would be fun to ask members of the fanbase to join the band onstage to play some of the string-and-horns arrangements we'd recorded on the album, instead of filling in those melodic parts on guitar or piano. I'd done similar things with musicians, dancers, and other random stage-performer volunteers over the years; the community always loved it. Hundreds of eager players volunteered via email, and we picked four or five volunteer musicians for each city. The payment for volunteering onstage was the usual crowdsource currency: free tickets and guest list for friends; merchandise, backstage beer, hugs, high-fives, love. The fans knew the drill. The first few shows worked out perfectly.

Then a French horn player wrote me an open letter on her blog, saying that while she was tempted to join the tour, she felt that the lack of payment was unethical. The blog post went viral, the *New York Times* ran a story, and within days a controversy had blown up.

And gotten distorted, to boot. A lot of critics on the Internet were starting to claim that I'd made a million dollars and I wouldn't pay my band.

Actually, I *did* pay my band; they were all on salary, which meant they got paid even on their days off. As for the volunteers, they had volunteered. No one had anticipated that their performances were going to be seen as political statements. They'd understood the deal when they volunteered, and just wanted to play music.

The initial Kickstarter controversy regarding digital panhandling, which was just dying down, began anew, and now things were darker. Now I was not only begging my fans for money, I was also exploiting musicians in a tawdry search for free labor. It got mean. Gawker, the celebrity news and gossip blog site, referred to my use of crowdsourcing as "the smoke-and-mirrors tactic of a grifter." A blogger from the *New Yorker* wrote, "Amanda Palmer's hustle becomes a half-real and half-symbolic version of the competition to scrape a last dollar from the hides of the desperate."

The noise was mostly from people who had never heard of me before and knew nothing about me—or the fanbase. My Twitter feed and blog comments, usually sources of comfort and community, were now also filled with people who were only visiting to voice their outrage. A classical musicians' union started a petition against my unethical crowdsourcing. The day after the *Times* article ran, I received an email from a professional violinist who'd worked for years with my hometown's symphony orchestra that opened: "Amanda, you ignorant slut…" and went on to tell me what a terrible person I was, on top of being an untrained, unprofessional, shitty musician.

That hurt. It all hurt.

After a week of this, I threw up my hands and decided to pay the volunteers. It seemed like a harmless solution: They'd be happy to get an unexpected $100 for their time (though some of them gave their surprise paychecks to charity, twittering and blogging that they'd volunteered and wanted to keep it that way). My stressed-out band and I could stop fielding hate bombs in our Twitter feeds. And we could all get back to work.

In the aftermath, a familiar feeling lingered, a leftover from my statue days. The whole controversy was pretty... *GET A JOB*. But we were all, in our own ways, *doing* our jobs.

Everybody on the sidewalk who interacted with The Bride was in the arena with me, engaged in the strange exchange. And everyone at my shows—whether onstage, or volunteering, or in the audience—was happily exchanging: favors, flowers, dollars, music, hugs, beer, love, whatever. But the critics were neither with us on the sidewalk, nor with us at the shows. They were yelling from their car windows, or from behind their laptops. They couldn't see the exchange for what it was: a process that was normal for us, but alien to them.

A short time later, as the outrage was dying down, a paradox struck me that seemed to get at the heart of the matter: What if I'd simply SOLD the chance to come play with the band onstage by making it a package of the Kickstarter—an item for purchase, like a $25 CD or a $10,000 art-sitting? What if I'd *charged* $100 for the opportunity to come and play trombone live onstage with my band?

I didn't need to do an experiment to find the answer; The Polyphonic Spree, an orchestral indie band, had already done it for me. They launched a Kickstarter that same month and offered a $1,500 option to come onstage with any instrument and join the band for a few numbers. They limited the number of packages to ten, and sold every one of them.

There was no controversy.

Why not? The conclusion I came to was that people are comfortable as long as there is money flowing in ANY direction, whether from the artist to the volunteer, or from the volunteer to the artist. People can understand a price tag, no matter what it's stuck on. But some can't understand a messier exchange of asking and giving—the gift that stays in motion.

I thought back to my statue days and the **GET A JOB** critics, who didn't feel very far off from the people calling me a beggar when I decided to take help directly from my fans.

It said, something, I think, about the fundamental discomfort people have around the artist—or the person—who *asks* for direct exchange.

A big part of the reason artists feel so squeamish about standing behind their own cash registers is a direct response to the fact that many *customers* feel squeamish about *seeing* them there. Nobody would have yelled **GET A JOB** at the ticket-taker outside a gallery door if The Bride had been on view for a dollar a pop. It seems that, over time, artists and audiences alike have become accustomed to a legitimizing agent, a transactional middleman to throw professional fairy dust over the exchange. The times are changing.

It's a 180-degree turn from the eighties and nineties, when most exchanges with big musicians were entirely indirect, and involved—at least in my case—getting on your dirt bike, cycling to the mall, walking into the record store, and exchanging your $9.99 for a physical album, which was rung up for you by an indifferent clerk who had absolutely nothing to do with the artist who created the music.

All buskers—and artists, and people—have different degrees of comfort with asking. Some buskers have perfect three-minute pitches in which they yell at a crowd to please give as much as possible (and watching a master at work is a treat—it's a part of their craft). But my friend Jason Webley, who busked for years with an accordion, refused to put his case out for money…he didn't like the idea of being coin-operated. So he would play for half an hour, build a crowd, and then he'd sell CDs for $5 at the end of his show, not accepting any donations. If somebody generously tried to give him a twenty instead of a five, he'd simply thrust four CDs at that person.

Everybody finds their own path for letting other people help.

. . .

Who's allowed to ask? Well, technically, anyone. And the Internet makes it possible for *anyone* to ask for *anything* with a signal that can potentially reach anyone else online. The flipside, however, is that you also can't limit who hears your plea or control who sees your crowdfunding page.

A freelance fine artist once reached out to me over Twitter with the link to his crowdfunding page, asking if I'd help spread the word that he was asking online for help with his medical bills. He'd had a stomach operation, and there were complications keeping him from working. His was a typical tale from the failing American health system—a family, kids, a house, a sudden illness, not enough insurance coverage, mounting medical bills, and potential bankruptcy and impending foreclosure.

I hesitated to help.

I'd recently seen some articles blasting a Canadian couple who were trying to crowdfund their dream of moving to Scotland. Some of the press was nasty, calling them "bizarre" and printing headlines like, "We'd love to live in Scotland. Canuck pay our air fares? Canadian couple launch online bid to fund dream," while the online comments (as often happens) were even worse:

Are you kidding me? These scroungers want people to pay for their luxuries while we have so many people with a real need that could be helped. SHAME ON THEM!

I can't believe they have the brass neck to ask for others to finance their dream. Everyone has dreams, you just have to work towards them and not expect others to foot the bill.

Someone actually commented (I'm not kidding):

GET A JOB

They raised only a few hundred dollars, and from the interviews it sounded like they actually *had* expected total strangers to get excited about their dream. If they'd raised thousands of dollars from friends and family who were happy to have a formal mechanism through which to help them, it wouldn't have been a sad story at all. It would have been a cause for celebration. But the story was kind of sad because they didn't realize how futile their asking was.

So when I saw the email from the artist needing stomach surgery, there was a part of me that cringed, fearing that he might be asking an invisible crowd, crowdsurfing into an empty room. I sighed and shared the link, ready to be disappointed.

Within twenty-four hours, he'd made his goal of $10,000 from what looked like a tight-knit community of forty or fifty friends and family.

And as I looked at his success, I realized that I had been thinking like the trolls, standing on the periphery, judging.

Who can know? He risked, his crowd helped. He asked, he got. There was no reason for me to be skeptical. The only people who can really judge if a request is fair are the ones being asked—the ones who have the relationships are the ones who understand the complexity of the situation.

Unfortunately, some people try to use crowdfunding not understanding this concept, hoping that somehow there's magical "free money" out there. *There isn't.*

Effective crowdfunding is not about relying on the kindness of strangers, it's about relying on the kindness of your crowd.

There's a difference.

.   .   .

When I came across the work of Walt Ribeiro, a composer/arranger on YouTube, it delighted me: he takes current pop songs and arranges them orchestrally using computerized instruments. He'd uploaded his arrangements of Adele, Radiohead, and MGMT and they'd gotten hundreds of thousands of views, but as often happens with popular digital content creators, the hit tally wasn't translating into real money. Walt wanted to make a record with a real orchestra but couldn't figure out how to make it happen.

I had another fancy show coming up with the Boston Pops Orchestra, and I reached out to Walt over Twitter, got his email, and asked if he would be game to do an arrangement of "Poker Face" by Lady Gaga for the concert at Symphony Hall. He was beyond game. We chatted about crowdfunding; we became friends. His arrangement rocked.

When Walt emailed me a few months later excitedly telling me about his new Kickstarter campaign, I happily plugged it and thought that he would easily achieve his goal of $7,000. I twittered about it, I blogged about it, I told the story of this nice arranger/orchestra dude who was embracing the future of music and trying to Kickstart his orchestra album.

His Kickstarter didn't get funded. It more than didn't get funded: it only raised $132 of a $7,000 goal, from three backers. I was one of them.

Hundreds of thousands of people had enjoyed Walt's work on YouTube, but he hadn't cultivated a long-term relationship with them, he hadn't yet built a bridge of exchange between himself and his potential supporters.

There isn't always a crowd from which you can fund. Sometimes you just don't know until you jump.

It also appeared that my enthusiasm for somebody else's project held little or no sway with my own fans. Some clicked the link, they looked, they decided it wasn't for them, they moved on. I could boost the signal, but I couldn't build the bridge.

Which, as I thought about it, wasn't a *bad* thing. It made me consider one of the reasons I loved my fanbase so much: they are wholly independent and have their own unassailable, discerning tastes. They weren't looking to me as a leader to follow blindly, there to dictate their choices. They were looking to me as a connector, a coordinator, which was the role I wanted.

Standing *above* everybody is lonely—I knew that from experience. I liked the idea of being *with* everybody.

(Two years on, Walt is still working on his arrangements and just launched a Patreon.com page. He has eighteen backers. I'm one of them.)

. . .

My friend Sxip Shirey is a crazed multi-instrumentalist composer with a huge white Albanian Afro who used to tour with small punk circuses as their live one-man band. His music is absolutely entrancing, but it's miles from mainstream. Sxip's been touring for almost twenty years as an MC and impresario: he's a connector, a carny, a lover of food, whiskey, randomness, people, and laughter.

He never landed a record deal with a label, but he wanted to make a high-class official recording of his music, so he decided to crowdfund. He surpassed his goal of $20,000 with the help of 531 backers. Most of these people were Sxip's friends and fans from New York, and a few hundred people from other states or countries who had seen him on tour over the years. I'd estimate that Sxip had, at one time, probably shared a drink with at least 37 percent of his backers. They just wanted to help him make his record and . . . Be Sxip.

Sxip's Kickstarter proved a theory I'd had, but never tested.

Beyond the basic CD option for $20, he didn't give many details of what he was going to give the crowd. He just asked them to trust him.

These were the descriptions of his Kickstarter backer levels:

Pledge $1 or more: All backers will get SOMETHING!

Pledge $20 or more: You will receive my new CD with beautiful art. I will sign it and you will be SO PLEASED at the surprise gift that is ALSO sent with it. It will be worth it!

Pledge $50 or more: You will get my new CD and OH MY!! There are TWO extra surprise gifts in the same parcel! You have a lot to listen to now! Call your mom or other family member. This is a day to remember!

Pledge $1,000 or more: Damn, oh shit...just you wait...be calm beating heart...oh...oh yes...oh YES...JUST YOU WAIT, seriously. My hands are sweating just thinking about. Seriously.

Pledge $2,000 or more: Call me, it's important. we need to plan this out. It won't be simple but it will be worth it!

Pledge $3,000 or more: Oh My God, for YOU, I'm gonna...BRING...DOWN...THE...THUNDER!!!!!

He reached a total over $21,000. Most (350 people) bought the $20 package and another seventy-six bought the $50 package, while fifty-nine bought the $100 package. Two people bought the $1,000 package.[8]

My theory: one of the biggest reasons people usually want to help an artist is because they really want...to help an artist. Not get a fancy beer cozy. If they make the decision to help, they will help at the level at which they are able, no matter what token, flower, or simple thank-you awaits them at the other end.

I emailed a pal at Kickstarter to see if they had any hard evidence to support this, and indeed, they had the numbers: Since Kickstarter began, 887,256 backers have asked for the artists to refrain from sending them any kind of reward—which represents a little over 14 percent of their user base.

Sometimes people just want to help. You never know until you ask.

---

8. I emailed Sxip to ask him what those people wound up with. In one case, at the request of the backer, he arranged a piano composition orchestrated by the backer's wife, and performed it for them live at Joe's Pub in New York City. I'm sure they got their money's worth.

The night my Kickstarter campaign closed, at the stroke of midnight on May 31, 2012, I threw a free celebration party in Brooklyn. I announced it ninja-style on Twitter and on the blog the day before. A few hundred people gathered in a parking lot with a rented sound system, pizza, booze, and spontaneous circus performances, and we counted down the final hours in style.

A friend loaned us a gigantic plastic tank—to create a human-sized aquarium—and I paid a handful of artists to source dozens of phone books. They spent three days gathering them and handwriting, each on a separate yellow page, the names of the over twenty-four thousand backers. My band and I donned old-fashioned swimsuits, sat in the life-sized fish tank on the back of a truck, and began ripping every page out of every phone book and thanking every backer individually by holding each page up against the front wall of the tank, where a camera was recording a live webcast.

After we held up each page, we'd crumple it up and drop it to the floor of the tank. By midnight, we were sitting chest deep in an ocean of crumpled yellow-page names; it was glorious, and a few of us even went for a yellow-page swim.

When we mailed out the physical album to thousands of backers a few months later, we included a single random yellow-page surprise with each order. Someone started a "find your yellow-page person!" database online.

Two years later, people are still finding each other.

When they do, they tell me. And I tell everybody else. The net keeps tightening.

• • •

Here are three Kickstarter stories.

An indie musician named Deakin from the band Animal Collective presold a limited-edition CD and other rewards through Kickstarter in connection with his trip to a festival in Mali, Africa, and to support an anti-slavery charity there. He raised about $25,000 from a few hundred people. Then he dropped off the face of the earth: no communication, no record, no nothing. He never posted anything to the backer update page, and his backers started to grumble after a while.

In the backer-only comments, which are visible to the public, you can see the story slowly unfold. They start out excited, then patient, then everybody starts wondering what the hell is going on. A year in, people begin asking if they can please get their money back. But there is nobody to ask: the ship had been abandoned by its captain. Then comes the anger. They were miffed, but mostly because they'd been abandoned as collaborators.

The backers started to complain that they been "duped"; they begged for information, they resented the fact that he was off making a new album with his band. One backer posted: *I gave this to my boyfriend as a fucking gift... which was never delivered. Ungrateful fuck.*

A couple of years later, he gave an interview in which he explained that he'd been struggling with making the album, confirmed that all the money had made its way to the charity, and promised to deliver when he could. But there were still a lot of unhappy backers.

If Deakin had sent out a message to his backers saying:

Hey guys! So sorry but the recording fell through, here's why, and here's some pictures from my trip, and here's a deep, personal story of what I saw while I was there... how do you feel if I just send you some signed photos instead?

...I think his crowd might have been less upset.

John Campbell is the creator of a webcomic called "Pictures for Sad Children," who ran a Kickstarter to produce a hardcover collection of his work and raised $51,615 from 1,073 backers. After reaching his goal, making the book, and fulfilling many of the orders over the next year and a half, he posted a long, rambling blog piece about affluence, capitalism, and consumerism, and included this announcement:

> I shipped about 75% of kickstarter rewards to backers. I will not be shipping any more. I will not be issuing any refunds. For every message I receive about this book through email, social media, or any other means, I will burn another book.

He also posted a video of himself burning a copy of the book. It looked like he was having a meltdown, and was out of resources (both in the money and energy departments) to complete fulfillment of his backers' book orders. But here's the interesting thing: If you look at the backer comments, his supporters weren't actually all that angry. Most seemed worried about his well-being more than anything else.

His backers *rallied*. Most showed a high level of concern for the artist—you could tell that this was a community, not a soulless storefront. One backer offered to make a digital version of the book to send to those who hadn't received their packages. Another set up a "Sad Children Book Club," posted his own email address, and offered to serve as the intermediary post office for anyone who wanted to donate their book to someone who'd missed out.

Three months later, another artist named Max Temkin stepped in, drove to John's house to collect the unfulfilled books, and paid the shipping fees out of his own pocket to get the remaining books to their backers.

There are patrons everywhere. The point, though, is that even though John fucked up royally and did the unthinkable—Insulted his fanbase! Burned his own book!—at least he communicated. And *that* act—no matter how dark the story had become—kept him connected with the crowd.

Josh Ente is an artist living in a part of New Orleans that was devastated by Hurricane Katrina. On his block, there was a collapsing, abandoned house, and he launched a Kickstarter to fill it with thousands of colored bouncy balls. He raised about $3,000 in backing from about two hundred people, but after everybody's accounts had been charged, the city got an anonymous complaint and threatened to arrest him if he went forward—even though he had approval from the homeowner and the city permits department. There's no reverse switch on Kickstarter—you can't automatically refund people once their credit cards have been charged—but Josh couldn't stand the idea of leaving people hanging.

So he got in touch with every person who funded the ball pit and offered them a choice: he would pay them back individually, by check, or put their money towards the charity of their choice. He even ran into an old friend at a party a few months later and gave him cash straight out of his wallet. Here's how it broke down: about 40 percent asked for their money back, 40 percent sent it on to charity, and 20 percent said, *Just put this towards your next art project.* Josh had already spent the starting capital to build the project; he'd already bought the bouncy balls. Which means he paid all of those people back—and donated to all those charities—out of his own pocket, at a loss.

I wondered what he did with all the balls, so I asked him. His response: *I was able to intercept them before they were delivered; as far as I know they're still in a warehouse in Dallas waiting for me to pick them up. I also had two hundred pool noodles that were supposed to be used for safety padding on my porch for almost two years before I gave some to a Mardi Gras float and some to a Viking funeral.*

. . .

My relationship with my fans is like a friendship. I have faced a slew of screwups over the years: accidentally double-booked shows, mail-order albums that shipped five or six months late. But most of the time, if I explain the backstory and the behind-the-scenes logistics of the situation, the audience stands with me. I've apologized tons of times. The only thing I must not do is break the code of honesty and steady, forthright contact. You can fix almost anything by authentically communicating.

◦ ◦ ◦

The most expensive bundle package of the Kickstarter was the ten-thousand-dollar "art-sitting and dinner," for which I promised to draw your portrait or vice versa...or whatever (clothing optional). Two people bought it. I delivered the first one in Washington, DC, and brought Neil along.

Nobody got naked. Instead, Neil and I painted a mural on a bedroom wall belonging to the unborn baby incubating in the belly of the Kickstarter backer, Chanie. We created a surreal scene featuring a moon-man playing the piano and a killer rabbit in a hot-air balloon while Chanie and her husband sat on the floor of the empty nursery, chatting with us about bad films, sibling feuds, and local politics. Then we took them out for Indian food.

I delivered the second art-sitting in Perth. The backer's name was Yana, and it wasn't until I met her at my public concert the night before that I realized I knew her from Twitter. We'd been casually communicating for years...and I realized she'd brought food backstage to a show a few years before.

Yana's hard to miss. She was born with achondroplasia. In her late twenties, she's four foot six inches tall, and she's undergone ten operations to lengthen her arm and leg bones. After she gave me a tour of her folks' cozy suburban Australian house and the backyard jungle where she'd adventured as a kid, we all sat down for a home-cooked feast, during which I chatted happily with her younger brother Sebastian and her French mum and British dad about everything from homesickness to the new Australian prime minister, Tony Abbott (nobody was a fan). I felt very at home; they were such a loving, warm family. And I was so impressed by Yana, how confident, self-possessed, and funny she was. She'd studied music business in college but was working shifts in a hospital, and she seemed determined to not let her condition get in the way of her happiness—she exuded positivity.

After the family meal, Yana bundled up a canvas, blankets, and brushes into boxes that I helped carry across a street and a soccer field. She had it all planned out: she wanted to pose nude in the park where she'd played as a child. I told her that if we got arrested, it would probably be the most cred-building event in my life since I was jailed in Amsterdam for doing a ninja gig in the wrong place at the wrong time.

Yana wasn't a natural exhibitionist, but as soon we settled into a shady gazebo near the playground with nobody around, she took a deep breath and shed her clothes. I picked up a paintbrush.

Her body was a beautiful landscape of snow-white skin, her legs and arms covered in constellations of scars from her surgeries. As I focused on sketching her outline, I felt a quiet, profound sense of honor. I'm an amateur painter, and completing a passable likeness took two hours, which included a couple of close calls in the indecent exposure department. One old man wandered over to us and asked us what we were doing, as Yana dived under the blanket.

We're art students, I lied earnestly.

Yana shared the stories of her life: about how she was constantly ill as a result of her condition, and about Jeff, her best friend, who had turned her on to my music years ago.

We were both hospital babies, she told me. *We never had to justify ourselves to each other.*

Jeff had died the month I launched my Kickstarter. Yana had bought the art-sitting as a sort of parting gift to his memory. I didn't ask where she got the money.

Everybody always looks at me, she mused, as another passerby wandered too close and she grabbed the blanket, . . . *but never for the reasons I want.*

I kept messing up her eyebrow.

Everybody I know, I said, *especially the performers, has such a complicated relationship with being looked at. But seriously, I cannot imagine what yours is like.*

It's hard, said Yana.

I erased and redrew, thinking about how we judge one another. Was I trying to make her more beautiful? I shook off the thought and kept trying to get her left eyebrow to at least look like an eyebrow.

. . .

I'd sold thirty-four Kickstarter house parties for $5,000 each—anywhere in the world—and promised to deliver within eighteen months. I laid out some guidelines, having already sold and successfully delivered a handful of them as part of my *Amanda Palmer Goes Down Under* record. No more than fifty people. They could happen anywhere (outdoors, indoors, anywhere in the world, and I'd pay my way there) but they couldn't be publicly promoted shows. The package included about $1,000 worth of merchandise as well: the vinyl, the high-end art books, the record player, and so on.

Very few people could afford the price tag of the party, so only about five parties were sold to single individuals; the rest were impressive efforts of community trust. Facebook groups started, volunteers coordinated to pool funds, find locations, and whip the parties into shape. From South Africa to Israel to Canada to Germany to Australia, total strangers trusted one another. When I showed up at the parties, there were often three hosts: the person who volunteered their house, the person who volunteered to throw down the five grand and trust that forty-nine people would kick in $100 each, and the person who dealt with potluck logistics. These hosts often became friends with one another through the very act of combining their efforts. It was an innovation in collectivist fandom that I'd never seen before.

Eric, my manager, wears about eighteen different hats—including making himself personally available on email and Twitter to thousands of fans who had questions about the Kickstarter. He was in charge of being the liaison for all thirty-four house party contacts. He juggled my travel schedule, along with my booking agent, to make sure I could hit all thirty-five cities while I toured—hopefully not having to zigzag or backtrack too much. It was an exercise in organizational Zen. (At the time this book goes to print, I've delivered thirty-three. The last one, in South Africa, remains undelivered. They've been really understanding…they've even uploaded a song-video to YouTube about how much they're looking forward to it.)

* * *

Delivering the house parties felt like cresting a peak of crowdsurfing or couchsurfing. As I bounced back and forth on a regular basis between playing for a crowd of 1,500 in a standing-room-only theater one night and fifty people in a living room the next, I realized what the difference really meant.

An official show in a club or a theater is repetitive work: soundchecks, dressing rooms, testing lights. The environment is set up to do business, not art: security checkpoints; cash registers ringing open and slamming closed; bored bartenders loudly scooping ice into drinks, waiting for you to finish your screaming and swearing so they can clock out.

At a house party, everybody improvises and cobbles together a space; there's nobody who doesn't *want* to be there. Dogs and kids run freely, curfews don't exist, strangers become real friends under the magical umbrella of a unique, shared experience. The music is important—I always play for at least an hour or two—but it isn't the absolute center of the evening. Nor am I, the so-called star, the center. I slink back and watch as people warm to and bond with each other.

Throughout the post-Kickstarter year I got better and better at the house parties, which took place in cleared-out wheat barns in rural Germany, illegal basement speakeasies in London, suburban backyard barbecues all over the States, the UK, and Australia. Something surprising happened every night, and I started to enjoy the feeling of absolute uncertainty. No matter what happened, I twittered, instagrammed, and blogged the results. The crowd followed along.

The Tel Aviv house party featured a pole dancer and a rendition of one of my songs sung in Hebrew by the entire group—they'd all rehearsed a translation. On a remote hillside in Oslo, the whole party engaged in a game where everybody took turns drawing on an easel provided by the host, and one by one described the best and worst things about the various Nordic towns they hailed from. I got a pretty thorough education in Norwegian-Swedish rivalry that night, along with a great massage from a bearded man who, hours later, set up a DJ tent and blasted music into the dawn as the fire pit died down.

At a party in Nashville, a girl asked her parents' permission to graffiti the outside walls of their guest house; fifty people attacked the huge structure with spray-paint cans. A few weeks later, a house party in Chicago picked up the theme and we spray-painted an entire garage.

I fell into the crowd at every event, talked late into the night over wines and beers, and freely discussed what was on my mind. I got pulled aside a lot, told a lot of dark stories, held (and was held by) a lot of people. Arriving at a house party in the carpeted basement rec room of a family home in Ashburn, Virginia, I asked my party host if there wasn't, perhaps, a giant closet available. I explained to the fans that I'd played a show at Lincoln Center in New York City the night before and been soundly clocked on the head by a metal lighting rig pole that hadn't been securely fastened, that I'd sustained a minor concussion and was going to need a cuddle—preferably a horizontal one. We dragged a futon into a giant walk-in closet, which was stocked with three racks of theatrical dresses and costumes.

A bunch of musicians had brought their instruments along to my party, so after taking requests for an hour or so, I invited them all to join me in some impromptu Nirvana covers—moshing included. I then announced I was hitting the closet, leaving the party to happily rage in my wake. I figured it'd take about two hours to get quiet time with everyone if they joined me in the closet one at a time. I misjudged: I was in there for four hours—but, man, I heard some stories. It was like *Spoon River Anthology* live. By the end of the night I had heard about two impending divorces, about the deepest fears of a nine-year-old girl (the child of one of the guests), and about losses secretly mourned: the deaths, the cancers, the miscarriages, the abortions, all the secrets they carried beneath the sheen of the dancing and mayhem outside the closet.

I arrived one night at a remote house in the woods, a few hours outside San Francisco, filled with high school kids and their parents. Bill was the dad who'd organized the party, and he welcomed me and my friend Whitney, who had driven me to the party, like long-lost family members into the already-jubilant festivities. Home-cooked food abounded, homemade beer flowed, and everyone sat together on the living room floor, playing instruments and sharing songs. In the kitchen, Whitney and I agreed that we were experiencing a classic case of Family Envy. How was it possible that all these seventeen-year-olds wanted to HANG OUT with their parents?

I took my plate of cake and fruit outside onto the porch, smelling the redwood trees and watching the kids take turns igniting a ten-foot-tall metal sculpture that blew fire out the top. I talked with Bill, the Perfect Dad.

His teenage daughter had died the year before. He showed me her paintings. He told me the party was for her, in a way; it was a celebration of her life. Later in the night, I played a song called "Lost"—which was on the Kickstarter record the party had helped to fund—on the living room piano while the entire gathering, young and old, linked arms and formed a kick line, singing along. I couldn't believe they all knew the words.

It all felt so real.

. . .

The Kickstarter album had taken a few months to record; Jherek, Chad, Michael, and I spent a solid month in Melbourne between practice rooms and a recording studio bringing my preciously hoarded songs to life in full-band color. Only one song was recorded on solo piano ("The Bed Song," which took at least two dozen takes to get right); the rest were awash with accompaniment, created by all three members of the band, who brought their sounds and structural ideas to the table. Michael programmed the drum loops. Chad spent hours finding the right synthesizer sounds. Jherek created beautiful string-and-horns arrangements for five of the songs and we hired local musicians to come into the studio for a few days. We twittered for a glockenspiel at one point. I named the album *Theater Is Evil*, which I changed to *Theatre Is Evil* (the British spelling) by a popular demand that arose the day I announced the album title on Twitter, and the Brits and Americans took up arms against one another. No bloodshed was necessary: they took a vote, and the British won.

A few weeks before the album was officially released in stores and hit the fans' mailboxes, the whole band and road crew of five embarked on a mini-tour to deliver the Kickstarter art parties we had sold, which were backer-only events limited to two hundred and fifty people held in strange little galleries, pop-up art spaces, and small clubs. The community would commune, the band would play a special acoustic set, and the original album art would be displayed on the walls. I'd hired about thirty-five painters, sculptors, and photographers—mostly friends of mine—to create work inspired by the lyrics of the songs. Every artist was paid $500 per piece of artwork, and we shipped all the art to the parties, which were held in New York, Berlin, LA, San Francisco, Boston, and London. We put together a variety of gift bags for the attending backers that included blindfolds, surprise CDs, custom stationery, and in most cities, a locally purchased used book. The morning of every art party gig I popped into a used bookstore, buying about three hundred used books (it felt like a giant supermarket sweep) and hauling them over to the venue.

A few days before the first art party, I got the random idea to let the fans draw on me—I'm never sure where these ideas come from—and texted my assistant, SuperKate, to buy a package of markers to pass around. Washable if you can find them, but maybe do some tests. I'll probably be sweaty, it's summer.

The people in those rooms were my fan-family, I had faith in them. They'd trusted me to deliver an album, and letting them draw on my naked body was a gesture to show that I trusted them right back. At a couple of the parties, I prepared to strip but decided not to if the winds in the room just didn't feel quite safe enough. We tried different drawing utensils on different nights: one of the first nights was kind of a disaster since we could only find tiny, cheap drugstore markers that didn't write well on clammy flesh. Everybody tried their best to draw on me, but it mostly felt like being stabbed by fifty pointy little forks. We all had a sense of humor about it. One night we used paintbrushes. Another night we tried finger painting. That was interesting.

Every one of those nights—with my arms wide, closing my eyes and letting the fans draw on my body—felt like a final exam in trust.

There was that feeling again, the same one I'd had standing in front of Felix and Michelle's doorbell at midnight: an electrifying combination of fear and a tenacious, underlying trust that refused to take no for an answer.

It reminded me of the shiver you get in the split second after leaving the edge of a diving board, knowing that your every pore is about to experience a shocking, full-body sensual assault: you brace... with joy. Nakedness with strangers is such a powerful feeling, even when—*especially* when—there's no sex involved. I squeezed my eyes shut, outstretched my arms, much like I had done as The Bride, and felt every vulnerable inch of flesh exposed to the room. Every paintbrush, finger, or marker that touched my skin—even if it hurt or was shockingly cold—felt like a loving caress. Some people didn't dare venture away from my arms; some happily drew designs right on my tits and outlined my pubic triangle with flowers. I laughed and allowed them to decorate with abandon.

It was a question to the crowd, really, in the form of my own naked body.

I trust you this much.

Should I?

Show me.

. . .

I took a short break from touring to do some yoga. There was barely any cell service at the retreat, but I walked up a hill one day to wave my phone at the sky and download a few days' worth of text messages. One was from Anthony.

He'd been to a doctor, he said.

They'd misdiagnosed him up to now.

It was cancer.

Bad cancer. Leukemia.

They've given me six months, tops, he texted.

It's over, beauty.

My head stopped working.

I walked down the hill. The yoga teacher, Nigel, and one of my other new British yoga friends, Max, were sitting on a stone wall, laughing in the sun. Max was playing a Spanish song on his guitar.

They could see my eyes were red and beckoned me over. I didn't want to avoid them. I wanted to tell them. But how could I explain this? They barely knew me, let alone knew who Anthony was and what he meant to me. They'd probably think I was being a drama queen. They probably wouldn't believe me.

I just got a text . . . I said. *I think my best friend is going to die.*

I looked at them, and they looked at me. They saw me.

Nigel reached his hands out and held me. The sobs came from the bottom of my gut. I stood there, rocking in Nigel's arms, so happy that these two strangers—of all people—were the ones I'd encountered.

We stood there for a few minutes, saying nothing, while I cried into Nigel's neck and then calmed down. Max offered to play me a song on guitar, and I sat on the wall, holding Nigel's hand and losing myself in the sound. Then the reality of it would hit me again.

Anthony is going to die.

I had to leave.

I was barely able to think. I walked to the pay phone in the retreat office and called Neil collect.

Anthony just texted. The doctors told him he's going to die in six months, Neil. I have to get home. Fast.

Oh god. My love, I'm sorry.

I need your help. I have no cell service here, just the pay phone. Can you help me? Can you help me change my ticket?

Yes, yes of course I will. And you mean... He hesitated. *You're fine to let me pay for it?*

Of course, I said. *It's fine... I'll pay you back.*

I'd rather you didn't pay me back, Amanda. Just let it go. I love you. Now let me hang up and see if I can book you a flight. When do you want to leave?

First thing in the morning, the earliest flight you can get. I love you, too. Neil?

Yes?

I'm sorry, I said. *Thank you. Thank you for helping me. I'm sorry.*

Amanda, he said, *listen to me. I want to help. I know how much Anthony means to you. I want desperately to help. All you have to do is ask.*

I hung up the phone and packed my bags, feeling blank and blurry. The next morning, before leaving for the airport at sunrise, I walked off the retreat property, into the woods, to find a stick.

• • •

The trip back to Boston took about twenty-six hours—a bus ride, a ferry, two planes. When I got to the first airport, I walked catatonically into a news shop and bought a blank journal, sat down at the gate, and started writing. Everything I could think of that Anthony had ever told me, every piece of advice, every stupid skit we'd made up together, every memory, no matter how small. I boarded the plane and kept writing, unable to stop.

That ink flowing to the blank pages of that book was my lifeline, my IV, my only escape from collapsing. In that moment, I understood something about my writer husband that I'd never understood before. I had a small glimpse into the act of writing something down as a direct, very viable escape from pain. I had no desire to publish this writing; I wasn't thinking about an audience. I just needed to do it, or else I'd weep and not be able to control myself. For the first time, I experienced the physical truth of what it felt like to dwell in the act of creation as a direct escape hatch from an unbearable reality.

If I stopped writing and started thinking, I'd start crying and wouldn't be able to stop, or make sense of my thoughts, so I kept the pen to the paper and barely lifted it for the entire journey.

. . .

Neil picked me up from the airport, and together we drove to the hospital. We sat for a moment in the parked car, and talked.

I can't leave again. I'm going to have to cancel the whole European tour, I said, staring out the windshield onto the gray wall of the hospital garage. *And the Australian and the New Zealand tours. I can't go, not while he goes through this.*

My mind started to race. *It's already on sale, Neil... thousands of tickets have sold. Jesus, honey, this is going to be so fucked. The fans will get it. But it's going to lose tons of money if I reschedule, and I won't be earning anything... and... the band... I'm going to need to give them some money to bridge the gap... they're all going to be out of work on three months' notice, I need to pay them, and—*

Darling, slow down, slow down. First of all, don't worry about the money, Neil said.

I'm not worried about the money, I said. *You'll help cover it, right?*

Of course I will. Wait, hold on... He looked skeptical. *You mean you're fine just letting me help?* he asked.

Yes. Honey, I'm more than fine. This isn't like last year when I hit the black spot. This is easy.

Why is this easy? he asked.

It's impossibly easy . . . I said. *It's Anthony.*

It hurt enough.

I got up off the nail.

. . .

The second time I saw Anthony cry was about ten years after I gave him the letter about Laura.

He needed chemo, they said. Thirty-six trips to the hospital, and he couldn't get there and back himself, because the side effects made him too tired to drive safely. His friends scrambled into action, and a carpool was organized so that everyone could take turns driving him to and from the treatments.

Neil seemed scared of my sadness, afraid that he was going to do the wrong thing, say the wrong thing, react in the wrong way. But I could feel how much he really wanted to help, to see me. Neil and Anthony had become a lot closer, but I still didn't know if Neil understood what he meant, how big it was. All I wanted was to plug Neil into my brain and show him the entire history of our friendship. The love.

All my life, Anthony had been my go-to, the person I'd gone to with every sorrow, every problem, every heartache.

The only person I really trusted to understand how I felt about Anthony's cancer was Anthony, and I couldn't call him and collapse. That was out of the question; he had cancer. Asking for his help on this one wouldn't really be fair. I felt a kind of loneliness I'd never felt before.

I was driving him home from one of the first treatments. We were on the freeway, and I was deliberating whether I should drive in the slow lane (he was feeling nauseated and fragile) or the fast lane (he also wanted to get home and back to bed as soon as possible). It had been a relatively normal drive for the first ten minutes—you know, as normal as it can be when your friend-who-had-just-been-given-a-death-sentence is sitting silently next to you steeped in chemicals and you're trying to maintain a stable state of mind. We were approaching a patch of traffic.

Get off, he said.

You want me to exit here? I mean, I can. But…

GET OFF. GET OFF. And he tried to grab the steering wheel and pull the car over to the right.

HEY! Hey. Hey. I snapped. *Watch it. Seriously. Don't kill us.*

Then he hit the glove compartment. Really hard.

I don't want to go through this, Amanda.

And his voice choked and his fist hit the glove compartment again. And again, and again.

I DON'T WANT TO GO THROUGH THIS.

I felt my eyes sting and took a giant breath.

I DON'T WANT TO GO THROUGH THIS.
I DON'T WANT TO GO THROUGH THIS.
I DON'T WANT TO GO THROUGH THIS.

He hit the dashboard so hard it frightened me.

And he started to cry.

He wiped his eyes and sounded so weak, and so tired.

I don't want to go through this, Amanda.

I breathed in and out again. I put my hand in his and kept my eyes on the road.

I know.

I know.

I know.

There was nothing else I could say.

I didn't want to see him like this, I didn't want to fuck up, I didn't want to say the wrong thing.

And I felt dark and selfish. I didn't want him to be sick. I didn't want him to fall apart.

I wanted him to take hold of me and help me. He always had.

But this was it. He was breaking down in front of me. Which, I realized, was the ultimate act of trust and love.

He was asking me to see him.

Not as my mentor, not as the guy with all the answers, but as himself.

Human. Afraid.

He'd been taking care of me all my life.

It was my turn.

* * *

I hadn't really talked about Anthony to the fans before. He was the magic friend behind the curtain.

My close friends all knew The Anthony Deal, but now I had to talk about him on the blog and to Twitter. It was a shitty reason for introducing someone (*Dear Everybody, meet my lifelong best friend and mentor! He's dying, probably!*), but otherwise there was no way to explain why I might have to postpone all the upcoming shows.

Launching the Kickstarter gave me a new level of pride in the fanbase, but the outpouring of support they showed when I told them about Anthony and his cancer was astounding. They truly held me up, sending me love, but more than that, sharing their own stories and pain, past and present: parents with cancer, wives with cancer, teachers with cancer, children with cancer. I didn't feel alone.

Neil and I had been about to head to New York, but instead we canceled our move and rented a house in Cambridge, near Harvard Square, so we could be on hand. Neil offered to cover the whole rent there, and for the first time, his wanting to help didn't send me into a fit of anxiety. The money, and who was covering the rent, didn't seem to matter as much as the cancer, which was all I could think about. Neil was paying, I was paying, whatever.

I rejiggered my schedule and tried to leave town only when necessary to deliver the remaining house parties, then came home to drive Anthony to and from chemo when it was my turn in the carpool. I got used to the routine: pick him up, drive to the hospital, take a parking garage ticket, walk him up to the ninth floor, wait for his treatment to start, bring him a sandwich, sit and wait while they prepared and administered the chemicals while Anthony lay in the hospital bed, go get the car four hours later, drive him home.

Neil joined the carpool, too, and sometimes we'd drive in together. Then we'd sit in the treatment room or go for walks to the hospital cafeteria while Anthony dozed off.

First they said he had six months, I complained. *Then they said it was a sixty percent chance that the chemo would save him. Then the guy today said it was more like a fifty-fifty chance. What exactly are they basing that on? I mean, if his type of cancer is that rare… doesn't it sound like such a perfectly random bullshit number? Fifty-fifty? Really? They expect us to take that seriously?*

Neil was silent. He'd spent the entire night before researching T-cell leukemia online. Then he said, *I don't know. If we believe the Internet, it's much worse than that. More like a five percent chance, darling. Who knows what the truth is. I think fifty-fifty means what it means. He might survive, and he might die. And they don't know.*

Somewhere inside, I had no doubt he would survive. He *had* to survive: he was Anthony.

We picked him up, we drove him in, we sat, we waited.

The chemo made him tired.

Sometimes, sitting next to him as the clock ticked, I'd start feeling confused and guilty about the choices I was making. I'd finally released my Kickstarter record, and instead of touring, promoting, and connecting with the fans, I was staying at home, sitting in a hospital, watching a bag of chemicals drip into my friend's arm.

But then I'd look at him, sleeping there.
Fifty-fifty.
Anthony.
He had loved me more than enough.
He had loved me way beyond enough.
I would give him everything.

THE BED SONG

Exhibit A:
We are friends in a sleeping
   bag; splitting the heat,
we have one filthy pillow to
   share.
And your lips are in my hair.
Someone upstairs has a rat
   that we laughed at,
and people are drinking and
   singing bad "Scarborough
   Fair"
on a ukulele tear.

Exhibit B:
Well, we found an apartment.
It's not much to look at:
a futon on a floor,
Torn-off desktop for a door.
All the decor's made of milk
   crates
and duct tape
and if we have sex
they can hear us through
   the floor.
But we don't do that anymore.

And I lay there wondering:
   what is the matter?
Is this a matter of worse
   or of better?
You took the blanket, so I
   took the bedsheet.
But I would have held you if
   you'd only . . .
let me.

Exhibit C:
Look how quaint and how quiet
   and private;
our paychecks have bought us
   a condo in town.
It's the nicest flat around.
You picked a mattress and had
   it delivered

and I walked upstairs
and the sight of it made my
   heart pound.
And I wrapped my arms
   around me.

And I stood there wondering:
   what is the matter?
Is this a matter of worse or
   of better?
You walked right past me and
   straightened the covers,
but I would still love you if
   you wanted a lover . . .
And you said:
"All the money in the world
   won't buy a bed so big
   and wide
to guarantee that you won't
   accidentally touch me
in
the
night . . ."

Exhibit D:
Now we're both mostly
   paralyzed;
don't know how long we've been
   lying here in fear . . .
too afraid to even feel.
I find my glasses and you turn
   the light out;
Roll off on your side like
   you've rolled away for
   years,
holding back those king-size
   tears . . .

And I still don't ask you
   what is the matter . . .
is this a matter of worse or
   of better?
You take the heart failure;
   I'll take the cancer . . .

I've long stopped wondering
   why you don't answer . . .

Exhibit E:
You can certainly see how
   fulfilling a life
from the cost and size of
   stone
of our final resting
home.
We got some nice ones right
   under a cherry tree;
you and me lying the only way
   we know.
Side by side and

still
and cold.

And I finally ask you: what
   was the matter?
Was it a matter of worse or of
   better?
You stretch your arms out and
   finally face me . . .
You say:
"I would have told you
If you'd only asked me
If you'd only asked me
If you'd only asked me . . ."

—from *Theatre Is Evil*, 2012

I remember seeing Yana again, at the Kickstarter house party in Melbourne. It had been over a week since our nudist park escapade, and she looked a little ragged. I'd seen her in the front row of my official theater concert the night before, her chest pressed against the lip of the stage, getting smooshed by a few hundred people behind her. The hostess of the house party was a drummer, and her grunge band was playing in the backyard while everybody ate picnic food and nursed hangovers from the show the night before. I bumped into Yana outside the bathroom. She'd flown all the way from Perth to come to the Melbourne concert and house party. She looked sad.

Yana! How are you doing? I asked.

It's been a hard week. Symptoms of all sorts, she answered, in a voice that seemed like it didn't want to elicit any pity.

Is it just physical? I asked. *Body stuff? Or is there other stuff going on?*

I'm fine, she said, shrugging. *It's been a brutal week, with all the travel. Just dealing with all sorts of shit.*

I hugged her, then rejoined the party, talking to the guests, watching as people took turns sharing songs they'd written on guitars and ukuleles. My band came by with the tour van and flocked to the potluck food. I was about to play for the whole crowd in the garden and ducked back into the house to put on some makeup.

I made my way into the hostess's bedroom, where I'd left my suitcase, and sat down in front of a cracked mirror. As I tossed my ukulele onto the bed, I saw a pile of clothes in the center of the room that seemed to be moving. I looked closer. The pile of clothes was Yana. She was lying on the floor, wrapped in a blanket.

Damn, girl. You doing all right down there? I asked. *Don't you want to lie on the bed instead of the floor?*

No . . . I'm good, she said.

Really? I asked.

Yeah. Just need to rest.

I put my hand on her cheek and looked down at her. I knew those eyebrows so well. I still wished I hadn't fucked them up so much in the painting.

Feel better, okay? I whispered. She shut her eyes and I pulled the blanket over her shoulders. Then I went back to the party.

. . .

I got to Berlin a few days ahead of the Kickstarter art party, and started noticing the same girl and guy everywhere I went in the city. They struck me as nice enough, albeit a little overenthusiastic, the first few times I ran into them. Which I did, seemingly coincidentally, in every spot where I happened to be eating or hanging out in Prenzlauer Berg, even though I was eating in pretty random neighborhoods and staying with different friends with no mention to Twitter of my specific whereabouts. Every time I ran into them, we'd say hello, and take another picture together. By the fourth time, I'd figured out that somehow they were *following* me, maybe even waiting for me at a distance to see where I was headed in a taxi. It was creepy. There was nothing *threatening* about this couple—they were sweet—but it seemed to me like they'd crossed a line.

The Berlin art party was held in a bunker-like pop-up gallery called Platoon, and the night had been electrifying from the start. The commissioned album art fit perfectly on the vast cement walls; the gallery staff were all thrilled and offered to kick in a bunch of free beer; there were some spontaneous last-minute guest performers, including a ragtag marching band I knew from the States called Extra Action, who happened to be playing a show a half a block away. I'd seen on Twitter that they were in town and invited them to come busk in the parking lot, and they made a perfectly ecstatic racket with their brass horns, banging on their beaten-up instruments, shouting into their megaphones. We passed the hat for them and everybody threw in a few euros.

The gallery fired up a barbecue. My German is still pretty fluent, and I danced between speaking German and English, running around in my kimono with my glass of wine, bringing requests to the DJ who was set up on a few milk crates, eating a vegan sausage as the sun set. Thrilled.

The band and I took our places in the middle of the gallery to play our acoustic set and a local string quartet accompanied us. At the end of the set, I took off my stage dress and invited the crowd to decorate me with marker. I wound up using a beautiful photograph of that moment for my TED talk, accompanied with a suggestion: that if you ever wanted to experience the visceral feeling of trusting strangers, I recommend this exercise—especially if the strangers in question were drunken Germans. The night, the venue, the bands, the fans—everything felt perfect in that moment.

A tipsy girl squeezed right up to me, saying something incomprehensible, painted a star on my nose and staggered away. People started markering one another's faces and arms. One overbearing American was gently escorted away by the crowd because he was getting a little too racy with his marker. I laughed. It was like the street all over again: the crowd was taking care of me, an army of love police. Once I was thoroughly drawn on, which only took about two minutes, I volunteered to do something I hadn't been planning on, but was happy to do given the mood: take pictures with people.

But only for like one minute, you motherfuckers. I laughed above the din, as someone handed me another wheat beer. *I'M NAKED!*

The couple who had been stalking me around town was in attendance at the art party, and as a photographer friend jovially agreed to grab people's cameras to take photos, they stepped up. They flanked either side of my naked body, and while we posed for the photo, the girl slid her hand behind me and thrust her fingers between my legs.

It was a sudden, startling violation. Caught up in the crazed moment of the photo frenzy and the blaring music and the laughter, I shifted my body, whacked her hand away, and grabbed the next person who'd been waiting.

I was so irritated. But, I told myself, I was fine.

Later that night, I didn't feel fine. I felt very shaken up. I went to my bus-bunk and texted Neil.

I had a nasty run-in with a pervy fan tonight, post-markering. I think I need my husband for a second.

I lay there with the phone on my chest. Neil texted back.

Hello, brave wife. I'm sorry. Do you need to talk?

Yeah, actually I think I do.

Only when I called him did I let myself collapse a little. Talking to him made me feel better.

Shit's going to happen, I said. *Right? And it's not like I haven't done a million pieces of naked physical performance art and had lots of sex with lots of people. But man... what a skeezy thing to do. She ruined the perfect magical everything. Or... maybe she was an important part of it. Maybe I should actually be grateful.*

I'm not sure I follow you, darling, Neil said, in a British way that suggests that he's listening but is sometimes baffled by me.

I mean... she's the extreme exception to the rule, right? I've been trusting people for years, and it's all come to this moment, where I lay myself literally bare and then she sticks her hand in my vadge and breaks my heart. But maybe she has to, right? To drive the cosmic point home.

And what point would that be?

*I **trusted** them, Neil,* I said, feeling a lump growing in my throat. *I guess the point is, there is no trust without risk. If it were EASY... I mean, if it was all a guaranteed walk in the park, if there wasn't a real risk that someone would cross the line... then it wouldn't be **real** trust. Now I know it's real. She proved how much I **could** trust everybody else. Her stupid drunk move just reminds me how safe I am. Like, there's a set of statistics I just need to accept and there's a definite one percent* *probability that when you trust people like that, someone will fuck with you. Is that crazy? Am I stupid? I feel stupid.*

You aren't stupid. He sighed. *And I don't think you're crazy. I think maybe you just trust and love people extremely easily, and that gets you into trouble sometimes.*

It does. On the other hand, I said, *it got me married to your ass.*

That's a very good point, he said.

●　●　●

I was recently in the Bay Area at a small back-garden hot tub where I've been going for years with a local friend. The property is private, but the backyard is a kind of gift from the owner to the community. He prunes the beautiful little Japanese garden, keeps the tub clean, and maintains a little shower and places for people to leave their clothes. Only women are allowed to attend alone; if a man goes, he must be accompanied by a woman. There's a passcode-locked door, and if it starts to feel like the rules are being broken, the owner just changes the passcode and starts the trust cycle over again. Talking is not allowed. People do yoga on wood platforms under towering trees.

I was naked in the dimly lit changing shed, freshly showered and about to get in the tub, when a naked girl on her way to put her clothes back on caught my eye and recognized me. She took in a quick breath and remembered we weren't supposed to speak, so she flailed her arms at me in a way that indicated, *I KNOW YOU! I LOVE YOUR MUSIC.* I flailed back and then opened my arms to her, asking for a hug.

She stepped towards me, and we embraced; two silent, naked strangers who didn't feel like strangers at all.

●　●　●

"What is REAL?" asked the Rabbit one day, when they were lying side by side near the nursery fender, before Nana came to tidy the room. "Does it mean having things that buzz inside you and a stick-out handle?"

"Real isn't how you are made," said the Skin Horse. "It's a thing that happens to you. When a child loves you for a long, long time, not just to play with, but REALLY loves you, then you become Real."

"Does it hurt?" asked the Rabbit.

"Sometimes," said the Skin Horse, for he was always truthful. "When you are Real you don't mind being hurt."

"Does it happen all at once, like being wound up," he asked, "or bit by bit?"

"It doesn't happen all at once," said the Skin Horse. "You become. It takes a long time. That's why it doesn't often happen to people who break easily, or have sharp edges, or who have to be carefully kept. Generally, by the time you are Real, most of your hair has been loved off, and your eyes drop out and you get loose in the joints and very shabby. But these things don't matter at all, because once you are Real you can't be ugly, except to people who don't understand."

—*The Velveteen Rabbit* by Margery Williams

. . .

Once I canceled my tour, and explained why, Anthony started getting *fan mail*. Girls in Denmark knitted him socks and mailed him chocolate. People in Russia sent him books. A collection of fans in Boston folded him a thousand origami cranes and framed them in a giant glass box. All over the world, people were sending him their love and well wishes. He was amazed. He started a Facebook page.

What did you do to them? he asked.

I loved them. And they love me. And I love you. So they love you.

He'd been writing up some memoirs about his childhood and daily emotional struggles, and I needled him to self-publish them. A few of his friends who were also writers stepped in to help, and he put out a book called *Lunatic Heroes* and set up shop online. It actually sold really well.

The best marketing plan in the world, he said dryly. *A terminally ill author.*

I kept darting out of Boston for occasional out-of-town appearances and batches of house parties—trying never to be away for longer than a week at a time. People started asking about Anthony everywhere I went, bringing me little gifts to pass on to him. I'd carry them home.

Staying in the Harvard Square rental house with Neil, while the world seemed to keep turning without me, was hard. I didn't have the things that usually made me happy and strong. The crowds. The constant love from uncomplicated strangers. The signings. I missed it. It made me feel selfish.

My band waited patiently and found other work.

Everybody waited to see which way the fifty-fifty was going to fall.

*   *   *

We were safe in bed, and I thought up a game.

I'm going to ask, I said, *and you answer.*

Okay, said Neil.

What are you afraid of? Like really, truly afraid of?

Getting old.

Okay. What else are you afraid of? Be specific.

Getting old and losing my memory, he said, and added, *and not being able to write anymore.*

Okay. What else are you afraid of?

You leaving me alone, he said.

I hugged him.

Okay. What else are you afraid of?

Not being able to have sex anymore.

I shuddered. *Okay. What else are you afraid of?*

Being ugly. Not being attractive enough to hold your attention.

This game went on for a while.

Then we traded.

What else are you afraid of? he asked.

Turning into an actual drunk someday, I said.

Okay. What else are you afraid of?

Losing control at some point and going off the deep end and hurting someone beyond repair.

Okay. What else are you afraid of?

Everybody hating me, I said.

What else are you afraid of? he said. *Be honest.*

People thinking I just married you for your fame or money.

Okay. What else are you afraid of?

My friends thinking that everything the critics say is true but nobody having the balls to tell me. People actually thinking I'm a cheap bitch who doesn't think about anybody but herself.

Oof, dear. Okay. Anything else?

I swallowed. *People thinking I don't work hard enough. People thinking I'm a shitty musician who just tweets all the time. People thinking I'm an ugly, flaming narcissist. People thinking I'm a fake.*

He drew me close into his chest.

Oh, darling. You're really very worried about what people think, aren't you?

I buried my face in his armpit.

Ya think?

. . .

The next time I saw Yana was a long while after the Melbourne house party, when I returned to Australia to work on this book. I'd taken a ten-day residency at the Sydney Festival, playing a show each night in their wooden, stained-glass, merry-go-round-esque Spiegeltent, and was trying to make progress on the book during the daytime. The publisher's deadline had become suddenly breakneck, but the shows had been booked months in advance, so I juggled a monastic schedule: wake, yoga, coffee, write, play show, sign, sleep, repeat. Yana, along with a small group of hardcore Australian fans from different cities, had tickets for the entire run of ten shows, and they'd bonded over the Internet and became a clan of friends. Yana dropped me an email just as I arrived, asking if I'd have time for a cup of coffee. I told her that I was antisocially buried in the book, but not to take it personally. I said I'd see her soon, at the shows, and looked forward to giving her a hug.

On my way to soundcheck one day, I saw Yana and a group of five or six fans by the fountain near the tent, and I went over to say hello. Yana seemed out of sorts; she wasn't acting like her warm, friendly self. I couldn't tell if she was angry at me, or just in a globally dark mood, and though I didn't address it at that moment, I felt bad. Maybe I'd screwed up my priorities. Maybe I was a jerk for saying no to the coffee.

I brag endlessly about my real friendship with my fans, I thought, *but maybe I'm full of it. Maybe I'm just a fair-weather friend who takes what she wants when she needs it and scampers away.*

My inner Fraud Police bristled.

A few nights later, after the show and signing, I was sitting in my underwear behind my computer, answering the last of the day's tweets and emails and about to retire according to my book-marathon bedtime of one a.m., when I saw some troubling tweets in Yana's Twitter feed. I read back through her recent Twitter history, and it was clear that something was wrong—she was posting dark, vague, and despairing sentences. I emailed her to ask if she was okay. She sent back a single word:

suicide.

For a moment, all my compassion fled, and I was just *pissed*. There was no way I could go to bed now. And then I was instantly ashamed of my reaction. I wrote back, and stayed up emailing with Yana and texting with another fan-who'd-become-a-friend, Carolyn, who knew her and who had also seen the tweets. She offered to go check in on Yana at her youth hostel.

I've had fans threaten suicide at me. In 2004, back when my personal email was still posted on the band website, there was a girl who sent me a few emails in quick succession threatening to kill herself if I didn't write back. It was my first foray into that kind of darkness with a fan over the Internet, and I wrote her long, life-affirming emails for several days. Wrong move. That just encouraged her to send me weirder, more intricate threats. I finally figured out that the best thing to do was to send her the phone number for the Samaritans and otherwise ignore her. She kept sending me suicide threats, several a week, for an entire year. I blocked her email.

But Yana was different. I *knew* her. I'd spent real time with her. We emailed that night about her mom and dad and brother, about life, about death, about needing to be seen. I told her we could grab a quick walk together after the show the next night. I tried not to feel manipulated. Life happens. I finally went to bed at around three in the morning, after getting a text from Carolyn that Yana had come down off the figurative ledge and was also heading to bed.

The next night, after the show and signing, Yana and I left the festival grounds and took a walk to a park. I'd spent time with her, true, but I'd never walked around with her in public, where people stared. I noticed the way people looked at her and her four-foot-six stature as she moved through the world. I wondered what it must feel like to have the gaze of the world fixated on you because of the shape of your body. Inescapable. I remember how I'd been impressed by Yana the first few times I met her. She seemed so absolutely fearless, so embodied, so totally comfortable with herself. I sat and listened while she poured out the stories of the past few months. She'd told me she'd been suicidal since after getting into a scuffle with the management of the hospital where she was working, doing patient intake administration. They'd tried to force her out of her position, but they wouldn't level with her about the reason why.

They wouldn't tell me what was wrong, she said, blinking back tears. *I was great at my position. I was really good at my job, Amanda. Everybody in the ward loved me. And they refused to tell me what was wrong.*

And that's what made you suicidal? I asked, wiping her teary cheek with my sleeve. *There's got to be more. I know that losing a job is super-stressful. But it sounds to me like it was about something more than that. Why did it hurt so much?*

Yana didn't say anything, but it suddenly occurred to me *exactly* why something like that would hurt Yana so much. It was the story of her life—and I'd just witnessed it as we walked from the tent to the park, through the festival of people who stared at her body and then quickly glanced away. Who gawked at her, but never said anything. She'd lived her whole life having to cope with people looking at her the wrong way, but never addressing it.

They wouldn't tell me what was wrong.

They were looking at her. But they weren't seeing her.

We left the park and started walking along the waterfront, and as Yana spilled out more of the background of her story, we wound up on the topic of government assistance. She'd been eligible for disability benefits for ages but had refused to take them. Her parents encouraged her not to.

Why? I asked.

Because I don't really have a "real" disability. I'm just short. I can do things that everybody else can do. I can work, I can drive, I'm educated. My parents insisted, when I was growing up, that I was absolutely like everybody else. Short, for sure, but not different. And the way they see it, if I take disability from the government, it's like admitting failure. Like defeat. It's like saying, "Yes! You're right! I'm a cripple!"

Her comment from the park echoed in my head. I thought about all the shit this girl had had to go through in her life, the ten operations, the stretched bones, the medications, the people staring in the park, the bosses and co-workers who wouldn't tell her what was wrong.

You and I have one giant thing in common, Yana, and I just noticed it, I said. *Have I ever told you about my marriage problems? And how I refused to take any money from Neil until Anthony got sick and I had to cancel this year's tour?*

No.

You're in for a lovely treat. Want to walk me home?

. . .

It had been over thirteen weeks of chemo, and they couldn't tell us yet what the outcome was going to be. There was talk of a bone marrow transplant. And if they did that, an even smaller chance of survival. We all got used to living in the cloud of unknowing.

One day Neil and I were sitting in the hospital on either side of Anthony, who had just fallen asleep because the chemicals had hit him.

He's out cold, I said.

Yep, said Neil.

I don't want him to die, I said.

I know, said Neil. *Neither do I.*

I don't want you to die either, I said.

I'm not going to die for a while, darling.

Good, I said.

You know, I'm quite proud of you and me. We've managed to learn how to take care of each other, Neil said, *even if our marriage is a bit of a mess at times.*

Yeah.

We sat in silence for a few minutes, looking at Anthony's chest rising and falling, his head propped up on the white hospital pillow.

You really love him, don't you? said Neil.

Yeah, I answered. *I really do. He taught me everything.*

The liquid dripping into his arm from the metal rack above was crystal clear, and I had a hard time looking at it without remembering that each bag, according to the doctor, cost $10,000. It always made me think about my friends without health insurance, and how hard I'd fought my parents when, just getting out of college and broke, I hadn't wanted to pay for my own. The battle had lasted months. They wound up offering to pay for half of it. I resented it but paid for the other half. God, I was so cavalier when I was twenty-two, so asleep and so ungrateful. I looked at Neil.

I really love you, too, I said. *I actually, truly do. You know that, right?*

Yes. I think I do.

It's funny, I said. *Anthony taught me that.*

What's funny? Taught you what?

The love stuff. You. Taking your help, so we could be here. The whole deal.

Neil looked at sleeping, snoring Anthony. Then he looked back at me.

And then he smiled. *He taught you how to love. You taught me how to love, and how to be loved. I suppose it's all a bit of a circle, isn't it?*

I reached over and squeezed Neil's hand.

We're turning out good, darling, I told him. *We're getting it.*

• • •

"I suppose *you* are real?" said the Rabbit. And then he wished he had not said it, for he thought the Skin Horse might be sensitive. But the Skin Horse only smiled.

"The Boy's Uncle made me Real," he said. "That was a great many years ago; but once you are Real you can't become unreal again. It lasts for always."

The Rabbit sighed. He thought it would be a long time before this magic called Real happened to him. He longed to become Real, to know what it felt like; and yet the idea of growing shabby and losing his eyes and whiskers was rather sad. He wished that he could become it without these uncomfortable things happening to him.

—*The Velveteen Rabbit* by Margery Williams, again

• • •

I called Anthony from the road. I was in someone's backyard, in Canada, away from home for a few days to deliver a few house parties. He was getting more and more tired. The chemo was wearing him down. And he wasn't always answering my texts. Sometimes it took a few days to get him on the phone. I worried.

Remember the sin-eater? he asked.

Yeah.

Cancer, same thing. I'm growing on the inside. There's more room. It's all coming at me. The only way it works is if you act like a sieve, he said.

A sieve? A kitchen sieve? Like a spaghetti colander?

Yes, clown. And I'm having to do the same thing with the cancer. More room, bigger space. It's all the same.

I'm not following you.

Everybody keeps talking about "fighting" the cancer, he said, *everybody keeps telling me to fight for my life, to fight the disease, and how their uncle won the battle against cancer and their cousin won the fight against cancer and blah blah blah blah.*

Okay... and?

I'm not fighting, he said. *It's already inside me... and I'm not going to fight. I'm going to be a good host, let it pass through me... resist nothing. Sieve. Let it all pass through.*

I get you. But it's all a metaphor anyway. Be careful about saying that... you might piss people off. So many people are so proud of their cancer fight. That's just their way of thinking about it.

The fight doesn't work, beauty, he said. *It's like the haters and the Internet shit you deal with. Let them in, love them, let them go. No fight. Like I said. Sieve. Befriend every dragon. You get it.*

Yeah. I get it.

I'm gettin' off the phone now. Can't keep talking. Too tired. Gotta take this cancer-ridden body to slumberland. Say the magic words, my girl.

I love you.

•   •   •

As time wore on, the hardest thing was the relentlessness of the fifty-fifty. We hung on every word from the lips of every doctor trying to figure out if Anthony was going to escape the death sentence. I didn't want to plan anything I couldn't cancel, so I just stopped thinking about the future altogether. It was late winter in Boston, and the cold and the paralysis of the schedule seemed to be sucking the life force out of everything. I tried to write music, but I failed. I felt empty and lazy and uninspired.

I was invited to talk at TED, and that gave me something nice and distracting to freak out about.

There was also a tired smear of hurt left in my heart from the volunteer musician controversy. The worst of it had dialed down, but the wounds were slow to heal, and I found myself occasionally stumbling across Internet lists of how I was one of the Ten Worst People Ever. I took comfort in preparing my TED talk, sitting in Anthony's study, reading him my talk drafts on his chemo-recovery days and pacing around the basement of our rental house, flailing my hands around to an imaginary TED audience consisting of dirty paint cans and boxes of books.

After a few months, the fog started to lift, ever so slowly.

The chemo was working, they said.

My friend wasn't dead...yet. He might be okay.

I did the TED talk, and people liked it. My life was starting to grow back, people on the Internet seemed to be tired of hating me and had moved on to being outraged about Miley Cyrus's decision to twerk. Spring was coming.

Neil and I flew home from our week at TED, back to Anthony's side, and I started feeling better for the first time in months.

. . .

The feeling didn't last long.

I was sitting in the café of Porter Square Books in Cambridge, mundanely answering some emails over a coffee and some Vietnamese soft rolls, when several people suddenly twittered at me to say that there had been unexplained explosions at the Boston Marathon, at the finish line, which was only about eight blocks from the Cloud Club.

It's bad—it's real—bomb went off. Here at marathon.

Within minutes, just how bad became clear. More tweets came in. People had lost limbs.

I drove home, sat down at my computer, and didn't get out of the chair. I was glued to my Twitter feed, sharing every piece of relevant information coming from the news, every update from my virtual community on the ground, and every outpouring of concern and love from the rest of the world. People who were at the marathon site shared their shock and fear and sadness, and told us what they were seeing. Everybody wanted to help one another.

I twittered over five hundred times that day.

Neil was out of town.

I called Anthony. Laura had been near the finish line, cheering on a friend. She was safe. He was tired.

As evening closed in and I was still in the chair, a painfully graphic photo of one of the victims was uploaded, and I shared it, with a warning. There was a collective outpouring of grief and anger and confusion—people commenting in real time about how it made them feel.

At that moment, I found myself thinking that I wanted to be in a space where people were physically all together, communing, stilling themselves and feeling the massive disruption in our city and the impact of all the blood, debris, and senseless loss of life. I felt alone. Sitting at home alone on the Internet just wasn't doing it for me. People sent tweets asking if I could get everybody together at a park, or in a square, but there was a police mandate against any public gatherings, because the bombers were at large.

I typed a message to Twitter:

We can't gather. Illegal. But how about a few moments of silence. I need it. Does anyone want to join me?

My feed exploded with a rousing "YES, please." It was 8:55 p.m., so I set the minute of silence for nine o'clock exactly, and asked people to find a good spot, and do whatever they needed to do to get ready. I lit a few candles, counted down with the Twitter feed, set my iPhone timer, and at nine on the dot, closed my eyes.

Seconds later, Neil's visiting cousin Judith came through the back kitchen door, looking as emotionally exhausted as I felt. We hugged. I gestured at the laptop on the kitchen table and said:

Hey… it may sound a little weird but… I'm holding a moment of silence on the Internet.

Judith knew me. She got it. I closed my eyes again and sat in silence, with Judith—and with my online community—until the timer went off.

Everybody sent love and peace back and forth. I sent the people around me in Boston a wish for a safe, unafraid night's sleep.

. . .

The next days were filled with a steady onslaught of unsettling images and news. The manhunt for the alleged bombers—two young brothers. The city lockdown, during which planes were grounded, trains were canceled. I was supposed to play a show in New York; getting there seemed unlikely. I found myself obsessed by the horror of imagining what makes a person do something so terrible, and imagining the pain of the victims, suddenly legless. I heard about Dzhokhar Tsarnaev, the surviving alleged bomber, a nineteen-year-old they finally found hiding at the bottom of a boat, and who—I found out through the news on NPR—had been a friend of my friend's highschool-aged kid. I heard the story about how they hijacked a car and tried to make their way to New York. It was all close to home.

A few days later, after a yoga class, I went back to the same café I'd been sitting in when the news of the bombing hit, and blogged a stream-of-consciousness mishmash of thoughts about my life, the lives of my friends, and about the teenager at the bottom of the boat, in the form of a free-verse poem.

```
You don't know how to stop picking at your fingers.
You don't know how many Vietnamese soft rolls to order.
You don't know how things could change so incredibly fast.
You don't know how little you've been paying attention until
    you look down at your legs again.
You don't know how to drive this car.
You don't know how precious your iPhone battery time was
    until you're hiding in the bottom of the boat.
You don't know how to mourn your dead brother.
You don't know how claustrophobic your house is until you
    can't leave it.
You don't know the way to New York.
```

There were thirty-five such lines. I didn't think it was a great poem. It was just a collection of my own feelings and impressions. The coincidences. The blender. The dots.

I called the blog "A Poem for Dzhokhar." The fans read it, and within a few moments sent back tweets and comments of understanding; a lot of them had been online with me the night of the bombing. But three hours later, the blog post had gotten over a thousand comments, and the poem was being linked to on right-wing news sites as an example of liberal evil. Some critics of the poem (who weren't all strangers, by the way; some were within the fanbase) asked:

How could you be so insensitive? How dare you shamelessly promote yourself by writing a poem about this?

One news website said it was "the worst poem ever written in the English language." A television news commentator that night called it, "Amanda Palmer's love poem to a terrorist."

There was nothing about loving terrorists in the poem.

The onslaught continued over the next few days. There were two thousand comments on the blog, almost all of them hate-filled and outraged. Strangers started posting limericks, suggesting with or without humor that I should have my own legs blown off. Blog comments included sarcastic haikus and limericks, some of which were competent parodies of my own poem, and some were more along the lines of:

```
Roses are red
Violets are blue
Fuck you fuck you
Fuck you fuck you
```

And in response, my own readers posted their own poems about empathy and non-violence. Then someone told me it was national poetry month. Timing is everything.

My Twitter feed was filling up with angry comments so fast I couldn't even keep up with it. And I stopped wanting to—it hurt too much. People were calling me a monster.

In the aftermath of the bombing, one journalist and mother of a son said on the radio that her initial reaction had been motherly worry for the bomber. And another local journalist wrote an op-ed wondering if this trend of empathy had gone too far.

Wondering if this trend of empathy had gone too far?

To erase the possibility of empathy is to erase the possibility of understanding.

To erase the possibility of empathy is also to erase the possibility of art. Theater, fiction, horror stories, love stories. This is what art does. Good or bad, it imagines the insides, the heart of the other, whether that heart is full of light or trapped in darkness.

. . .

Here is one successful recipe I have used to deal with haters, trolling, bullying, and other manifestations of critical voices. We all have them.

Take the scathing article, hurtful office gossip, or nasty online comment.

Hold it in your mind.

Now imagine the scathing article, hurtful office gossip, or nasty online comment being aimed at the Dalai Lama.

Now imagine the Dalai Lama is reading or hearing the scathing article, hurtful office gossip, or nasty online comment.

If it helps, you can get specific here and think up something like: *HEY DALAI LAMA! UR DUMB AS SHIT & UGLY & BALD & WHO DO U THINK U R TRYING TO FREE PEOPLE?? FUCK U*

Or, if that isn't working for you, a subtler approach:

Dear Dalai Lama. With all respect, I find your approach to peace highly problematic. If you would stop narcissistically meditating and pretending to "help" people, perhaps you would actually be a force of good in the world. Sincerely, a former fan.

Now imagine the Dalai Lama's reaction. He may smile, frown, or laugh—but he will undoubtedly feel compassion for the author of the scathing article, hurtful office gossip, or nasty online comment.

You can substitute the compassionate/holy/serene being of your choice. It may work to use Jesus, Joan Baez, Yoda, or your kind-eyed but strong-as-an-ox great-aunt Maggie.

Rinse and repeat as needed.

• • •

About a week after I wrote the poem, I turned thirty-seven. I was in Seattle to deliver a handful of Kickstarter parties. It was hard to leave Anthony, but I was happy to leave Boston for a few days. Neil came with me for the start of the trip, so we could celebrate my birthday together.

I was miserable, visibly drained, and verging on a shade of depression that I hadn't felt since my blackest college years. I was tired of feeling hated. Tired of explaining myself. Tired of thinking about it. Tired of Anthony being sick and not knowing whether he would live or die. I didn't even want a birthday. It seemed pointless and unnecessary.

We hadn't made any plans for the day in Seattle except to not do any work—and to stay away from the Internet, which was still roiling with hateful comments and bomb limericks. Things had gotten bad. Someone had just suggested on Twitter that I should have a bomb shoved up my cunt.

When we woke up on the morning of my birthday, it was freezing cold, dark, and slashing down rain.

So what do you want to do today, birthday girl? Neil asked lovingly.

I dunno, I said. *Stay in bed. Vanish. Die.*

Well if you're going to die, let's eat first. I'm hungry. Would you like some lunch?

No.

We found a quiet little Japanese restaurant, where I sat with my sunglasses on, feeling sorry for myself, and staring into my miso soup.

Darling, Neil said. *It's going to blow over. Trust me. I've never seen you this unhappy.*

Sorry.

Is there nothing we can do? Let's do something nice, okay? We could try to find a place to get you a birthday massage. Want a massage?

I looked up from my soup. Neil. He was trying so hard. He was so kind.

I'd taken a few flights that week, and my back hurt. And my neck hurt. And my head hurt.

Yes. I'd love a massage. That'd be wonderful.

I left to go to the bathroom, and Neil started typing into his phone. When I came back, he said, *I found a massage place right near here and booked online, using a little form! Isn't the Internet amazing?*

Uh-huh.

Two hours later we showed up at an antique office building, slightly early for our appointment, and rapped lightly on the propped-open door before entering. I dried my eyes and tried to look like not too much of a mess.

The massage therapist, who was pretty and tattooed, was eating a salad out of a takeout container. We had barely said hello when she took a deep breath, looked me deep in the eye, and said, *I have to talk to you.*

Okay . . . I said, taken aback. *With Neil? Without Neil?*

He can wait out here. It'll just take a second. She pointed to a chair in the hallway outside her office and Neil sat down to wait.

She led me past her massage table into her back office, where a small recording-studio setup—complete with a digital piano and a microphone—took up one corner of the room.

Oh my god, I thought. *She's going to play music for me. Oh NO . . . wait . . . maybe she's going to ask me to record backing vocals in exchange for my massage? I don't know if I can handle this right now.*

We sat down.

So . . . hi, she said. *How are you?*

I was still trying to hold back tears. I took off my sunglasses.

Honestly? I'm pretty raw, I said. *I'm sorry. It's . . . my birthday. And it's been a really rough week.*

She handed me a tissue.

Happy birthday, she said. *Listen, I couldn't work on you without talking to you first; it felt unethical. I know who you are. I know who*

Neil is. And when I got his email a few hours ago saying that it was your birthday and you two wanted to come in for massages, I thought my friends were playing a practical joke on me.

She wasn't smiling. She took a deep breath.

I'm a songwriter, and I was following that whole thing with your volunteer musicians. And I have to tell you...I've written some... really, really horrible fucking things about you on the Internet. Like really horrible. Whole long blogs about what a bitch you are and how much I despise you and everything you do. They were so horrible that a few weeks after I posted them, I deleted them because I felt so bad. And if you could read what I'd written, you'd just be...I don't know.

I sat there, stunned. This was not a good birthday.

I'm not proud of what I did, or what I wrote, she said. *I'm really not. But I couldn't have you just come in and lie on my table, without you knowing. And if you want to go ahead and cancel, I totally, totally understand.*

I looked at her.

I looked up at the ceiling, thinking:

Is the universe shitting me?

I said:

I'm really, really glad you told me. Honestly...I don't want anything more in this world than to get on your table.

Okay, she said. *Let's do this.*

So there I lay, for an hour, letting the tears leak out of my eyes and onto her massage table, while she wordlessly ran her hands gently all over my body. She rubbed my arms, my hands, my back, my feet, my face in a ritual of total forgiveness, at least in my imagination. And I wasn't even sure who was forgiving whom.

I felt her elbows dig into my hips. I felt her knuckles separating my ribs. I breathed deeper. I felt her fingers dig into my neck, trying to release all the stuck, metallic tension.

I closed my eyes.

Every tweet telling me I was fucking worthless, every blog comment telling me to shove my vain head up my own ass, every piece of blog criticism I'd read that labeled me as a self-serving, greedy, superficial attention whore danced in my mind as her hands swept over my body, slowly and reassuringly. Almost lovingly.

She was like a saint, this woman, come to absolve me. Forgive me. Forgive herself. Forgive everybody. I didn't know what she'd written about me. I'm sure it was horrible. I didn't care. I'd read enough. I'd had enough.

Not a single word passed between us for the entire session. I didn't care that she could see me silently crying, soaking the towel under my head.

After an hour, she leaned over and said quietly,

We're finished.

Then she opened her hand, laid it on my heart, and whispered into my ear,

Happy birthday.

Then she left the room.

I got up and blew my nose. I felt exhausted. But light, like something substantial had been lifted out of my insides. I put my underwear on. Then my shirt. Then my pants. She came back into the room, said nothing, and handed me a cup of water.

I drank it, and we stood there, looking at each other for a minute. She broke the silence.

You're really good, she said, looking me right in the eye, *at receiving.*

And I looked back into her eyes, deeply, for the first time, and saw a lot of sadness in there.

She looked tired. Hurt.

And you, I said, *are really good at giving.*

That broke her.

She grimaced and her eyes filled with tears.

We stood there, just looking at each other.

So . . . I said, *you're a musician? I saw the piano.*

Yeah, I'm a singer-songwriter. Can I give you my CD? Consider it a birthday gift.

I took the gift.

LOST

I lost my wallet
I lost my wallet
And I'm lost, dear
I swear I had it
I had it on me when we got
    here

Let's go to Vegas
Let's get a karaoke back room
I'll never find it
I wanna shout into the
    vacuum:

That nothing's ever lost
    forever
It's just caught inside the
    cushions of your couch
And when you find it
You'll have such a nice
    surprise
Nothing's ever lost forever
It's just hiding in the recess
    of your mind
And when you need it
It will come to you at night
Oh!

I miss the yellow
I miss the yelling and the
    shakedown
I'm not complaining
I got a better set of knives
    now

I miss my drummer
My dead stepbrother
And the pit crowd
And Chuck and Matty...
If they could see me, they'd
    be so proud

But nothing's ever lost
    forever

It's just caught inside the
    cushions of your couch
And when you find it
You'll have such a nice
    surprise
Nothing's ever lost forever
It's just hiding in the recess
    of your mind
And when you need it
It will come to you at night
Oh!

The wake is over
We gotta leave because they
    said so
I want to tell you
I want to tell you
But you're dead, so...

Golden light
So way up high
So wave good-bye
Tonight you'll find:

That no one's ever lost
    forever
When they die they go away
But they will visit you
    occasionally
(Do not be afraid)
No one's ever lost forever
They are caught inside your
    heart
If you garden them and water
    them
They
make
you
what
you
are

—from *Theatre Is Evil*, 2012

After the Birthday Massage Of Absolution, Neil flew home from Seattle, and I rented a car and drove off to spend the night and share some wine, Thai food, and friend-commiseration time with Jason Webley on his houseboat.

I woke up the next day ready to drive three hours to Portland for a six p.m. collectivist-style house party at someone's home on the outskirts of town. I had a few hours to kill before I embarked, so I went to a café in Seattle to work and check my email. As I was ordering my coffee, I got a text from Eric, my manager, asking me to call him.

I'd just received a death threat through the website.

It's probably just a crazy person, Eric said. *We don't know. We're trying to track down the email ISP. Can you get to a local police station? It needs to be reported, and we can't call it in. You need to go.*

I refused. It just seemed too silly.

What was the threat, exactly? I asked.

You don't want to know. And we don't want to send it to you. We don't want to worry you.

Seriously . . . what did they say?

They said they were going to find you and kill you. I'm not going to tell you the details. They're disturbing.

I looked around the café. I'd just twittered my location. Was my life going to turn into a stalking nightmare? It wasn't impossible: some crazy chick had driven her car into the side of the singer of Pearl Jam's house. It was almost definitely just a random crazy person. Anybody can email a death threat. But as I washed my hands in the café bathroom a few minutes later, I noticed they were shaking.

The three-hour drive to Portland took seven because of traffic, and somewhere around the Columbia River crossing, I lost it. A

John Lennon song came on the radio and I lost it even more, crying as I drove along.

When I finally arrived at Susan's house, everybody was already drinking and carousing on her porch and, as I crossed the lawn, they gathered around me and applauded. Someone thrust a beer in my hand. Susan, the hostess, was a loving eccentric who used to work designing animated film sets and now handcrafts intricate jewelry and headpieces using wood, plastic flora, and rhinestones, and makes her living selling them on Etsy. She crowned me with a bejeweled antler headdress. I looked at all of them.

Hi, everybody. Thank you all for coming, and I just wanted to apologize if I'm in a totally fucked-up mood tonight. I just drove seven hours and I've had a terrible, terrible week. Did you guys follow the poem thing?

They all nodded solemnly.

It's been... I don't want to bring the party down, you guys. But I just...

Someone asked, *Amanda, do you need a hug?*

I nodded.

Susan said, *You're here now. We get it, Amanda.*

And they did. The wine flowed, the food was shared, I talked with everybody, I felt at home. I got into long conversations about empathy, violence, love, and pain with handfuls of strangers at a time. The sun set. I went into camp-counselor mode and organized a group parlor game called Mafia in Susan's shag-carpeted basement.

I didn't tell them about the death threat until much later that night, playing ukulele in the basement, all of us crammed in and huddled on floor pillows and cushions.

I couldn't tell if people in Portland, a land of extroverted hippies, were just inherently warm and wonderful, or if something about my breakdown had in turn broken down everybody else's defenses, but strangers were hugging, laughing, and singing together off in corners, and somewhere a neck-rub circle had started. If they were doing it all just for me, I didn't mind. It worked.

The party continued on into the night, and I bowed out on the early side, hugging people good night on my way to bed.

Susan followed me upstairs and showed me to my room, taking us on a detour through her studio, an enchanted wonderland of sewing machines, pincushions, and glittering piles of gems and objects-in-progress. She went off to find me a clean towel for the morning. Then she all but tucked me into bed.

This is my daughter's room, she said. *She's off at college now, and she is in agony over missing this party. But she'll be so happy you slept in her bed. I'll see you in the morning. I'm making muffins.*

I gazed at her.

Thank you, Susan. For everything.

You've had a rough one, honey. Feel better, okay? She pulled the blanket over my shoulders, closed the door, and went back out to the party.

I shut my eyes and let the day disappear as I drifted off to sleep, feeling more loved, understood, and safe than I'd thought possible.

. . .

The chemo worked, they said.

Anthony was okay.

At least, they said, *for now.*

He was okay *for now.*

He'd beat the fifty-fifty, but the cancer might come back within the next few years. Impossible to tell, they said.

I held my breath and rescheduled my postponed tour dates, announcing very cautiously that my friend had made it out of the woods but might be chased back in...who knew. The fans were, as usual, totally understanding. They rebooked their flights, remade their plans, and got ready to come see me...six, eight, ten months later than planned.

A couple of publishers had approached me to see if I wanted to write a book.

Neil and I packed up our Harvard Square rental house. I hadn't been writing any songs. Usually when I was angry or upset about something, it made for great writing material—a perfect therapy to shake the demons out. But the controversies, the bombing, the cancer... it didn't make me angry or upset anymore. It just left me feeling tired and empty.

Anthony was still battling symptoms and on all sorts of medications, and our walks resumed, but they weren't as long; he was always tired.

I kept thinking that his cancer prognosis should be this ongoing celebration of cheering, aliveness, fireworks, and popping champagne. But there was the lurking specter that it might come back, and everybody was just too exhausted to be jubilant. Even Anthony. He was driving his own car again, and I was tagging along on a trip to get his blood tested, which he had to do every few weeks. He was grumpy. He had a crushing headache from the steroid medication. They'd dropped his dose too quickly. A car in front of him was in the wrong turning lane, and he leaned on his car horn and didn't let up.

Jesus, I said, *take it easy on humanity. We're not even in a hurry. Who cares?*

Who taught this clown to fuckin' drive? He leaned on the horn again and the light in front of us turned red.

FUCK, he said. We sat there, unmoving. He was fuming.

You know... at least you're alive, I said optimistically. *Remember when you were dying? Eh? Remember dying?*

I'd rather be fucking dead than have this crushing headache. I've had it with people. I don't care that they're all in pain. I hate everybody.

You're such a hypocrite. I laughed. *What about compassion for all?*

He turned and looked at me. *Don't argue with me when you know I'm wrong.*

You're not wrong. You're just being a dick.

Well look at you, little miss fucking enlightened. Then he finally smiled at me.

You know what I always say, beauty. If you want to know what you believe, ask the people you taught.

• • •

I got a book deal, I told Neil grumpily. *I'm going to write a book about the TED talk. And all the . . . other stuff I couldn't fit into twelve minutes.*

He was writing at the kitchen table and looked up with delight.

Of course you did.

They're paying me an actual advance, I said. *I can pay you back now.*

That's wonderful, my clever wife. I told you it would all work out.

But I've never written a book. How could they pay me to write a book? I don't know how to write a book. You're the writer.

You're hopeless, my darling, he said.

I glared at him.

Just write the book, Amanda. Do what I do: finish your tour, go away somewhere, and write it all down in one sitting. They'll get you an editor. You're a songwriter. You blog. A book is just . . . longer. You'll have fun.

Fine, I'll write it, I said, crossing my arms. *And I'm putting EVERYTHING in it. And then everyone will know what an asshole I truly am for having a best-selling novelist husband who covered my ass while I waited for the check to clear while writing the ridiculous self-absorbed nonfiction book about how you should be able to take help from everybody.*

You realize you're a walking contradiction, right? he asked.

So? I contain multitudes. Can't you just let me cling to my own misery?

He looked at me.

Sure, darling. If that's what you want.

I stood there, fuming.

He sighed. *I love you, miserable wife. Would you like to go out to dinner to maybe celebrate your book deal?*

NO! I DON'T WANT TO CELEBRATE. IT'S ALL MEANING- LESS! DON'T YOU SEE?

I give up, he said, and walked out of the room.

GOOD! I shouted after him. *YOU SHOULD GIVE UP! THIS*

*IS A HOPELESS FUCKING SITUATION! I AM A TOTALLY
WORTHLESS FRAUD AND THIS BOOK DEAL PROVES IT.*

Darling, he called from the other room, *are you maybe expecting
your period?*

*NO. MAYBE. I DON'T KNOW! DON'T EVEN FUCKING
ASK ME THAT. GOD.*

Just checking, he said.

I got my period a few days later.

I really hate him sometimes.

. . .

Seeing each other is hard.

But I think when we truly see each other, we want to help each
other.

I think human beings are fundamentally generous, but our
instinct to be generous gets broken down.

The Bride taught me more than I realized, and I still learn from her.

Sometimes people would only toss a penny into my hat. I'd still
always give them a flower. That was the rule. Sometimes I used the
flowers to thank people for helping me: the value was not fixed by
outside entities.

The flower always had *a* value, but it was never an *absolute* value;
sometimes it was a twenty-dollar flower, and sometimes it was a free
flower. But it was *always* a gift.

The money was a gift. And the flower was a gift.

And often, though it had already been paid for, be it with a
quarter or a five-dollar-bill, the value of the flower would increase
the moment I handed it over to its buyer—and as we held each
other's gaze, I could feel the value rising, like an emotional stock
ticker. The value of the gift rises in transit, as it is passed from hand
to hand, from heart to heart. It gains its value in the giving, and in
the taking. In the passage.

When I became a musician, the music worked the same way.
Once I allowed people to share the songs, and there was no fixed

price enforced by the label (or the store, or any other broker), things changed. People trusted me, and one another, more than before.

I kept faith. Giving away free content, for me, was about the value of the music becoming the *connection itself.*

It was about the value coming from the taker of the flower, the hearer of the song, the heart of the beholder. Being painted white and standing on a box, the crowdsurfing, the Kickstarter, ringing a stranger's doorbell in the middle of the night: I no longer see these things as risk. I see them as acts of trust.

I think the real risk is the choice to disconnect. To be afraid of one another.

We make countless choices every day whether to ask or to turn away from one another. Wondering whether it's too much to ask the neighbor to feed the cat. The decision to turn away from a partner, to turn off the light instead of asking what's wrong.

Asking for help requires authenticity, and vulnerability.

Those who ask without fear learn to say two things, with or without words, to those they are facing:

I deserve to ask

and

You are welcome to say no.

Because the ask that is conditional cannot be a gift.

· · ·

How do we create a world in which people don't think of art just as a *product,* but as a *relationship*?

As art returns to the commons and becomes more and more digital, uncaged, freely shareable, we need to figure out how people can sustain a new artistic ecosystem. The Internet is wonderful, and crowdfunding has opened up new worlds of possibility. There are terrific new tools, but they're only tools. They'll improve, they'll go away, they'll evolve, but even the perfect tools aren't going to help us if we can't face one another. If we can't see one another.

The entertainment industry, reflecting the world at large, has been obsessed with the wrong question: *how do we MAKE people pay for content?* What if we started thinking about it the other way around: *how do we LET people pay for content?*

The first question is about FORCE.

The second is about TRUST.

This isn't just about music.

It's about *everything.*

It's hard enough to give fearlessly, and it's even harder to receive fearlessly.

But within that exchange lies the hardest thing of all:

To ask. Without shame.

And to accept the help that people offer.

Not to force them.

Just to let them.

. . .

I decided to go to Australia to write the first draft of this book all in one breathless, two-month marathon. Neil was planning to come for the first three weeks, but the book deadline was barrelling towards me, and he saw the terror in my eyes. I had no idea how I was going to juggle being with Neil for three weeks while simultaneously turning myself into a book monk who did nothing but write for ten hours a day. We had tried getting things done together while being in the same space and failed miserably—and this was an extreme case.

I can tell you're freaking out, Neil said, about a month before the trip. *I'm not going to come. Just go write your book. If anyone understands a writer's need to tell everybody to sod off, it's me.*

You're serious? It means we won't see each other for almost three months.

I'm serious. All I ask is that you make me feel loved and reassured. You're not always good at that. In fact, you were terrible at it when you were making your record there two years ago.

Was I really that bad?

Yes, darling. You were awful. You went days without texting, weeks without calling. Then again, I took all that time and wrote a really good book.

Right? But to be fair, I'd warned you, I argued. *I told you I was going to disappear into my recording cave.*

He looked at me and said nothing.

I felt like such a selfish failure of a human being. A Bad Wife.

I'll try harder this time, I said.

• • •

Ben Folds, a piano-slaying, songwriting friend of mine, wrote a song called "Free Coffee" about the irony of being showered with certain kinds of help once you don't need it as much. It's a kind of Murphy's Law. Let's call it Ben's Law: Once you're a well-known artist who can afford to buy coffee, some percentage of the independent coffee shops you walk into will be staffed by a fan who will offer you free coffee. You will want to scream, *I DON'T NEED FREE COFFEE! I CAN FINALLY AFFORD COFFEE, I COULD EVEN BUY LIKE TWO HUNDRED COFFEES AND NOT FEEL THE FINANCIAL STING* or *NOW? **NOW** YOU OFFER ME FREE COFFEE?* And you will realize you're staring down the barrel of your past, being offered free coffee by a previous incarnation of your barista self, the one who worked at Toscanini's and had $26 in her bank account. And you will look at yourself and remember how you used to give free coffee to the people you admired and liked, to your friends, to your family, to the old professor of yours who walked into the shop and barely recognized you.

And so you will take the coffee, because the truth of the matter is that your acceptance of the gift IS the gift. And if you're not in a hurry, you will also draw the barista a picture, or draw a picture for his friend who's a huge fan, or tell her about the Ben Folds song. And when he's not looking, you leave a ten-dollar bill in the tip jar. Because you can. And because you remember how fucking amazing it used to feel to empty out the tip jar and see a ten-dollar bill.

The gift must always move.

. . .

I finally wrote a new song. I realized, while I was writing it, that it had been almost a year since I'd written...anything. Not since the Kickstarter launched, the band hit the road, the cancer hit Anthony, the bomb hit the marathon, and my whole plan fell apart. I hadn't been spending very much time by myself. I'd been spending it with the fans, with Neil, with Anthony. I hadn't even wanted to connect the dots. There were too many. And collecting them was hard enough.

I find it really hard to write around people, physically. Even Neil. I'm too self-conscious. One day while we were still in the rental house in Cambridge, I got an idea for a new song. Neil was writing in the house. Though he was two rooms away, I still felt like finding privacy was impossible. I went outside into the corner of the garden of our rental house with my ukulele, and tried to see what would happen. The garbage collectors came by to pick up the recycling and waved hello. I went and hid behind the neighbor's garage.

Behind the garage, I wrote a song. The year. The hurt. The hate. The fans. Anthony. Blender setting = 1.

I recorded it into my phone. I called it "Bigger on the Inside."

. . .

Our first job in life is to recognize the gifts we've already got, take the donuts that show up while we cultivate and use those gifts, and then turn around and share those gifts—sometimes in the form of money, sometimes time, sometimes love—back into the puzzle of the world.

Our second job is to accept where we are in the puzzle at each moment. That can be harder.

I know people who support their spouses, their families, or their recovering/destitute/unemployed friends. When speaking off the record, sometimes they say they resent it. They have an uneasy feeling of obligation.

And I know others who are rich in the same kind of wealth or power, and who make an art of being able to help those around them. It takes a lot of work to get it right.

On the other side, I know people who *accept* support from their friends, families, or spouses but really can't get comfortable with it; they avert their eyes, they refuse to discuss, they feel a huge shame. Others accept the help offered to them with grace and humility, and announce with a smile that they're living at home while they figure shit out. Humor is key.

Some days it's your turn to ask.

Some days it's your turn to be asked.

. . .

Neil was going to take me to the airport to catch my flight to Australia.

I had spent as much time as I could with Anthony before I left. He was doing better, finally off the last dose of steroids and cancer drugs. He had just been to the hospital, where he'd had a battery of tests: he was officially in remission and getting ready to self-publish his second volume of his memoir-stories.

We went for a long walk around Lexington that ended in our regular coffee shop stop. The kid behind the counter asked for my autograph and told me he'd just emailed my TED talk to his mom. He tried to give me my coffee for free. I refused. Anthony rolled his eyes.

Mrs. Huge, he said, poking me in the ribs as we sat down. I took his cane and after whacking him with it, leaned it carefully against my coat, where it wouldn't fall over.

Ha, I said. *Mr. Big. You know I owe you everything? My whole soul? You don't owe me nothing,* he said.

I'll be back in April, I said. *Enjoy the evil, soul-numbing, sucking torment of the Boston winter.*

You're a pussy, he said. *There's no such thing as bad weather, just bad clothing choices. You just can't learn to wear a fuckin' sweater.*

He knew I hated it when he said that. And he said it every single time I complained about the cold.

I glared at him. *I hope it blizzards on you all winter. I hope you have to shovel ten feet of snow every day.*

Ha. YOU. YOUUUUU, he said, in his gravelly godfather voice, pointing at me. *YOU...I love. You helped me.*

I'm going to miss you, I said. *I'm so glad you're not dead. Have I mentioned that lately? That I'm so glad you're not dead? I am. And maybe I'll write about your sorry ass in my book.*

Make me famous, okay? he said, brightly. *Maybe I'll finally get some free coffee around here.*

I'm kind of afraid to write it, I told him. *I feel like there's all this pressure to get it perfect. It took me like two months to write the TED talk, and that was only twelve minutes, and even then I fucked up and went over and it was more like thirteen minutes, and I'm worried the book will suck, and it'll be convoluted and self-centered...*

Shut up, beauty, he said. *You're going to do great. Just tell the truth. And don't forget what I've always told you about people.*

You've always told me, like, seven hundred things, I said.

You can't give people what they want. But you can give them something else.

Ah.

You can give them understanding. Just tell the story. Tell it all. They'll understand. He smiled at me. *You'll be fine.*

I'm going to miss you. Please don't get cancer again while I'm away, okay? Please? Promise?

Can't promise that, beauty. But I can promise to love you. That'll have to be enough.

That's enough, I said.

I stretched over the café table to hug him.

It's enough.

.   .   .

Blake (remember him? the ex-boyfriend ex-white-angel statue?) emailed me this story.

Early on in my busking career I got caught in a summer rainstorm.

You know how it is sometimes in Boston, there will be a drop or two of rain and it's a fifty-fifty chance it will either clear up and get sunny again or just plain downpour. Eventually I made a rule for myself that if the bricks on the sidewalk got more than halfway covered in water it was time to get down and seek shelter, but this was my first real rainstorm. I knew my costume wasn't waterproof; the wings were largely made of papier-mâché, but I also knew the costume needed some improvement and figured if it got ruined that'd be all the more motivation to make a second version. So, the clouds rolled in and the raindrops came slowly, then quickly. The pedestrians tend to disappear as soon as the first few drops hit the ground.

It seemed like there was no one around, and I wondered what it would mean to busk in an empty square. So I stayed. I held a pose with my arms slightly out and down. Not the easiest pose, but one I could hold for quite some time.

I waited the rainstorm out, getting soaking wet, down to the core.

After probably only fifteen or twenty minutes of really heavy rain, the sun came out.

The rain stopped and the sidewalk started to dry.

I had really thought no one was watching, but for the next several minutes people came from all directions and they spoke to me, saying they had seen me in the rain and that they were touched.

I didn't really think it was that big of a deal at the time. It was an easy choice.

For the rest of my decade-long career, people occasionally came up to me and said they'd seen me in the rain.

• • •

As Neil pulled the car up to the departure gates, I looked at him, worried.

Are you sure you don't want to come? I said. *Maybe this is all wrong. Maybe you should.*

He helped me put my bags and ukulele case onto a luggage cart.

I love you. I'll see you in nine weeks, darling.

Maybe while I'm writing the book, I'll figure out my life. And our marriage, I said. *If I do, can I write about you and all your innermost personal details? Or will you divorce me?*

He sighed. *I won't divorce you. You couldn't get rid of me if you tried. It's like Anthony said. You hit me. I stay hit.*

I laughed.

It was freezing cold outside the airport, and the wind whipped at us. I didn't have gloves or a hat on, and was only wearing a thin coat, since I hadn't wanted to bring a heavy one to Australia.

He shut the back door of the car.

Just make sure you stay in touch during your book marathon, he said.

Promise. I'll miss you, I said, and put my freezing hands under his sweater, warming them in his armpits.

He gasped, then smiled.

I tucked my mouth into the crook of his stubbly neck, and whispered:

Thank you. Thank you for letting me go. Why are you so good to me?

I don't know, darling. Because I love you, I think.

We stayed in our hug.

I'm proud of you, he said. *I'm proud of you for finally letting me help. Even if it took Anthony getting sick for you to ask. I'm still proud.*

You know, I didn't ask for the money just so I could stay home with Anthony, I said, pulling out of our hug and looking at him. *I think I thought that, then. But I don't think that now.*

What do you think now?

I think I asked…because I trust you enough to let you help me. I mean it.

I love you, he said.

Then I turned away from him and pushed my baggage cart towards the glass automatic doors, looking behind me only once to blow him a kiss. He stood next to the car, waving. He looked happy. I believed him.

The glass doors slid open, and shut again behind me. I wheeled the cart over to the international check-in kiosk. I looked back through the doors, though the mess of people. He was gone.

Now I have to write a book, I thought. *How the hell am I going to do that?*

As I stood in the line, I realized I was crying. I wasn't really sure why. I knew the story, I knew what I had to say, but it all felt too disconnected, even though it wasn't.

I pictured Anthony sitting in the café, during the million-dollar Kickstarter day, looking at me and shaking his head, trying to be patient.

I thought about everything I was leaving behind. The cold, the winter, the cancer, the hate, the past year.

Can hate grow back if it goes into remission?

My brain started to flood with images as I stood there with my passport in my hand.

All the dots. The Kickstarter, the backlashes, the bombing, the poem, the house parties, canceling the tour, sitting on Anthony's hospital bed while the chemical bag dripped into his body, the TED talk, the massage girl. The book deal.

Neil.

All the nights I held him as he told me his secret childhood stories, all his fears and worries.

And all the nights he'd held me, when I was lost in my own paralysis of terror, afraid to take his help, afraid for Anthony, afraid that I was doing the wrong thing, afraid of looking weak to everyone. The Queen Of Asking, too ashamed to ask.

The fanbase, the chaos of complicated, creative ways we'd asked and helped each other, comforted and made space for each other. All the bizarre exchanges of money, songs, tears, food, beds, gifts, writing, stories.

All the people I had hugged. Touched. Who had touched me. All the little places we'd found strange solace in one another…the massive, connected, heartbreakingly human messiness of the whole fucking thing.

I wiped my eyes, took my phone out of my pocket, and sent Neil a text.

If you love people enough, they'll give you everything.

* * *

A few weeks after I arrived in Australia for the book marathon, I found myself walking through the packed and drunken streets of Melbourne during White Night, an overnight festival where pedestrians and revelers can wander freely throughout the city center all night long, until daybreak, as it explodes with performance, music, and artistic light projections illuminating all the downtown buildings.

After hours of wandering, happily lost, through the chaotic magic of the all-night museums and the churches filled with inebriated, ecstatic crowds of people, I was heading home when I spied a living statue working across Flinders Street, near the Town Hall. I can spot a living statue a mile away.

I walked across the street and watched him from a distance. He was crouched in a gargoyle pose; his body was completely purple in a costume that clung to his skin. His face was covered with an intricate handmade mask, which revealed just his eyes. It was decorated with little glued-on mirrors that made his muzzle look like a disco ball. He was majestic, dragon-like, beautiful. When a passerby put money in his cup, he un-froze and encouraged them to pat him as he made serpentine movements of pleasure. It was nearly dawn, and I wondered how long he'd been working there. I was tired, but I wanted to watch. I leaned against a tree across the sidewalk.

A group of drunken people stumbled over, jeering and laughing, and took a bunch of pictures of him. I felt my pulse quicken.

They stumbled away, and another group, drunker than the first, took over. Even though one of them gave him a dollar, the girl who went to pose with him shrieked so loudly I saw him flinch slightly. Then she took the can of beer she was holding and, giggling, tilted it above him, pretending she was going to pour it on his back. Her friends laughed loudly, and she darted away. Then they loitered in front of him, gabbing riotously and ignoring him.

I crossed the sidewalk, and as I crouched down and put in a two-dollar coin, I looked into his eyes. He came to life and then stopped for a moment. Then he lowered his head.

It was odd. He froze in that position and I stayed there on my bent knees, waiting to see what would happen.

Then his whole back started slowly shaking.

He raised his head back up and I looked into his eyes, which were brimming with tears.

We crouched there, for a moment, face-to-face.

I reached my hand out to touch his cheek, before taking him into my arms.

He buried his head in the crook of my neck, sobbing without a sound.

I closed my eyes. I tightened my arms around him. He tightened, too.

The drunken crowd who had just been tormenting him stared at us, and went silent.

We stayed, attached, on our knees, for what felt like two or three minutes.

I held him.

He held me.

He finally raised his head and looked at me through the slit in his mirrored mask, with his wet, red eyes. I felt his breath slow down.

I whispered in his ear:

Get back to work

…and I walked up the street without looking back.

BIGGER ON THE INSIDE

You'd think I'd shot their
    children
From the way that they are
    talking
And there's no point in
    responding
Cause it will not make them
    stop

And I am tired of
    explaining
And of seeing so much hating
In the very same safe havens
Where I used to just see
    helping

I've been drunk and
    skipping dinner
Eating skin from off my fingers
And I tried to call my
    brother
But he no longer exists

I keep forgetting to
    remember
That he would have been much
    prouder
If he saw me shake these
    insults off
Instead of getting bitter...

I am bigger on the inside
But you have to come inside
    to see me
Otherwise you're only hating
Other people's low-res copies

You'd think I'd learn my
    lesson
From the way they keep on
    testing
My capacity for pain
And my resolve to not get
    violent

But though my skin is
    thickened
Certain spots can still be
    gotten
It is typically human of me
Thinking I am different

To friends hooked up to
    hospital machines
To fix their cancer
And there is no better place
    than from this
Waiting room to answer

The French kid who wrote an
    email
To the website late last night
His father raped him and he's
    scared
He asked me
How do you keep fighting?

And the truth is I don't know
I think it's funny that he
    asked me
Cause I don't feel like a
    fighter lately
I am too unhappy

You are bigger on the
    inside
But your father cannot see
You need to tell someone
Be strong
And somewhere some dumb rock
    star truly loves you

You'd think I'd get
    perspective
From my view here by the
    bedside
It is difficult to see the ones
    I love
So close to death

All their infections and
    prescriptions
And the will to live at all in
    question
Can I not accept that my own
    problems
Are so small

You took my hand when you
    woke up
I had been crying in the
    darkness
We all die alone but I am so,
    so glad
That you are here

You whispered:

"We are so much bigger on
    the inside,
You, me, everybody
Some day when you're lying
    where I am
You'll finally get it, beauty

We are so much bigger
Than another one can ever see
But
Trying is the point of life
So don't stop trying

Promise me."

—released to the Internet in
    some form or another, 2014

Epilogue

I came back from Australia. I'd written way more material than I needed. I figured whatever was left over, I could blog.

Neil and I are still trying to figure out where we're going to live. The intimacy/commitment Venn diagram continues to merge. I'm trying not to keep score anymore. I'm learning.

Anthony stayed fine for a while, but at the moment that this book is going to press, he isn't fine. He stayed in remission for over a year; then the cancer came back. His doctors decided he should get the bone marrow transplant. He's going to have it within a few months. Nobody knows what's going to happen. He has a donor lined up, a perfect match, that person is a gift-giver of the highest order. The doctors say Anthony has a 40 percent chance of surviving, but who knows what that means. He's also back on chemo. I'm not touring very much, in case anything bad happens. He also helped me edit the book.

Lee is still running the Cloud Club. He also helped me edit the book. I've kept my apartment there. It's currently being crashed in by Michael Pope (who also helped me edit the book—and who is making a new, epic experimental film that will no doubt rope hundreds of volunteers into its vortex). And a few weeks ago my apartment housed an entire Bulgarian family.

Yana has a new job. The Australian government assisted her

financially during her recovery and unemployment status. She took the donuts.

Gus is still making ice cream at Toscanini's, but the Harvard Square branch closed permanently due to local construction. You'll have to go to Central Square to get a scoop of chicory root or bourbon black pepper.

Casey is also still living at the Cloud Club. She's painting and teaching art to preschoolers in Brookline.

Instead of getting yet another fish after Everything, Casey decided to adopt a cat from the Massachusetts Society for the Prevention of Cruelty to Animals.

She named her Something.

Afterword

by Jamy Ian Swiss

At the risk of stating the obvious, Amanda Palmer is a complex person. I can, at least, state this with some up-close-and-personal authority, knowing her as an artist, as a friend, and also now as a creative collaborator. I lent a hand and an ear when she was preparing her TED talk, and have spent much of the past year in the role of what she has dubbed her "book doula," helping her to birth this book in your hands. (It's all in the breathing.)

As passionate as the affection is that Amanda's friends and fans have for her, there are some outside those circles who seem to have difficulty understanding what makes her tick. When the media asked her to explain how her music Kickstarter became so successful, they came expecting answers about business plans and social media strategies.

But that's not where the answers will be found.

Her fans already understand that her relationship with them is inseparable from her art. Her remarkable songs and music are the artistic end product, but really, it is all a part of the messy dish that comprises her indefinable specialty: mixing, blending, cooking up, hosting, and serving a passionate stew of human connection.

Social media is not a separate piece of her. It *is* her—just as the songs are her, the music is her, the blog, the communicating, the hugging and hand-holding—the empathy is her. Her friend and mentor, Anthony, taught her the empathy part and much more, and she keeps trying to explain it to the rest of us, and acting on it when she is most severely tested—within her most intimate relationships or out in full view of the public eye. As I worked with her to help shape the book she was writing, we practiced everything she preaches in these pages.

In a culture that routinely sees creativity, art, and the human body as mere commodities, many find it difficult to grasp that there might be another point of view. Those who live in a world of cynicism and marketing can't quite wrap their heads around the idea that Amanda can be who she claims to be. That she can be exactly who she really is. That she can be that true, that authentic.

Perhaps, with this book, they can believe she is real.

A Note from the Author

I am, first and foremost, a musician. Writing a book was great, but I desperately want you to hear my music so I don't lose track of myself. I made a playlist of all the songs used/mentioned in this book, and I threw in a special "welcome to my actual life" page of my website for those of you who have just read this book without having any idea who I am or what my songs sound like. It all started with the Art Itself, and I hope the book leads you back there.

The playlist is free—you can take it, or pay what you want:

AmandaPalmer.net/TheArtOfAsking

The page also has a gallery of book-related pictures, and links to the artists mentioned in this book. And a link to the blogs that relate to the story, and my current blog. And, duh, the Email List of Gold.

The story continues. Come along.

Twitterfolk: I'm @amandapalmer. If you're talking about the book, please use #ArtOfAsking. Love.

Oh, and these guys: Neil Gaiman is at neilgaiman.com (and he's @neilhimself on Twitter). Anthony Martignetti is at camstories.net (there's some great free recordings of Anthony reading his memoir there. He's also @dramartignetti).

Acknowledgments

This book, much like my TED talk and other aspects of my life, was a crowdsourced effort.

I wrote it very fast and asked for a shit-ton of help. I will try to keep this entertaining so you'll actually read it.

First and foremost, I feel like my team gets slightly short-shrifted in this book, because it was way less complicated to write certain parts without including the gory details of how things function in AmandaLand. But so much of my work would be impossible without the small, dedicated collection of people who have my back every single day as I head off to work.

Case in point: the midnight-doorbell that I rang on the Lower East Side was only rung because Hayley Rosenblum, Queen Of Crowd Liaisons and longtime member of my office, was furiously scanning Twitter for good couchsurfing offers while I was on stage, stuck in a conjoined twin dress with Jason Webley. Hayley, you're a constant godsend.

My assistant, SuperKate Slepicka, was and is an indispensable part of my life and of this writing process. And is, as I write, double-checking the list of people who test-read this book and sending me reminder emails. SuperKate, I cannot thank you enough for being the ongoing, unshakeable, and unsung hero of my daily existence.

Eric Sussman started as a Dresden Dolls intern, became our tour manager, and now sits at the helm of the ship, steering and managing the rough and troubled waters of my whole, crazy business. He helped with this book enormously not just by reminding me (three times, in some cases) how much this-and-that Kickstarter package cost, but by holding down the fort and minding the shop while I Dropped Off The Face Of The Earth to write. Fist to chest, Eric.

And last but not least, Sean Francis has been with me longer than anybody. He has been my megaphone, my blog editor, my brain champion since the very beginning, my soul brother in constant, late-night, why-the-fuck-not ideas. Sean, I have no words. You know me like nobody else.

I'd like to thank everybody who backed the Kickstarter. Without you, this book may not ever have existed...or not quite like this.

I asked for help on Twitter (and on my blog, and on Facebook) *relentlessly* while writing every draft of this book. If you were there, you saw.

If I could list the number of Twitter, blog, and Facebook commenters that contributed to this book, even just for a word (I often went to Twitter as a hive-thesaurus, looking for a way to describe a concept), it would probably cover ten pages. I also went to the blog with questions and discussions that I sometimes used in the book, but more importantly, you guys inspired my brain and showed me patterns, presented great arguments, and went on this whole philosophical ride with me. Again, if you were there, you know who you are. To all of you on my blog and feeds, day in and day out, thank you. ((((((((((()))))))))). <3. no, <4. and for good measure,))<>((.

David Shaw rescued us a few times with last-minute technical support. Thank you, David.

I don't like to write in quiet places. I like to be around people. I started writing this book in a bar and finished it in a café. At this moment, I'm sitting at a wooden table in the McNally Jackson bookstore in New York City, nursing a cortado. I consumed a cubic-house worth of espresso and wine while writing this book, and darkened the corners of dozens of establishments, and I'd very much like to thank the ones I darkened frequently. In Melbourne: Arcadia, Grub Food Van, Atomica (who got an A+ for music selection, causing me to often dance while writing), Polly, Vegie Bar, 1880, Southpaw, Storm in a Teacup, and Thousand Pound Bend. In San Diego, where I traveled twice to work with Jamy The Book Doula, we owe thanks to Better Buzz and even greater thanks to the Hotel del Coronado, who saw me asking for crash space in the area and raised their hands, giving me the most opulent surf of all time, plus nice corners to write in. In NYC, many hours were spent in Cafe Gitane in SoHo, and many hours were spent here in McNally Jackson. And in Cambridge, there is only beloved Cafe Pamplona. Get the white gazpacho. It's incredible, it has grapes in it. (Unless it's winter; get the garlic soup.)

My housemates at the Cloud Club: Lee Barron our hermit-y captain, Michael Pope, Cassandra Long, Tristan Allen, Steve Martin (no, not that Steve Martin), Mali Sastri, Vessela Stoyanova, and Nate Greenslit—I really love all of you. Thank you for being my Art Family. And long live the Mystery Aesthetic.

Right as I was about to leave for Australia to work on the book, I walked into Trident, an independent bookstore in Boston, to use their bathroom. They'd laid *Daring Greatly* by Brené Brown out on the staff picks table. I'd seen her TED talk about vulnerability and loved it, so I picked up the book, figuring I'd probably have no time to read it. I toted it along to Australia, started reading it a few weeks into my own writing, and was completely shocked to see that she'd basically written my book for me—except from an academic perspective. When I got to the part where she quoted *The Velveteen Rabbit*, I gave up. I sent a text to my editor and literary agents saying BRENÉ BROWN HAS RUINED MY LIFE. SHE ALREADY WROTE MY BOOK. AND SHE STOLE MY RABBIT. But then I realized I should just take Rabbits and make Rabbitade. I invited her to write the foreword. Brené, thank you so, so very much. The work and research you are doing is changing the world.

On that note, this book would not have happened the way it did without TED. I'd like to thank Thomas Dolby for helping get my foot in the door for the original gig, and Bill Bragin, music connector extraordinaire, for advocating on my behalf. And I'd like to thank Chris Anderson, Mr. TED, who pushed me to say more than I wanted to say, but that made everything work. All the other incredibly inspiring friends, writers, and thinkers I've discovered and/or befriended—especially Jill Bolte-Taylor, Danny Hillis, Shane Koyczan, JR, Aimee Mullins, Dan Pallotta, Ron Finley, and Amy Cuddy—have all influenced and/or encouraged this book. I feel really lucky to have stumbled into this world. So thank you, Chris, and everyone working at TED, for everything you're doing.

I owe a huge amount of thanks to everybody who's ever hosted me—and the general list is too long for this book—but I'd like to thank a select few people who have gone above and beyond, or have given me a home and safe harbor while I was working on this book in particular. Danny and Pati Hillis not only opened their doors to me, but to my extended staff and friends, and are couch-hosts of the highest caliber (but also, we traded when Danny decided to move into OUR house for a while, so it's a fair trade all the way). Felix and Michelle popped into my life by answering a Twitter couch-call for a single night and I don't think any of us could have predicted that I'd be staying in their apartment for an entire week a few years later, writing about that very experience while listening to their Philip Glass vinyl collection on repeat. Thank you, guys. Thanks to Malcolm and Elaine for the Brighton crash space, the company, and the stories. The Cunningham/Siggs in Edinburgh have become a second family, as have John and Judith Clute in London. Kyle Cassidy, thanks for being as generous as you are with your house and your art. Thanks to Pascaline Lepeltier for giving copious amounts of wine and company to so many of us. Lance Horne, you've inspired pieces of this book and hosted parts of its creation in your kibbutz. Thank you.

In Melbourne, Peter Nicholls and Clare Coney have given me a real, true Australian home and made me part of their family, and I'm profoundly grateful. Rose Chong (and her employees, the Chongettes) in Collingwood have become another Home—thank you, Rose; you're another patron of Kindness and Random Beauty.

My Los Angeles family: Uncle Doug and Rita, thanks for letting us park in your house in LA while we edited, and for support and help over the years. Cousins Katherine and Robert, thanks for your always having a bed and a cookie for me when I come through town.

Melissa Auf der Maur has become a friend, cheerleader, couch-host and conspirator, thanks to an Icelandic Ashcloud and Twitter. Melissa, thank you.

Zoë Keating, my touring mate and confidant, is a constant source of inspiration to me at every level. Zoë, thank you.

Meow Meow, you are my mostly companion. Thank you for being my friend in Melbourne and beyond.

(And all three of you should hang out together. Please invite me. I'll bring wine.)

Jason Webley is always just the answer to everything. Thank you, Jason, for connecting the dots of my life before I even see them.

I wrote about a LOT of people in this book, including Jason, and I tracked most of them down for permission. They helped me get the facts straight, and in some cases they even rewrote their own dialogue. I hope I don't miss anybody. If I do, come yell at me for the next edition of the book. Gina Barrett was the TED speaker coach who I mention at the start of the book. E. Stephen Frederick, you're a Bride-Napper. Gus, may Toscanini's flourish forever (I still suggest you try my idea for a flavor called "Allied Invasion," containing chocolate, poppy seeds, rubble, and tears). Kathleen Hanna, thank you for letting me use your story. You're a Great Force in this world. Rob Chalfen, fish sometime soon. Alina Simone and Josh Knobe, thank you for being my oldest friends. Jacky, thank you, and thank your mum. Blake, thank you for sharing your statue reflections.

Edward Ka-Spel, you're still my hero. Let's make a record. Hera and Indiana, may we all meet in Iceland someday. Ron Nordin, thank you for helping me and so many other artists. You're a class act. Tom Wethern and Steve Gisselbrecht, until the next chocolate party. Beth Hommel, thank you for years of help. Emily White, thank you for your help as well and...are you sure you don't want another beer? And to Lorraine Garland and Cat Mihos, thank you for all the help you've given himself over the years, and, by default, to me. Frank Chimero and Maciej Cegłowski, thank you for leading me to Walden Pond and the donuts that awaited me there. Xanthea O'Connor? Take the fucking donuts. Sam Buckingham? Remind her, please. Ground control to Kim Boekbinder, may the force be with you. Thanks to Max Temkin for helping me out with John Campbell's story. Dear, dear Karen Mantler—expect the worst, accept the worst, demand the worst!!! At Kickstarter HQ, thanks are due to Yancey Strickler and Fred Benenson, for arming me with the facts (and an incredible tool). Josh Ente, thanks for letting me interview you, and thank you for being an awesome person. Courtnee, thank you for allowing me to share our moment with the world. And Yana...you've been brave to begin with but so fucking brave to let me share our story in this book. Thank you.

To Ayelet Waldman and Michael Chabon, thank you not only for letting us get hitched at your house, but for letting me camp out and edit my last draft. And thanks to the *Harvard Lampoon* for providing me an editing office, Katy Perry, and some bourbon.

I've been given real gifts on a deep level from my many, many yoga teachers, especially from the Baptiste family: Baron, Gregor, Claire, Troy, Pilar, and Emily...namaste, motherfuckers. And right near home, thanks to Glen Cunningham at Sadhana for constant reminders to stay awake and compassionate with myself and everyone else.

I'd like to give a cosmic shout-out to all my musical collaborators, without whom I'd never have done anything, especially my musical soul-brother Brian Viglione. Thank you for years of inspiration, Brian. Sloth Power. And to the Grand Theft Orchesta: Michael McQuilken, Thor Harris, Chad Raines, Jherek Bischoff, and our producer, John Congleton. Thank you, guys, so much for making music with me. The Danger Ensemble: Steven, Lyndon, Tora, Kat, Peta, Katie, Mark…thank you for the art. And my regular touring crew over the years: Jaron "Steak" Luksa, Dave "Psycho" Hughes, Jeff Maker (dot com), Laura Keating, and Katie Kay…thank you for all the support on the road. I'd like to thank Felice, Vickie, Kevin, Aleix, Sarah, Dana, Damien, Jessica, and Jared at Girlie Action for going on the Kickstarter adventure: thank you, guys, for everything you did to help us. Ditto for Mike, Nick, Machete, and everyone at Famehouse. Art-felt thanks to Andrew Nelson for creating such beautiful Kickstarter packaging. Thanks to Wes for years of merchandising help. Matt Hickey has been my faithful booking agent for over ten years, and without him I'd be lost. Thank you, Matt. Huge thanks as well to Bex Majors, who books me in Europe. And thanks to Ted Harris, who keeps me on the right side of the law.

I owe MASSIVE thanks to the people who actually test-read sections of this book and provided valuable feedback, caught errors, suggested changes, and saved my ass from saying the right thing the wrong way or the wrong thing the wrong way or whatever you know what I mean. Seth Godin went above and beyond the call of duty in suggesting cuts and tweaks to the first draft of the manuscript. Thank you so, so much, Seth. I don't know why you're so goddamn nice. Jason Webley and Michael Pope saved me from myself in several spots. Maria Popova, Kambriel, Len Tower Jr., Lisa Oberteuffer, Andrew O'Neill, Cormac Bride, Mike Masnick, Whitncy Moses, Kandace Schultz, and Bob Rosenthal all provided heartfelt encouragement and insight. Seriously, I cannot thank all of you enough for slaving on such a tight schedule to help me make this book. Thank you.

A lot of artists—helmed by the cover photographer, Allan Amato—contributed to the painting/party that culminated in the cover of this book.

Thank you to Geeta Dayal for all her encouragement in the author department.

I want to thank Ben Folds for constantly encouraging my writing and being an awesome friend.

And I want to thank Steve Albini. Just because I can. Here's a hug, Steve Albini.

This book also would not have been A Real Book if I hadn't had the help of literary agent Merrilee Heifetz at Writers House, who has lovingly held my hand while I traipsed into BookLand. Many thanks to you and to Sarah Nagel for all the work you've done.

Emily Griffin, my editor at Grand Central, has been the picture of patience and understanding while I've wrestled with this thing, and was the first one to come to me after the TED talk was released, asking *BOOK?* You're holding the answer in your hands, Emily. Thank you for all the love, work, thoughts, and edits you've poured into this book. Your faith in me is not taken for granted. Thank you, thank you. And to Megan Gerrity, our production editor, and to all of the team at Hachette who are putting this book onto shelves—Jimmy Franco, my publicist, and all the people in the art department— thank you.

Fiona, thank you for being the picture of patience while I slaved on my edits...your help and love means more than you know.

My parents, the whole wonderful motley collection of them: Kathy, John, Jack, Donna, Elaine...thank you all for raising me, helping me, and taking care of me, all in your own ways. I love you. And to my sisters Alyson and Lisa, thank you for sharing your stories and lives with me. I love you both. And to my half brother, Alex, and my brothers-in-law, Cees and Todd: I love you guys. To my stepchildren Maddy, Holly, and Mike...I love you, too.

To Anthony, and Laura: our hearts and our stories are entwined. I love you both so much.

Jamy Ian Swiss came into my life shortly before I was invited to TED and offhandedly offered to give me a hand with my talk. When I called him up and shared my initial ideas and first drafts, he dug in, and hasn't left my side since. His role as my Unofficial Talk Doula—sometimes staying on the phone for three hours while we hammered out the perfect way to put things—expanded into his role as my Official Book Doula. Together we sat at tables, flew back and forth across America several times, talked on phones, shared drafts, cut ideas, added ideas, and cut them again. He went over every single sentence in this book with a fine-tooth comb and has been an absolutely indispensable and essential part of this process. Kandace, his partner, was incredibly understanding as we worked weeks, then months, later than originally scheduled. Thank you, Kandace. And Jamy: I cannot thank you enough for your work on this book. It means everything to me.

And lastly.

My husband, Neil Gaiman, not only allowed me to put the intimate details of our marriage into the blender of this book on a low setting, he encouraged me, advised me, held me, and propped me up—and let me go away, when I needed it—through every single phase of the writing process. He took my first manuscript, pen in hand, and suggested massive cuts. I trusted him and, for the most part, took every suggestion. He put his own writing-life on hold for the last, mad week of the book edit, helping me to birth the very last draft when every hour counted. This book would not be the same without him, at any level.

Neil, you are the love of my life.

Thank you.

Thank you.

Thank you.

THE UKULELE ANTHEM

Sid Vicious played a four-
   string Fender bass guitar
   and couldn't sing
And everybody hated him except
   the ones who loved him
A ukulele has four strings;
   but Sid did not play
   ukulele
He did smack (and probably
   killed his girlfriend Nancy
   Spungen) . . .
If only Sid had had a ukulele,
   maybe he would have been
   happy
Maybe he would not have
   suffered such a sad end
He maybe would have not done
   all that heroin instead
He maybe would've sat around
   just singing nice songs to
   his girlfriend

So play your favorite cover
   song, especially if the
   words are wrong!
'Cause even if your grades are
   bad, it doesn't mean you're
   failing!
Do your homework with a fork!
And eat your Froot Loops in
   the dark!
And bring your Etch-A-Sketch
   to work!
And play your ukulele!

Ukulele small and fierceful!
Ukulele brave and peaceful!
You can play the ukulele too,
   it is painfully simple!
Play your ukulele badly, play
   your ukulele loudly!
Ukulele banish evil!
Ukulele save the people!

Ukulele gleaming golden from
   the top of every steeple!

Lizzie Borden took an axe,
   and gave her mother
   forty hacks
Then gave her father forty-one,
   and left a tragic puzzle
If only they had given her an
   instrument, those Puritans
Had lost the plot completely
See what happens when you
   muzzle
A person's creativity, and
   do not let them sing and
   scream
(and nowadays it's worse
   'cause kids have automatic
   handguns)
It takes about an hour to teach
   someone to play the ukulele
About the same to teach
   someone to build a standard
   pipe bomb
YOU DO THE MATH!

So play your favorite cover
   song, especially if the
   words are wrong!
'Cause even if your grades are
   bad, it doesn't mean you're
   failing!
Do your homework with a fork!
And eat your Froot Loops in
   the dark!
And bring your flask of Jack to
   work!
And play your ukulele!

Ukulele, thing of wonder!
Ukulele, wand of thunder!
You can play the ukulele too!
In London and down under!

Play 'N Sync and play Jacques
  Brel!
And Eminem and Neutral Milk
  Ho...tel the children!
Crush the hatred!
Play your ukulele naked!
If anybody tries to steal
  your ukulele, LET THEM TAKE
  IT!!!!!

Imagine there's no music,
  imagine there are no
  songs
Imagine that John Lennon
  wasn't shot in front of his
  apartment
Now imagine if John Lennon
  had composed "Imagine" for
  the ukulele
Maybe people would have truly
  got the message

You may think my approach
  is simpleminded and
  naïve
Like if you want to change
  the world, then why not
  quit and feed the hungry
But people for millennia have
  needed music to survive
And that is why I promised
  John that I will not feel
  guilty

So play your favorite
  Beatles song!
And make the subway fall in
  love!
They're only $19.95, that isn't
  lots of money!
Play until the sun comes up!
And play until your fingers
  suffer!
Play LCD Soundsystem songs on
  your ukulele!!

Quit the bitching on your
  blog!
And stop pretending art is
  hard!
Just limit yourself to three
  chords!
And do not practice daily!
You'll minimize some
  stranger's sadness
With a piece of wood and
  plastic!
HOLY FUCK!!! It's so fantas-
  tic!!! Playing ukulele!!!
Eat your homework with a fork!
And do your Fruit Loops in
  the dark!
Bring your Etch-A-Sketch to
  work!

Your flask of Jack!
Your vibrator!
Your fear of heights!
Your Nikon lens!
Your mom and dad!
Your disco stick!
Your soundtrack to *Karate Kid*!
Your ginsu knives!
Your rosary!
Your new Rebecca Black CD!
Your favorite room!
Your bowie knife!
Your stuffed giraffe!
Your new glass eye!
Your sousaphone!
Your breakfast tea!
Your Nick Drake tapes!
Your giving tree!
Your ice cream truck!
Your missing wife!
Your will to live!
Your urge to cry!
Remember we're all gonna
  die!!!!
SO PLAY YOUR UKULELE!!!!!!!!!

—from *Theatre Is Evil*, 2012

336   *Amanda Palmer*

About the Author

Amanda Palmer is a world-renowned singer, songwriter, activist, director, and blogger who first came to prominence as one half of the internationally acclaimed punk cabaret duo The Dresden Dolls.

She is a fellow at the Berkman Center for Internet & Society at Harvard University and has shown her underwear on Australian television. She currently avoids living in places including Boston, New York, and Melbourne with her husband, author Neil Gaiman, who is easily embarrassed.

Palmer's TED Talk, "The Art of Asking," which she presented at a 2013 TED conference, has been viewed at least 8 million times around the world. You can visit her website and blog at AmandaPalmer.net.